All rights reserved. No part of this publication may
be transmitted or reproduced in any form or by any
means without prior permission from the publisher.

© Roli Books, 2012
© For individual articles rests with JP Losty, Ratish
Nanda, Salman Khurshid, and Malvika Singh

Roli Books Pvt. Ltd.
M-75, G.K. II Market, New Delhi-110 048, India.
Phone: ++91-11-40682000
Fax: ++91-11-29217185
Email: info@rolibooks.com. Website: rolibooks.com
Editor: Neelam Narula
Picture Research: Aditi Ghosh
Production: Naresh Mondal, Sanjeev Mathpal,
Jyoti De, Shaji Sahadevan

ISBN: 978-81-7436-861-4

Printed and bound by EIH Press, India

Fig. 1 (Following Pages): THE ID PROCESSION OF AKBAR II WITH CHARLES METCALFE, Late Mughal style, c. 1815. Panorama of a durbar procession of Akbar II (1806-37), on the occasion of the Id or after Ramadan. The emperor is followed by his sons, by the British Resident (Charles Metcalfe), high officials both Indian and British (including William Fraser and Ahmad Bakhsh Khan), the Queen and the Queen mother, as well as by troops including detachments of Skinner's Horse. The royal procession includes elephants carrying the royal insignia (sun, umbrella, fish standards, etc.), camels, horses, gun-carriages, and palanquins. The large basket contained the royal pigeons.
Opaque watercolour and gold, 16 x 238 cm. British Library, London, Add.Or. 888.

His Majesty the King of Dehli proceeding in full State to the Eedgah or place of Sacrifice to celebrate the Festival of Sacrificial Festival — It is in Commemoration of the intended Sacrifice by by by by Abraham of his son Isaac —

The Emperor   Heir Apparent

of the Eid ool Koorban or &c / The Umbrella and Servaul

ent Sons & Relatives / The Resident Assistant & Commandant of Escort

Delhi

Delhi
Red Fort to Raisina

Edited by
J.P. Losty

Salman Khurshid
Ratish Nanda
Malvika Singh

Concept
Pramod Kapoor

Lustre Press
Roli Books

The Royal Nalkee or (5) Royal Guards
Covered conveyance car-
ried by men.

(11) The Queen Mother Resident's Escort from

...signia of Sovereignty

The Pigeon House borne by an Elephant – The Flying of Pigeons constitutes a Royal pastime –

The Queen Consort

Fig. 2: MAHTAB BAGH by a Faizabad draughtsman, 1774. *Inscribed on the right: Malab Bague; Jardin que fait Alanguir dans l'interieur du palais pour ses femmes à Dely.* The Mahtab Bagh or Moonlight Garden in the Red Fort lay to the west of the palace garden, the Hayat Bakhsh, and was already in existence in Shahjahan's time (Blake, p. 42). It was largely ruined by an explosion when munitions were stored there by Ghulam Qadir in 1788, while Syed Ahmed Khan remarks that nothing remained but a broad canal.
Pen-and-ink and watercolour, 68 x 123 cm. Bibliothèque Nationale de France, Paris, Éstampes Od 63/11.

Fig. 3: THE MUGHAL EMPEROR SHAHJAHAN (1628-58), Mughal, c. 1650. Shahjahan is depicted at about the time of his entry into his new capital of Shahjahanabad in 1648. He enjoyed his triumph for only ten years before his illness precipitated a succession crisis and an all-out war between his four sons. He was dethroned by the victor, his third son Aurangzeb, and was imprisoned in the Red Fort at Agra where he died in 1666.
Opaque watercolour and gold, 22 x 15 cm. British Museum, London, 1920, 09-17, 0.13.16.

Contents

Introduction
JP Losty
11

Delineating Delhi: Images of the
Mughal Capital
JP Losty
14

Life in Shahjahanabad
Salman Khurshid
88

Architecture of Shahjahanabad
Ratish Nanda
148

Map of Shahjahanabad, 1846-47
160

Making of New Delhi
Malvika Singh
190

Bibliography
241

Notes
243

Index
246

Introduction

In 1648 the Mughal Emperor Shahjahan entered his new city in triumph and Delhi under its latest name of Shahjahanabad once more became the capital of India. Delhi had been the first capital of Muslim India after 1193, when each succeeding dynasty or sometimes even ruler built his own new city, but had lost its primacy after a devastating sack by Timur in 1398. It had been briefly the early Mughal capital from 1526 to 1556 but Akbar and Jahangir preferred Agra which Shahjahan had decided was inconvenient. The new city contained the *Qila-i Mubarik* (the 'Exalted Fortress' now known as the Lal Qila or Red Fort), the great Jama Masjid and other imperial and lesser mosques and the palaces of princes and noblemen, as well as mosques and shrines from the earlier Sultanate period. The remains of the previous cities of Delhi – their fortresses, palaces, mosques, shrines, tombs, madrassas, tanks and much else – were all around, stretching fifteen miles southwards to the earliest surviving Islamic buildings in Delhi, the Qutb Minar and its enclosing Quwwat al-Islam mosque. But with the decline of the Mughal Empire in the eighteenth century and the many sacks of Shahjahanabad and its palace during that period, all who could do so fled the city. Power and patronage shifted elsewhere, to regional capitals such as Lucknow and Hyderabad, and to the settlements of the East India Company, over which by 1774 Calcutta had established the primacy. Calcutta remained the capital of British India until 1911, when it was decided to move the capital to Delhi and to build a new city from which to rule India.

This daringly imaginative feat was in many ways comparable to the shifts of the Roman capital from Rome to Constantinople and of the Mughal capital from Agra to Shahjahanabad, and it had similar consequences. Both the Roman and British empires had at the time of the change of capital passed their prime. Shahjahan's reign and the early years of Aurangzeb's mark the apogee of the Mughal Empire as a great civilization, but their weak successors could not retain control and the empire disintegrated around them. Britain's imperial sunset had

Fig. 4: KING GEORGE V (1910-36), by a Delhi artist, 1911. George V was the first British monarch to visit India which he did as Emperor of India in 1911. During the Delhi Durbar on 11 December 1911 he announced the transfer of the capital of British India from Calcutta to a new city of Delhi.
Gouache, 20 x 16 cm. Victoria and Albert Museum, London, IS 44-1979.

already begun when Lord Irwin first took possession of Viceregal House in 1931. India was ruled from Lutyens' great house for only sixteen years before Britain gave up the struggle to retain control and India won its independence in 1947. Delhi became the capital of the new country and the first prime minister, Jawaharlal Nehru, addressed the nation from the Lahore Gate of the Red Fort in a symbolic reference to Delhi's own imperial past.

Over sixty years have passed since these great events and this year marks the hundredth anniversary of the re-establishment of Delhi as India's capital. This book celebrates the centenary with four essays on different aspects of Delhi's history. The present writer draws on the wealth of available drawings, plans, and historic photographs of Delhi to document the city's monuments and structure and to record for the first time the growth of a topographical school of Delhi artists. These early images are used also to illustrate the next two essays. Salman Khurshid writes on how Delhi's inhabitants lived and the quality of their life, their shops and bazaars and food, the ever visible presence of poets and musicians, mystics and saints, the festivals that the different communities celebrated and their processions that enlivened the life of the city. Ratish Nanda describes the construction of the Red Fort and Shajahanabad and the layout of the new city and teases out the aesthetic principles that underpin Mughal architecture. He draws interesting parallels between the construction of Shahjahanabad and that of New Delhi. Malvika Singh writes on the transfer of the capital from Calcutta to Delhi and what it was like to be in Delhi for the great durbars of 1902-03 and 1911-12 through contemporary descriptions and photographs and drawings. She describes the construction of Lutyens' and Baker's new buildings in New Delhi and the life that evolved in the new city, and from personal experience what it was like to live there in the early days of India's independence.

A recurring theme throughout all the essays is the continued sense of loss and regret at the physical destruction visited on the Red Fort and city by the British authorities in the aftermath of the Uprising of 1857. Partly in revenge and partly to ensure the security of the Fort from future rebellious cannons, all buildings within 450 yards of the Fort wall were demolished up to the steps of the Jama Masjid and the internal courtyards of the Red Fort destroyed, so that all connections between the individual buildings were lost and the organization of the palace and how it functioned became incomprehensible. The results of this vandalism were vividly documented by contemporary photographers. When so much has been lost the preservation of what remains becomes all the more important, and our writers draw attention to the dangers of uncontrolled development. Delhi is a city of international importance and deserves to be treated with the respect due to its glorious past.

The authors would like to thank Roli Books for the concept of writing on these different aspects of Delhi, their editor Neelam Narula, Aditi Ghosh and Maya Kurien for organizing the obtaining of images from different collections, and Naresh Mondal, Sanjeev Mathpal and Jyoti De for taking care of design and production. Special thanks are due to the British Library which has supplied so many of the images and to John Falconer in particular for facilitating this.

JP Losty

Delineating Delhi: Images of the Mughal Capital

JP Losty

A wealth of topographical drawings exist for Delhi in the first half of the nineteenth century, later succeeded by photographs taken by some of the finest pioneers of photography in India. The new city of Shahjahanabad inaugurated in 1648 by Shahjahan (1628-58) (fig. 3) and the remains of earlier cities of Delhi to the south contained a wealth of buildings that merited being included in any topographical survey but it is not until the middle of the eighteenth century that any such drawings are found. The reasons for the lack of this type of visual imagery are varied. Mughal artists in the reign of Akbar (1556-1605) had represented a few recognizable places in their illustration of the historical chronicles. These include the fortress of Gwalior in the second *Baburnama* of c. 1590, with its naked Jain statues in the Urva valley beneath, and the well-known representations of the construction of the Agra Fort and of Fatehpur Sikri in the first *Akbarnama* of 1590-95.[1] The representations otherwise of the Mughal fortresses at Agra or Lahore or Rajput hill forts such as Ranthambor and Chittor are generalized. The lack of a suitable naturalistic vocabulary for architectural representation is of course one reason why this should be so, as well as an ingrained emphasis for both Hindu and Muslim artists on the ideal rather than the real in art.

Mughal artists became increasingly confident in their powers of naturalistic expression under Jahangir (1605-27) and Shahjahan (1628-58). From these reigns are found representations of actual Mughal buildings such as Akbar's tomb at Sikandra in the *Jahangirnama* c. 1610 (fig. 5) and the mansions on the riverbank at Agra in

Fig. 5: A REBEL IS BROUGHT TO JAHANGIR OUTSIDE AKBAR'S TOMB AT SIKANDRA, Mughal, c.1618-20. This is one of the very few earlier Mughal paintings where it is possible to recognize an extant Mughal building. In April 1606 Jahangir rode out from Agra towards Akbar's tomb at Sikandra to try to apprehend his rebellious son Khusraw and his allies. Here one of the rebels Mirza Hasan is depicted being brought bound before the victorious emperor. The tomb was not actually finished until 1613 making its depiction here something of an anachronism.
Opaque watercolour and gold, 28 x 18.7 cm. Chester Beatty Library, Dublin, In 34.5.

Fig. 6: VIEW OF CHANDNI CHOWK FROM THE LAHORE GATE OF THE RED FORT, by Sita Ram, 1815. From the albums of drawings done by Sita Ram for Lord Hastings 1814-15. Having depicted the palace from the top of the Lahore Gate (see fig. 28), Sita Ram turned himself round and produced this view of the Chandni Chowk with the canal depicted running down the middle, and the Jama Masjid immediately (and wrongly) adjacent to the south. Lady Hastings' procession of elephants is heading along the street.
Watercolour, 35.2 x 51.3 cm. British Library, London, Add.Or.4827.

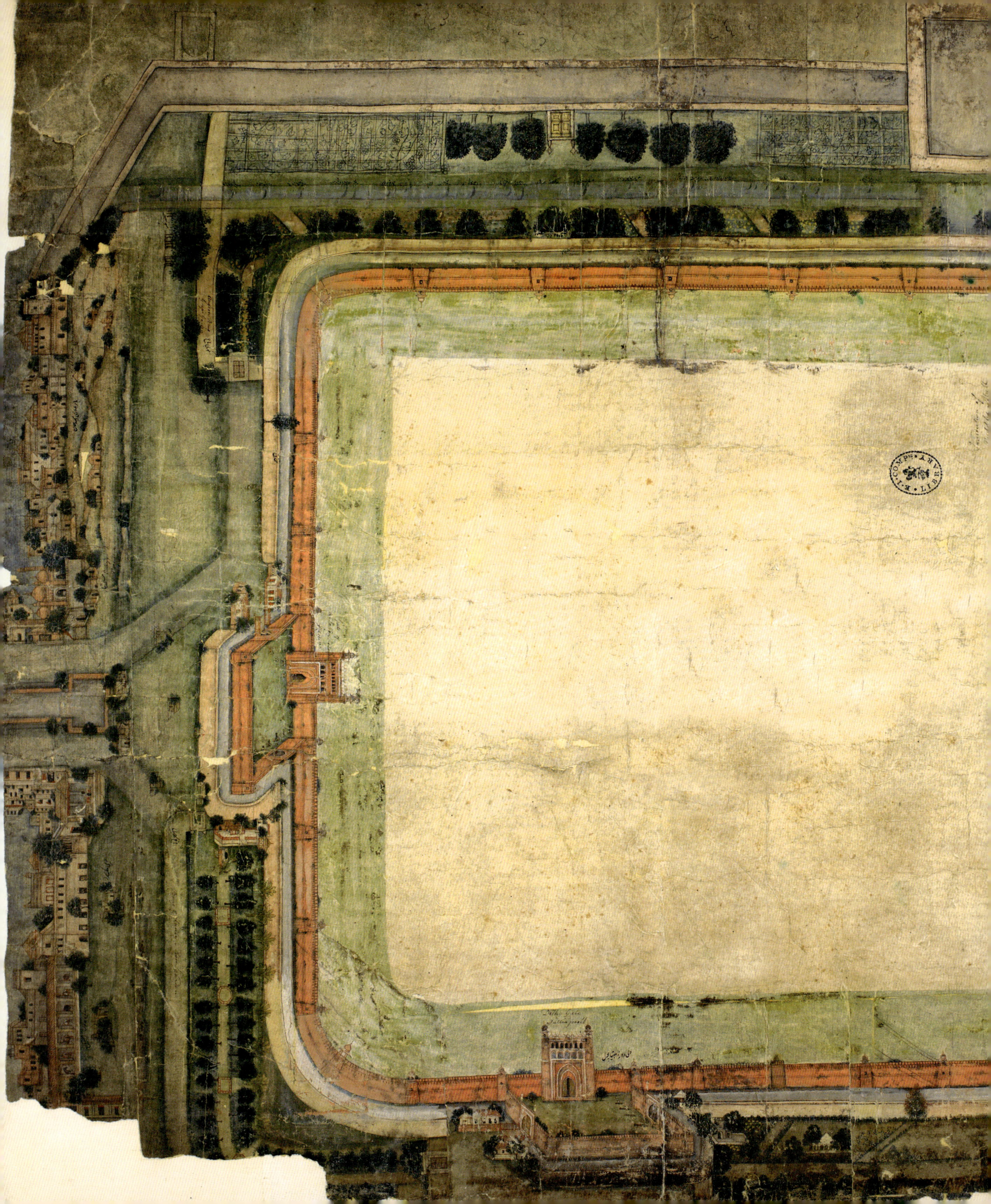

the *Padshahnama* from the 1630s.[2] These are still however incorporated as background into a narrative painting. It is also possible to recognize in the *Padshahnama* certain features of the Agra Fort in the 1630s that were later altered. The architectural arrangements of the old Diwan-i Am, wherein the emperor is depicted on high in the marble *jharokha* and his nobles below stand within the old wooden-pillared hall, were changed completely later in the decade. Other features of the palace, however, such as the terrace on which stand Shahjahan's new Diwan-i Khas and imperial baths opposite and the courtyard of the Diwan-i Am can still be recognized, even if the representations are highly stylized.[3]

The surviving paintings of the *Padshahnama* relate mostly to the first decade of Shahjahan's reign from 1628 and emphasize what he considered his greatest achievements in military and personal terms. Yet Shahjahan considered that his building works, which in these years included the Taj Mahal and the remodelling of the palace in the Agra Fort, were among the greatest achievements of his patronage. Although he apparently had architects bring him designs for their buildings which he would change to what he thought most appropriate, such designs never seemed to have resulted in any surviving drawings of the buildings.[4] It would seem that Mughal artists found the whole concept of architectural representation difficult. Certainly it took another century before any recognizable architectural drawings are to be found.

The earliest known plan of the Red Fort is a plan and elevation by the Mughal artist Nidhamal, c. 1750 (fig. 7). The layout of the walls is erroneously almost rectangular. Palace buildings and what is visible over the walls when viewed from outside are depicted in elevation round the edges of the design as if the walls had collapsed inwards. The interior layout, however, is blank, suggesting that what went on there within the *Qila-i Mubarik* ('the Sublime Fortress') was too other-worldly to be depicted in reality or to a mundane audience: 'the Emperor in his palace-fortress was the symbolic centre of a nested hierarchy: city, empire and universe.'[5]

Other such plans of forts are known similarly depicting the interior as a blank and the exterior walls with the palace buildings in elevation.[6] Thus when Europeans appeared on the scene in the middle of the eighteenth century

Fig. 7: PLAN AND ELEVATION OF THE RED FORT, DELHI, ascribed on the front to Nidhamal, Mughal, c. 1750. The walls, gateways and palace buildings of the Red Fort are depicted in elevation as are Salimgarh and the buildings on either side of the entrance to Chandni Chowk opposite the Lahore Gate. The Grape Garden to the north, Rose Garden to the west and the Imperial Garden to the south are all present, but the layout of the interior is left blank. The layout is also given an erroneous regularity – the Red Fort is an extended octagon, not a square, and the Khwabgah and Musamman Burj are not at the centre of the river wall opposite the Lahore Gate.
Opaque watercolour, 80 x 73.5 cm. British Library, London, Add.Or.1790.

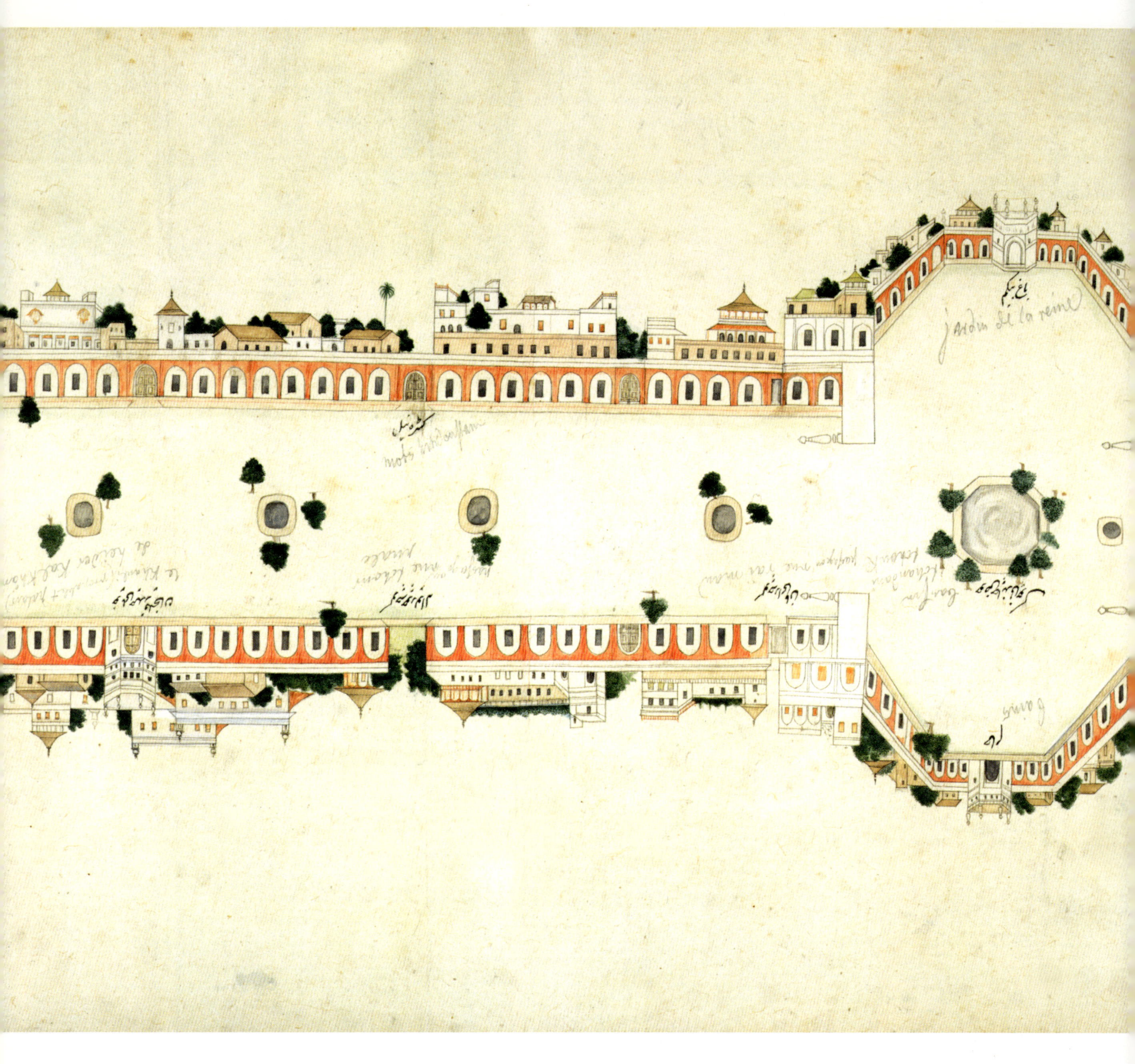

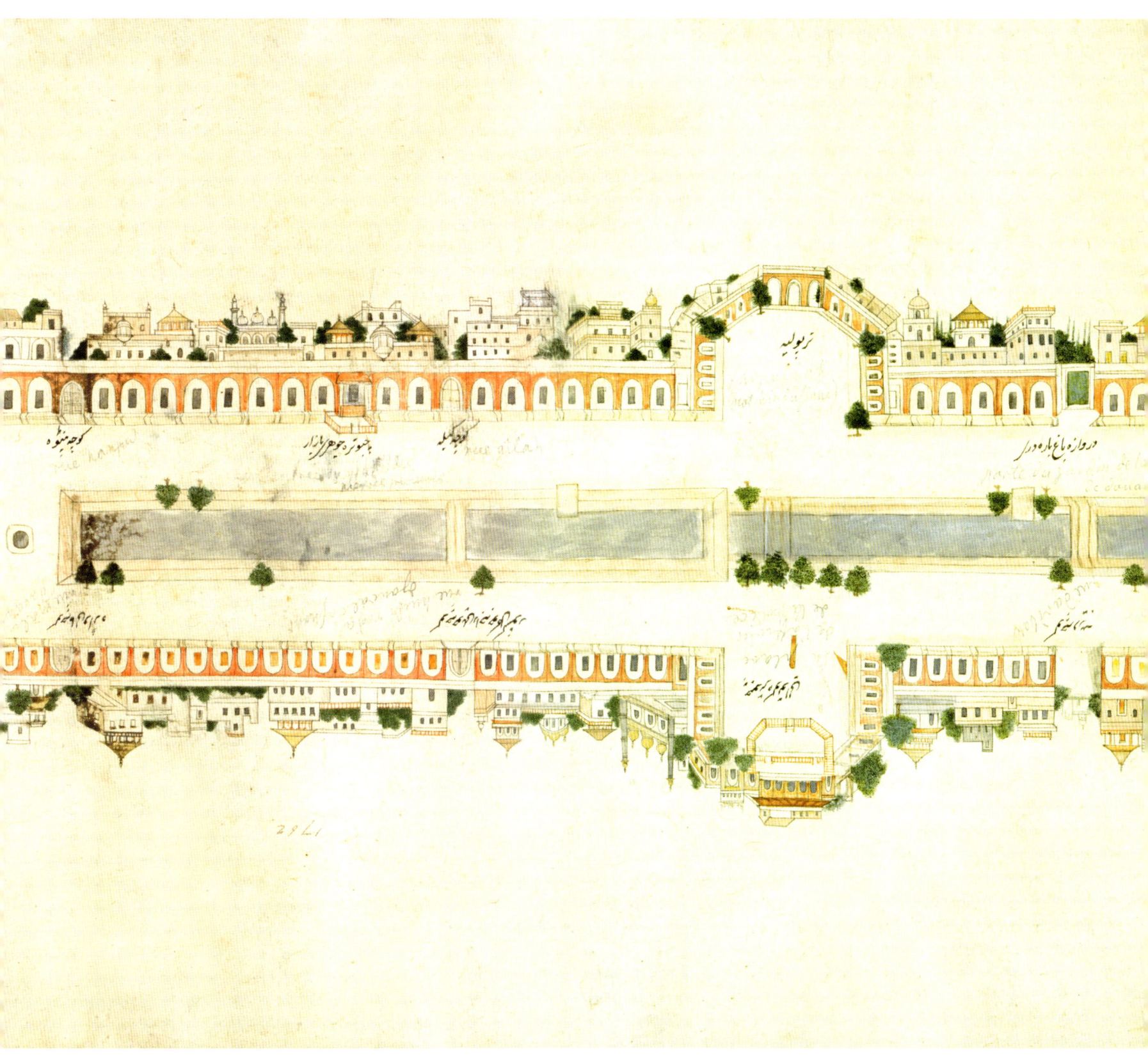

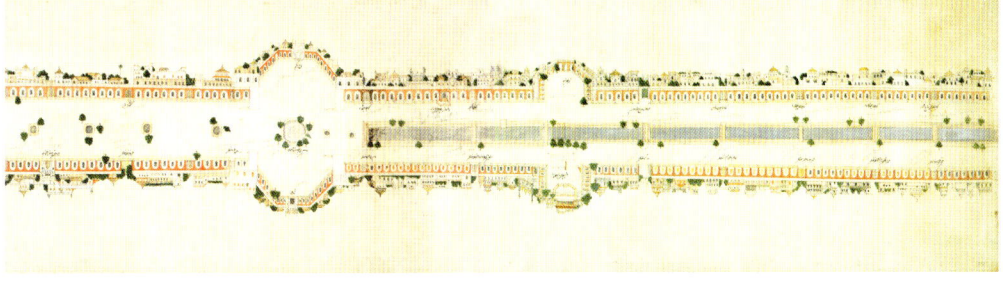

Fig. 8: PLAN AND ELEVATION OF CHANDNI CHOWK, by a Mughal draughtsman, c. 1774. This large plan is traditionally associated with the visit to Delhi in 1774 of Col. Jean-Baptiste Gentil. It shows the street and piazzas in plan, the buildings on either side in elevation with some indication of perspective, and the Fatehpuri Mosque at the end (not shown here) in bird's-eye view (erroneously the mosque has three domes). Inscriptions in Persian and French mostly indicate the side streets leading off. The Kotwali Chowk is noted, with the Tripolia gate opposite (where state prisoners were incarcerated, see cover), and likewise the octagonal Chandni Chowk with the Queen's Gardens (Bagh-i Begum) to the north and a baths (hamman) to the south. The canal of Ali Mardan Khan is shown running east from the octagonal Chandni Chowk, which was fed from a subterranean pipe from the main channel running though Jahanara's gardens.
Pen-and-ink and watercolour, 31 x 140 cm. Victoria and Albert Museum, London, AL1762.

Fig. 9: ELEVATION OF THE EAST FACE OF THE RED FORT, by a Faizabad draughtsman, 1774. Inscribed above: *Palais du Grand Mogol à Dely du coté du Gemma*. This elevation showing the east face of the palace in the Red Fort shows the limitations of Gentil's Faizabad artist. The Musamman Burj is not attached to the Khwabgah while the space between that tower and the Shah Burj has been filled with an erroneous imitation of the arrangements of the Khas Mahal at Agra.
Pen-and-ink and watercolour, 46 x 223 cm. Bibliothèque Nationale de France, Paris, Éstampes Od 63/3.

wanting records of buildings, artists took their earlier idea of elevations of buildings running along the walls or streets of their plans and enlarged them to fill the page. Another version of Nidhamal's plan and elevation of the Red Fort was produced for Col. Jean-Baptiste Gentil, a Frenchman in the service of Shujauddaula, the Nawab of Avadh (1754-75), when he visited Delhi in 1774 along with similar drawings of two important Delhi bazaars, Chandni Chowk and the Faiz Bazaar (figs 8, 10).[7] These show the streets in plan, the buildings ranged along each side in elevation, collapsed outwards, and key monuments such as the various mosques along both streets in bird's-eye viewpoint. Although no earlier versions of the two street plans are known, the fact that a version of Nidhamal's Red Fort plan was available for copying in 1774 along with them suggests that these are also copies of earlier plans. Even in the elevations there is considerable attention paid to detail and also to the suggestions of depth.

The Jesuit missionary Joseph Tieffenthaler, in his travels through India from 1743 on, also had similar topographical drawings done. These drawings were published in Berlin in 1786 and 1789 as part of J. Bernoulli's *Description Historique et Géographique de l'Inde*.[8] A similar story is revealed by a depiction of the Jama Masjid in Delhi c. 1778-79, done for Col. Deshaies de Montigny, an officer despatched from France on a mission to link the French with Indian powers disaffected with the English East India Company. Here the great mosque is drawn in plan and elevation, with the *iwan* collapsed outwards and the three walls of the courtyard with their gateways collapsed inwards.[9] A very similar drawing is in the collection made by James Chicheley Hyde, an officer in the Bengal Artillery, who was in Delhi from 1820 to 1826 (fig. 11). Among his other drawings are similar plans of the emperor's travelling house when in camp and of a summer house erected in the zenana for his children.[10]

In amongst the large collection of maps and plans in the Kapad Dvara collection in Jaipur, there is also a plan of the Red Fort in Delhi (fig. 22). This seems to have been prepared in the late eighteenth century. Like Nidhamal's plan and its copies, it shows the outer walls and the buildings upon them in elevation, as if collapsed inwards, and the interior buildings only in plan.[11] This seems to be the first plan of the Red Fort that shows the true shape of the perimeter of the walls, an extended octagon running north-south along the west bank of the river Yamuna with the upper three sides adjusted to accommodate the earlier fort of Salimgarh.

In contrast to these meticulously rendered plans done by Delhi artists, Gentil also had his retained artists from Faizabad prepare drawings showing flat but coloured architectural elevations on a much larger scale.[12] When Gentil reached Delhi in 1774, he had drawings prepared of buildings in Shahjahanabad similar to those which he had already of buildings in Faizabad and Agra.[13] The individual buildings are drawn very much larger than anything seen hitherto and are entirely in elevation – there is little or no suggestion of depth as found in his plans of Delhi streets. These large drawings include views of the Red Fort (fig. 9), some of the buildings and the gardens within it, (fig. 2) the Jama Masjid, the Tripoliya gateway (*see* cover), and palaces of the nobility in Delhi (those of Nizam al-Mulk, Raja Bahadur, Safdar Jang, and Muzaffar Khan) (fig. 104).[14]

These drawings do not, however, appear to be very accurate, suggesting Indian artists' continuing preoccupation with the ideal rather than the visual, as well as tending towards the imposition of unwarranted bilateral symmetry. This is clearly so where one of Gentil's drawings can be compared with the reality and with later drawings.[15] In the main view of the eastern elevation of the Red Fort, for instance (fig. 9), the Bengali-roofed pavilion that faces the length of the terrace beside the Shah Burj has been swung round through ninety degrees to face the river and a matching pavilion provided in an erroneous imitation of the arrangements round the Khas Mahal at Agra. Similarly, the four garden courts of what purports to be the zenana gardens cannot be accommodated within any surviving plan[16]. A view of a palace with an inscription linking it to the sixteenth-century ruler Salim Shah shows a building totally eighteenth-century in appearance.[17] All the other palaces of the nobility are depicted as having completely symmetrical façades and so on.

When he was based in Delhi from 1775 to 1780, Col. Antoine Polier, a Swiss also in the service of the Nawab of Avadh, had Mihr Chand, his retained artist from Faizabad, draw some of the great Mughal monuments.[18] Mihr Chand's version of the Taj Mahal is drawn from a horizontal, naturalistic viewpoint from across the river Yamuna and in strict linear perspective.[19] Other Avadhi artists such as Faizallah had used linear perspective earlier but from the high bird's-eye viewpoint, while he also played with multiple viewpoints.[20] In the architectural drawings done for Polier the perspective is totally consistent. Polier was himself an engineer and also an architect who had helped design the new Fort William in Calcutta and may have given his artist some helpful suggestions on perspective.[21]

Mihr Chand also drew for his patron two of the Mughal buildings of Delhi. His view of the Red Fort unlike the Taj Mahal is drawn from a high viewpoint and includes elements of the surroundings cityscape.[22] It is centred on the Musamman Burj and imposes a bilateral symmetry upon the northern and southern halves of the Red Fort that is not of course present on the ground. Conversely, this symmetrical approach works well for the Jama Masjid (fig. 12). Mihr Chand must have attended on Polier during his audiences with the Emperor Shah Alam II (1759-1806) and made enough notes to understand something of the layout of the axes of the Red Fort and its principal courtyards, but not how they all fitted together. Indeed, he may have been familiar with plans of the Red Fort such as that now in Jaipur (fig. 22), but felt compelled to impose an idealistic symmetry on the courtyards.

Other such architectural drawings in this period include those collected 1787-90 by William Stewart when deputy commandant of the escort to the Resident at Sindhia's court (figs 14-15). They are similar to the Gentil drawings in that the buildings are treated as

isolated elevations against a blank ground, but unlike them, this artist's drawings of the tombs of Humayun and of Safdar Jang are concerned with perspective and the effects of light and shade.[23] They are, however, something of an aberration in that they had no effect on artists for twenty years. Stewart was also a draughtsman and surveyor and would seem to have influenced local draughtsmen (two at least seem involved) to modify their style towards these very European architectural drawings.[24] These were the men who presumably had already produced Gentil's plans of the Red Fort and of the two Delhi streets (figs 8, 10) and were already used to drawing buildings in accurate elevation and in perspective, albeit in bird's-eye view.

During the second half of the eighteenth century, the Mughal capital remained a shadow of its former self, with little evidence of artistic activity. It was repeatedly plundered by marauders, while the emperors themselves were puppets in the hands of successive viziers and of the Marathas. In 1758, the year before his father's murder by his vizier, Mirza Ali Gauhar had fled to the east seeking allies against his father's many enemies (fig. 68). As Shah Alam II, he returned to Delhi from eastern India in 1772 (fig. 70). He was blinded and the imperial family abused by the Rohilla Afghan marauder Ghulam Qadir Khan in 1789 when searching for hidden treasure. When the East India Company took over Agra and Delhi in 1803 under the expansionist policy of the Governor General Marquis Wellesley (1798-1805), Shah Alam became a pensioner of the Company, his domain shrunk to the Red Fort in Delhi. Yet artists certainly had survived in the imperial city, since Mughal patronage began again almost immediately with three generations of the imperial family painted by the artists Khairallah and Ghulam Murtaza Khan. A few years later he was dead and a new Emperor Akbar II (1806-37) was installed (fig. 71).

When the new British administration had organized itself, the city and the surrounding territory were under the control of successive Residents, who also mediated between the government in Calcutta and the emperor in Delhi. These were for the first few decades experienced and senior men like David Ochterlony (in post 1803-06, and again 1818-22) (fig. 71), Archibald Seton (1806-11), and Charles Metcalfe (1811-18, and again 1822-27) who reported directly to the governor general in Calcutta. For much of this time until his murder in 1835, William Fraser actually managed the Delhi territory. They participated in the renewed court life of the palace, attending important durbars and taking part in imperial processions (figs 1, 71), and made themselves thoroughly

Fig. 11: GROUND PLAN AND ELEVATION OF THE JAMA MASJID, by a Mughal draughtsman, c. 1780. The drawing forms part of the collection of James Chichely Hyde (1789-1867) which was made in India from 1806 to 1837. Most of the drawings are contemporary with his stay in India, but there are a few which are similar to the plans of Delhi associated with Gentil in 1774 (figs 8, 10). This striking plan of the Jama Masjid shows the outer arcades and gateways all in elevation from outside and the great *iwan* in elevation from inside the courtyard.
Pen-and-ink and watercolour, 64.8 x 58.4 cm. British Library, London, Add.Or.3262.

at home in the Delhi environment (fig. 74). Ochterlony and Metcalfe both built themselves garden houses outside the city and lived there with their Indian consorts (fig. 37). Fraser kept a *bibi* in the village of Raniya, now in Haryana. They cultivated and indeed became friends with the principal inhabitants of the city (figs 46, 76, 78).

After the Company took over the Mughal capitals, large architectural drawings of the great monuments of Agra and its neighbourhood began to be produced in strict single- or two-point perspective. The buildings are isolated against a plain uncoloured ground and every semi-precious stone or coloured marble inlaid into their fabric is carefully depicted.[25] These are clearly not the artistic descendants of Gentil's drawings by his Faizabad artist, but rather of those draughtsmen who drew William Stewart's drawings in the 1780s. These men were not trained in the late Mughal figurative style, but as architectural draughtsmen, plan makers and similar. These were the indispensible men necessary for any building project, whether under Mughal or British patronage.[26]

While the basic artistic talent was there already, what seems to have precipitated the change in direction was the work of British topographical artists who visited Delhi in the 1780s and 1790s. William Hodges, the first professional landscape artist to visit India, got as far as Agra in 1783 but did not go on to Delhi in those dangerous times. Thomas and William Daniell visited both Agra and Delhi in 1788-89 (fig. 16). Both these artists published their work as aquatints when they had returned to London. Hodges' *Select Views in India* of 1786-88 with forty-eight plates was sometimes copied in eastern India when artists were looking for topographical subjects for their British patrons.[27] The book also influenced the development of the 'picturesque' Murshidabad style. The Daniells' *Oriental Scenery* was published in six volumes with 144 plates between 1795 and 1808, with ten views of Delhi. While its subjects were often copied in India, both by Indian and British artists, it had little influence on the development of any Indian style.

More influential in the development of this late Mughal topographical school was the work of Thomas Longcroft, who was influenced by his friend the artist Johan Zoffany to journey to India in 1783.[28] Longcroft visited Agra and Delhi in 1786. His most important drawing is of the Taj Mahal from the south-west done in 1786, which seems to have directly influenced the Agra artist who drew the monument from the same viewpoint in two-point perspective for George Steell.[29] Three of Longcroft's drawings of Delhi done in 1786 and 1793 are of immediate interest to us: the Jama Masjid, the Red Fort, and the Zinat al-Masajid (figs 17, 18, 19). Other than these artists, some surveyors in the Company's service must have visited the Mughal capitals around this time, since drawings of some of the monuments of Agra must have been circulating in eastern India for their subjects to have been included in sets of views by Murshidabad and Calcutta artists in the 1790s.[30]

Our Agra and Delhi draughtsmen at first seemed more concerned with documentation than with aesthetics. These drawings were necessitated partly as a consequence of the need to conserve the Mughal monuments of these cities. There is much correspondence for instance between London and Calcutta about the necessity to keep the Taj Mahal and Akbar's tomb in good repair and a committee was set up in 1808 precisely to do this.[31] In 1813 the Court of Directors in London requested plans of the buildings to be sent to London.[32] There is no trace now of any plan being sent, but the album of drawings of the Taj Mahal and Akbar's tomb, commissioned by George Steell, the executive engineer in Agra (1807-13), would seem to have been sent instead.[33]

Delhi itself fell within the Company's control but not the Red Fort which was still the preserve of the emperor. The first Residents, Ochterlony and Seton, treated His Majesty the King of Delhi as they called him with scrupulous deference. Seton for instance, in 1808 presented Akbar with a new set of scarlet hangings at the Company's expense to replace those fallen into decay in the Diwan-i Khas (fig. 87).[34] In 1809, on the drying up of the well in the centre of the courtyard of the Jama Masjid, repairs were effected to the decayed mechanism and stone work (fig. 19).[35] That same year the great gates of the fort, which had been damaged in a tumult earlier that year, were also repaired.[36] In 1817 the collapsed northern minaret of the Jama Masjid was repaired and the damaged courtyard repaved (fig. 19).[37] The canal of Ali Mardan Khan, which brought fresh water into the city from the hills to the north, was also repaired in 1821 (fig. 6).[38] In 1828, Col. Robert Smith of the Bengal Engineers repaired the top of the damaged Qutb Minar and famously added a Mughal-style cupola, which was taken down in 1847.

From about 1815 sets of views of the Agra monuments, done in the same clinical style as Steell's Taj Mahal, also sometimes include views of three of the monuments of Delhi: the Red Fort, the Jama Masjid, and the Qutb Minar.[39] The Daniells published no view of the Delhi Red Fort in their work. Two panoramic views of the east face of the Red Fort with watermark dates of 1808 and 1816, the latter a reduced version of the former, continue instead the format of drawings of elevations done by Gentil's Delhi draughtsmen (fig. 20). The earlier drawing is the only Delhi view in two volumes dedicated otherwise to the monuments of Agra and serves as a counterpart to a similar panoramic view of the Agra Fort. They both continue the moving panorama type begun by Gentil's artists but add some perspective so that they appear to have been taken from a single viewpoint centred on the Musamman Burj. The entire fort and palace and the southern part of Salimgarh are drawn parallel to and behind the picture plane without taking into account any effect of distance. The recession of the north-eastern wall is well handled, that of the south-eastern and southern walls much less so. The smaller, later view is better finished and also adds the trees of the Hayat Bakhsh garden. It needs hardly be stressed how important these two panoramas are in attempting to visualize all the palace buildings and courtyards in the Red Fort before their partial destruction in 1858.

The Daniells' views of the Jama Masjid and Qutb Minar were not precise enough in their rendition of detail to be of use to these early draughtsmen.[40] While Daniells'

Fig. 12: BIRD'S EYE VIEW OF THE JAMA MASJID, attributed to the Lucknow artist, Mihr Chand. While the details are sometimes inaccurate (the asymmetrical arches of the *iwan* for instance), yet the realistic view of the city includes the walls, the Ajmeri and Lahori gates linked by the Lal Kuan Bazaar, the Fatehpuri Masjid and the western end of the Chandni Chowk with the Golden Mosque of Roshanuddaula.
Opaque watercolour and gold, miniature 33 x 42.5 cm. folio 45.5 x 62.25 cm.
Museum für Asiatische Kunst, Berlin, I 5005, f. 2.

view of the *iwan* of the Jama Masjid is taken from an off-centre viewpoint, the well-known Agra artist Latif (fig. 19) imposes a strict bilateral symmetry on the monument in keeping with the overhead view done earlier by Mihr Chand (fig. 12). Similarly, the Daniells' view of the Qutb Minar lacked the precision needed by an Indian artist for the articulation of the surface of that monument. The topmost pavilion, reduced to an arch in the Daniells' view drawn in 1789, had fallen by the time the first of these Agra artists' views were taken probably 1815-17. This particular artist has difficulty expressing the volumes of the *minar* in his desire to capture the lovely alternating semi-circular and triangular flutings. A slightly later version by Latif from the same set as his Jama Masjid places great emphasis on the damage to the stonework, details which could have been learned only from personal inspection (fig. 21).

Mughal artists based in Delhi, who hitherto seemed to have painted only portraits and durbar scenes, were sufficiently impressed by these architectural drawings to want to undertake them themselves, but with a significant difference. Ghulam Ali Khan's view of the Diwan-i Khas in the Delhi palace of 1817 (fig. 87) is not simply an architectural study, but a complete picture with a foreground, background and sky, all rendered according to picturesque conventions. The building is depicted not as an isolated monument but as the residence of the emperor with the appropriate *shamianas* and *qanats* (renewed as we have seen in 1808 at Seton's insistence) which made the otherwise isolated pavilions of Mughal palaces inhabitable. He also introduced active participants into the scene instead of just casual bystanders, but at this stage in his career he clearly was not an experienced figure painter. This view became a model for later paintings of the Diwan-i Khas.

It is not however the earliest such view within the Delhi palace. Another artist using a more straightforward topographical style also attempted the same view about this time (fig. 23). Although lacking in the brilliance of Ghulam Ali Khan's version, this one is on paper watermarked 1809 so cannot be any later than 1815. It is one of a small group of Delhi drawings including also the exterior view of the Red Fort (fig. 24) which form part of the Hyde Collection referred to above. Their straightforward style may be linked to that of surveyors working for the antiquarian Colin Mackenzie of the Madras Engineers, who was surveyor general of Madras and from 1817 until his death in 1821 surveyor general of India.[41] He himself was in upper India during a leave period 1813-14.

The few Delhi drawings in the Mackenzie Collection include views of the ruins of Firoz Shah's Kotla and of the Quwwat al-Islam mosque at the Qutb complex. They are relatively straightforward views by artists trained originally in the Murshidabad/Calcutta style of eastern India but made to adhere both to Western concepts of perspective and to the ideals of the 'picturesque', a movement we shall be discussing shortly. With Mackenzie's collection it is sometimes difficult to ascertain which views are original done by either Indian or British artists and which have been copied later by his draughtsmen. These would seem to be Indian artists' copies of original drawings by Mackenzie.

With the emperor sitting more securely on his throne in Delhi, even though within the confines of his new straitened circumstances as the Company's pensioner, Delhi artists began to try to resurrect the city's imperial past. New versions of old paintings and manuscripts were produced that emphasized the emperor's links to his illustrious ancestors and were given to visiting dignitaries. A portrait of Shahjahan on the Peacock Throne produced in the early nineteenth century is typical of this sort of work.[42] Ghulam Ali Khan's painting of the Diwan-i Khas (fig. 87), which emphasizes that Mughal buildings were not moribund antiquities but still housed the emperor, is also a product of this movement, which seems to have begun with a school of manuscript production

Fig. 13: BIRD'S-EYE VIEW OF THE RED FORT, DELHI, by a Lucknow artist c. 1780-90 after the painting attributed to Mihr Chand done for Col. Polier. Col. Antoine Polier was based in Delhi from 1775 to 1780 and had his retained artist Mihr Chand draw some of the great Mughal monuments. His view of the Red Fort is drawn from a high, imaginary viewpoint and includes elements of the surroundings cityscape. It is centred on the Musamman Burj and imposes a bilateral symmetry upon the northern and southern halves of the Red Fort that is not of course present in reality. In this slightly later version, the surrounding cityscape is not shown. Shah Alam is shown proceeding from the Rang Mahal to the Diwan-i Khas.
Opaque watercolour, 29.2 x 41.5 cm. British Library, London, Add. Or.948

Fig. 14: HUMAYUN'S TOMB, by a Delhi draughtsman, 1787-90. The tomb of Humayun was built between 1562 and 1571 by two architects from Herat, Sayyid Muhammad and his father Mirak Sayyid Ghiyath. The drawing is one of two of Delhi monuments (see also fig. 15) collected 1787-90 by Lieut. William Stewart. The buildings are treated as isolated elevations against a blank ground, but are also concerned with perspective and the effects of light and shade. Stewart was a draughtsman and surveyor and would seem to have influenced the local draughtsmen to modify their style.
Braybrooke Loan no. 1, on loan to the Victoria and Albert Museum, Indian section.

for copies of the various histories of Shahjahan's reign.[43] In these for the first time are found images of Shahjahan's buildings as isolated monuments.[44] A particularly revealing sequence in one manuscript shows the major buildings on the processional way from the Fathepuri Masjid at the end of Chandni Chowk to the Diwan-i Am itself (fig. 52). This particular manuscript was given by the Emperor Akbar II in 1815 via his son Mirza Jahangir to the magistrate at Allahabad who had control of the imprisoned prince, neatly demonstrating the influential role such gifts were meant to play.[45] An interesting picture in a slightly later manuscript appears to show the arrangements of the imperial Hayat Bakhsh garden between the Shah Burj and the hamman in about 1830 (fig. 26). Stylistically these paintings are the forerunners of many sets produced in the 1830s.[46]

Two other artistic events of importance could have served as the catalysts initiating this change in Delhi topographical drawings begun by Ghulam Ali Khan in 1817. The first

Fig. 15: SAFDAR JANG'S TOMB, by a Delhi draughtsman, 1787-90. Nawab Safdar Jang inherited the governorship of the Subah of Avadh from his father-in-law Sadat Khan Burhan al-Mulk in 1739. When he died in 1753 his son Nawab Shujauddaula moved his body back to Delhi where he built for him in 1753-54 the last great Mughal tomb. It was based on the model of Humayun's Tomb, with a domed tomb square in plan centered in a char bagh garden. Like fig. 14, the drawing was done for Lieut. William Stewart when he was deputy commandant of the escort to the Resident at Sindhia's court 1787-90.
Braybrooke Loan no. 5, on loan to the Victoria and Albert Museum, Indian section.

was the visit to Delhi in 1815 of the Calcutta artist Sita Ram, the retained artist of Lord Moira, afterward Lord Hastings, governor general (1813-22), and of Lady Hastings. Sita Ram drew in ten volumes, each containing twenty-three large watercolour paintings, views taken on the Hastings' journey from Calcutta to Haryana and back. His views of the monuments of India are in a 'picturesque' style derived from William Hodges.[47] That is to say, the monuments are placed within their urban or landscape setting which is peopled with appropriate personages going about their business. Architectural detail and accuracy are sacrificed to overall aesthetic effect. Landscape and skies are drawn and coloured in accordance with picturesque conventions. One of the most effective of Sita Ram's thirty views of Delhi shows the Kalan Masjid with Lady Hastings approaching it to make a visit, a view that elevates a relatively small mosque into a towering edifice very much in the 'picturesque' manner (fig. 25). Similarly, his view of the Jama Masjid

Fig. 16: THE GOLDEN MOSQUE OF NAWAB JAVED KHAN, by Thomas Daniell, 1789. Thomas Daniell and his nephew William were the first professional topographical artists to reach Delhi in 1789. Their 144 aquatint views of India published as *Oriental Scenery* between 1795 and 1808 include twelve views of Delhi. Thomas's drawings done on the spot and washed within the next few months are often more interesting than the prints. This view is of the small Golden Mosque built in the name of Qudsiya Begum by Nawab Javed Khan in 1747 outside the Delhi Gate of the Red Fort (visible on the right).
Pencil and wash, 38 x 53.5 cm. British Library, London WD179.

clears away the clutter of buildings that surrounded it in the early nineteenth century and presents a monument isolated in its magnificence (fig. 81).

For reasons of protocol, being unable to agree how to meet the emperor, Lord Hastings did not himself go to Delhi but his wife did, taking Sita Ram with her. She stayed with the Resident Charles Metcalfe in the Shalimar Gardens north of the city, where he had built himself an agreeable garden house. Since it would have been inappropriate for her to visit the emperor herself, there are no views by Sita Ram of the palace buildings except that he got himself to the top of the Lahore Gate of the fort and drew the internal arrangements of the palace (fig. 28). Either the visit was very hurried or the awe and majesty which he felt emanating from the *Qila-i Mubarik* was too much for him, since the result is hardly accurate except for the top of the great arcaded *chatta* in front of him and the gardens on either side of it. He also turned himself round and drew the Chandni Chowk (fig. 6). Sita Ram could be a superb architectural draughtsman for detail, but this sort of view was clearly beyond his abilities for naturalistic expression and he reverted to a traditional kind of 'ideal view'. Among his other striking images are some of the earliest paintings illustrating the pre-Mughal cities of Delhi (fig. 96). It is interesting how Sita Ram's picturesque compositions are mirrored by photographers half a century later (compare figs 54 with 57).

The other artistic event of importance at this time was the work commissioned from Delhi artists by William Fraser and his brother James in 1815-16.[48] William Fraser worked with the successive Residents at Delhi from 1805 and became Agent himself (the post was downgraded from Resident) in 1832. For much of that time he was responsible for running the Delhi Territory. His brother James Baillie Fraser, a Calcutta merchant who was also a competent artist, visited his brother in Delhi in 1815-16 and commissioned him to have figures drawn by Delhi artists that he expected to be able to incorporate into his own views. This soon expanded into a much larger project of obtaining drawings of groups and individuals from Delhi and its neighbourhood as records of local life.

All these portraits are remarkable for the freedom of their poses and their engagement with the viewer (fig. 79). In the painting of the village of Raniya, however, the artist integrated people and their landscape and village setting in a way never before attempted in Indian painting, so that interest is scattered throughout the drawing. We do not unfortunately know who the principal artist working for the Frasers may have been. The letters and diaries of the brothers refer only to the 'artist' and never give a name, except only three paintings in a different style which they write are by the Patna artists Lallji and his son Hulas Lal.[49] While speculation has centred round the name of Ghulam Ali Khan as being the major Fraser artist, this was before the discovery of three ascribed drawings of 1817 (fig. 87) and 1822, which show him to have begun his career as a topographical artist with a very indifferent command of figural drawing. His earliest ascribed portraits, of Akbar II and his son Mirza Salim of 1827, bear no resemblance to the work of the major Fraser artist.[50] It is only with his paintings of James Skinner's durbar and farm at Hansi in this same year that he begins to exhibit the elegant stylisations and elongations that characterize his other work for Skinner and later patrons.[51] It is possible that he may have learned these stylized elongations at the feet of the major Fraser artist of the Raniya village scene.

Ghulam Ali Khan is most well known for his later portraits and durbar scenes, but he also may have been responsible for the transition in style from architectural drawings to a 'picturesque' style in which the monuments were placed in appropriate landscape or urban settings. Two such drawings ascribed to him are dated 1822. Both have inscriptions in Persian with a *nagari* transliteration and an English annotation which alone contains the authorship statement. As in his view of the Diwan-i Khas of 1817, people are going about their daily lives as part of the composition. One of these views (of which fig. 29 is another unattributed

Fig. 17: THE JAMA MASJID OF DELHI, by Thomas Longcroft (fl. 1780-1811), 1786. Longcroft came to India in 1783 hoping to make a living with his painting. However, he purchased an estate at Koil near Aligarh in 1787 and became an indigo planter, but continued to draw views seen in his travels throughout northern India. This impressive drawing of Jama Masjid was taken three years earlier than those of Thomas Daniell, and unlike him, Longcroft managed to include the entire structure in his view.
Pencil and grey wash, 39.5 x 66 cm. British Library, London, WD 2419.

version) is of the Red Fort seen from across the river Yamuna and focussed on the Asad Burj at the south-east corner of the palace, with oblique views of the river façade receding to the Shah Burj on the right and of the south-east angled wall of the fort receding towards the Delhi Gate on the left.[52] At least that is the intention, but it is evident that the artist has difficulty in suggesting the recession of the eastern wall with the palace buildings, but disguises it through raising up the ground on this side of the river. Ghulam Ali Khan may indeed have had a crutch of sorts for this view, since another undated drawing from the Hyde collection, from the same set as the view of the Diwan-i Khas above, is of a similar view of the Red Fort but with a watermark date of 1809 (fig. 24). It must be earlier than Ghulam Ali Khan's 1822 view. What is an innovation in both these views is the fact that there have been modern additions to Shahjahan's architecture, a feature we shall be returning to in a moment.

The other view dated 1822 and ascribed to Ghulam Ali Khan is one of the shrine of Bu Ali Qalandari at Panipat outside Delhi. Here his traditional viewpoint avoids the

Fig. 18: THE ZINAT AL-MASAJID MOSQUE, by Thomas Longcroft (fl. 1780-1811), 1793. The mosque was built by Aurangzeb's daughter Zinat al-Nisa Begum (d. 1710), a pious and learned lady, and she lies buried there. In Longcroft's view the city wall with its towers recedes north along the river Yamuna, leading to the Asad Burj of the Red Fort. The crenellated wall stretching out from the city wall enclosed the garden of a haveli that once belonged to Sa'adatallah Khan but in the nineteenth century belonged to Nawab Ahmad Bakhsh Khan of Firozepur.
Pencil and grey wash, 42 x 60.7 cm. British Museum, London, 1877.04-14.104.

perspective difficulties of his views of the Red Fort and of the Diwan-i Khas by being centred behind the woman in yellow in the middle of the picture, rather as in Latif's view of the Jama Masjid (fig. 19). By lowering the viewpoint he has also found it easier to handle the perspective of the sidewalls which appear to rise up as they approach the viewer and he has managed to achieve real depth in the painting.

Whether or not the attributions to Ghulam Ali Khan are reliable is neither here nor there: the fact remains that about this time a Delhi artist of genius decided to invent an entirely new concept of 'picturesque' views of Delhi. This new picturesque approach to the monuments of Delhi was immediately taken up by other artists and a topographical studio began operations about this time perhaps under Ghulam Ali Khan's direction or perhaps independently. Both the Panipat and the Red Fort views were immediately copied in a set dating from 1820-25 (fig. 29).[53] This view of the Red Fort shows even more clearly than

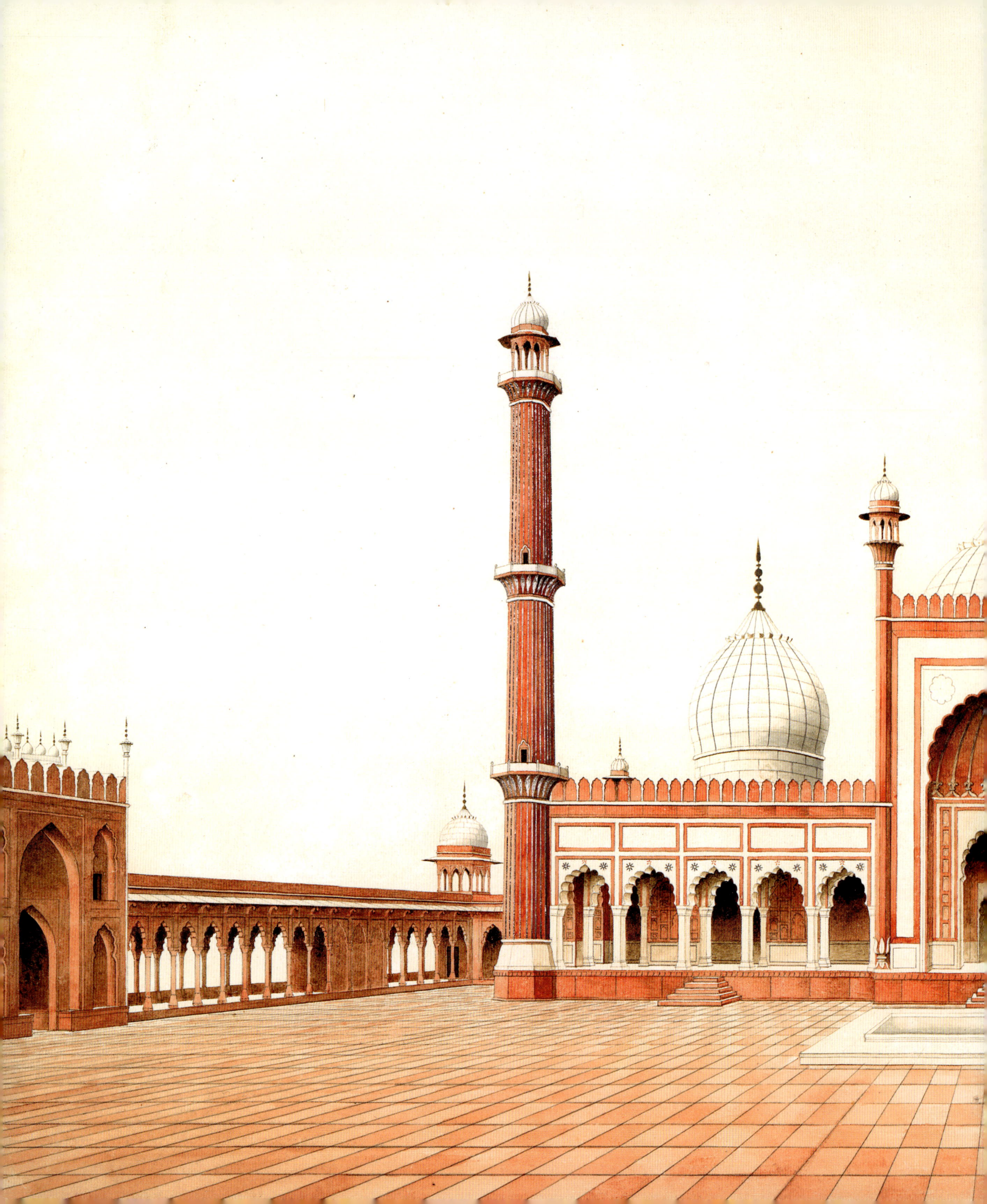

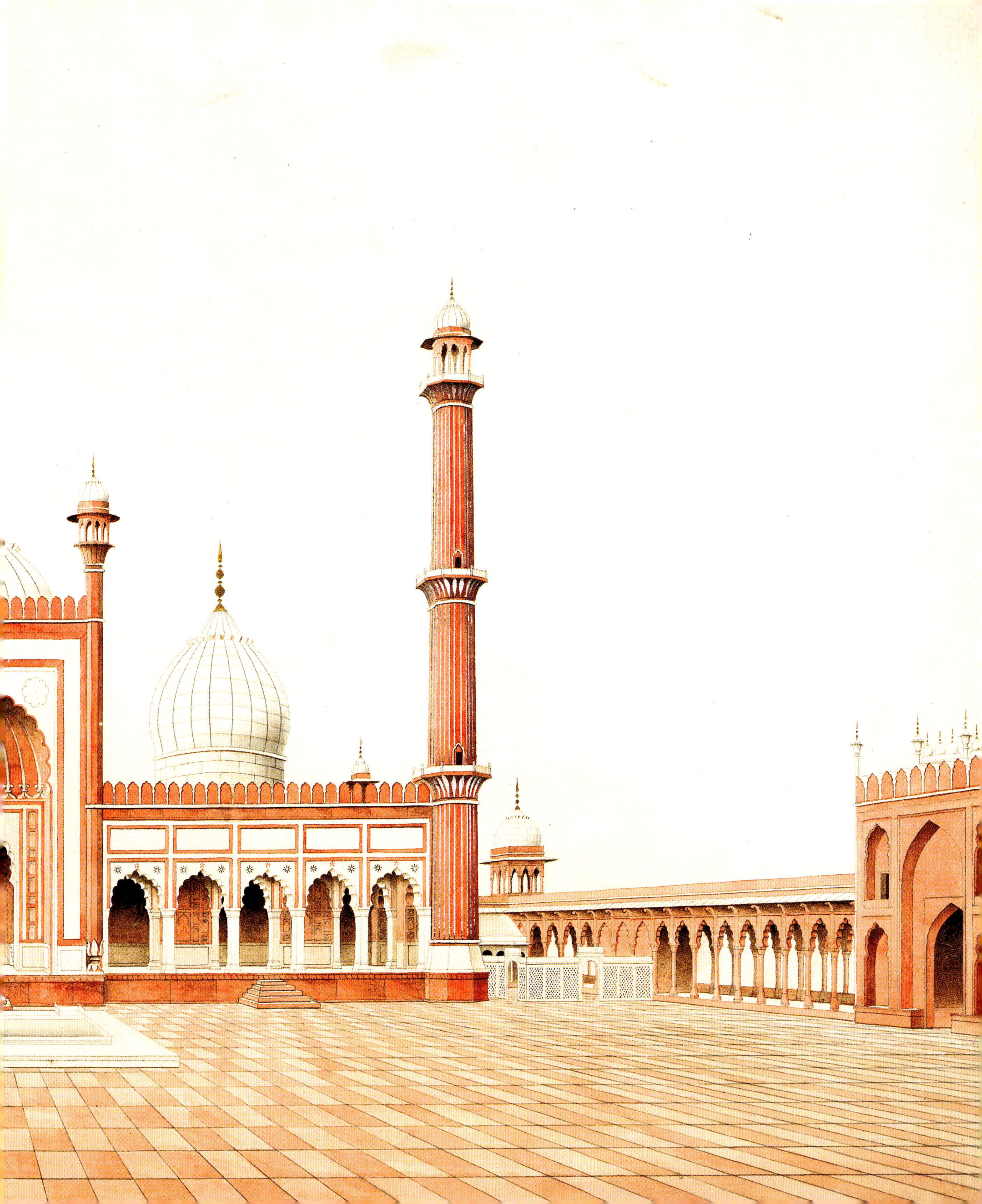

Fig. 19: THE JAMA MASJID, by the Agra artist Latif, c. 1820. Latif was one of the best known artists of architectural drawings in Agra as well as an architect. His drawings show the monuments in elevation against a plain background. Here he imposes a strict bilateral symmetry on the monument that is derived from earlier views of the Delhi palaces. The splayed effect of the side walls suggests that Latif was making use of a camera obscura. The drawing is from a set of twenty views mostly of Agra collected by John Bax (1793-1863) who was in the Bombay Civil Service from 1812 onwards. Latif was responsible for the design of the Mughal-style mausoleum of Col. John Hessing (d. 1803) in Agra, and according to Fanny Parkes in 1835 also 'inlays marble with precious stones, after the style of the work in the Taj' (Parkes 1850, vol. I, 418, 15 March 1835).
Watercolour, 53.5 x 71 cm. British Library, London, Add.Or.1806.

Fig. 20: PANORAMIC VIEW OF THE EAST FACE OF THE RED FORT, by an Agra or Delhi artist, c. 1820. The viewpoint is relatively high enabling one to see over the river wall and across the fort to the inside of the high southern and western walls, with the backs of the Delhi and Lahore gates and the Jama Masjid prominent in the distance. Shahjahan's pavilions are all visible along the wall: the Musamman Burj and Khwabgah in the centre with the Diwan-i Khas, to the right the hamman with the domes of Aurangzeb's Moti Masjid behind it, the Moti Mahal and Shah Burj, and to the left the Rang Mahal, the Chota Rang Mahal or Mumtaz Mahal with associated courtyards forming the zenana, and the Asad Burj.
Watercolour, 30 x 94.5 cm. British Library, London, Add.Or.540.

Fig. 21: THE QUTB MINAR, by the Agra artist Latif, c. 1820. This and the drawing of the Jama Masjid are the only drawings of Delhi by Latif in the set of architectural drawings mostly of Agra collected by John Bax by 1820. Standing 72.5 metres tall, the minaret was built as a celebratory victory tower as well as for its normal function to issue the call to prayer for the adjacent congregational mosque. It was begun by Qutb al-Din Aibak in 1198 and completed by his successor Iltutmish in 1215, although the two upper tiers were rebuilt at later dates. The topmost pavilion was reduced to an arch in Daniell's view drawn in 1789 and even this has now gone. Col. Robert Smith of the Bengal Engineers added a Mughal-style pavilion to the top in 1828. In this view Latif concentrates particularly on the damage to the stonework. Such defects or later additions were normally ignored by these artists who wanted to convey rather an ideal image of perfection.
Watercolour, 53.5 x 71 cm. British Library, London, Add.Or.1807

सलातीनोंकीहवेली

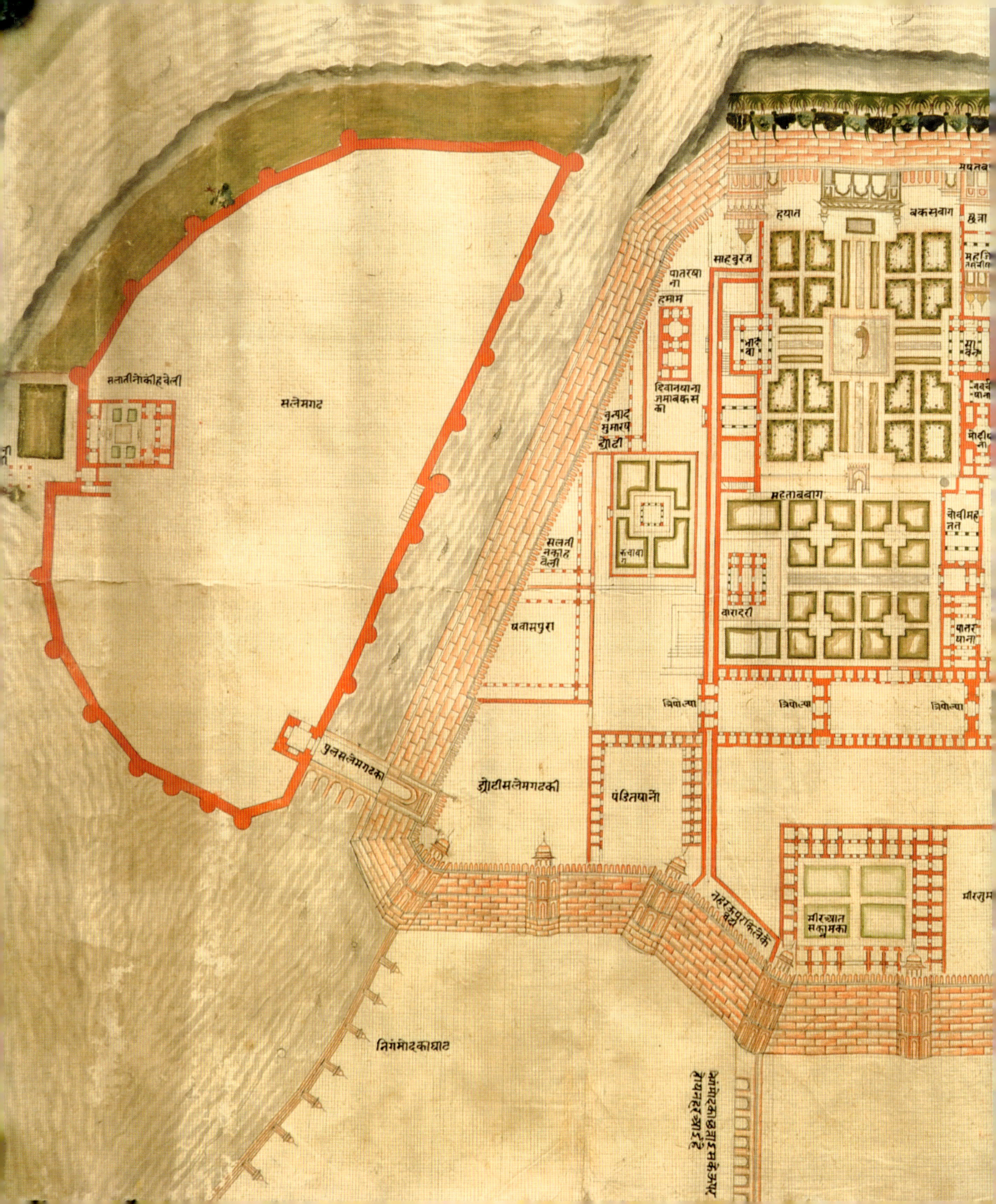

सलेमगट

पातरखाना
हमाम
साहबुरज
हयात बकसवाग बेजा
महर्रिसितस्वानेका
मर्दाना
जनानी
नौबत खाना
दीवानखाना जमाबखसकी
बुन्याद मुमारुषे रोटी
सुन्चावा
महताबबाग
नौबीमहल नत
सलनी निकाहहवेली
बवानपुरा
बारादरी
पातरखाना
पनसलेमगटका
त्रिपोल्या त्रिपोल्या त्रिपोल्या
ड्योटीसलेमगटकी
पंडितखानी
मीरआतसकूमका
निर्गमोदकाघाट
नहरकुएप्राकलेकी
मीररुम

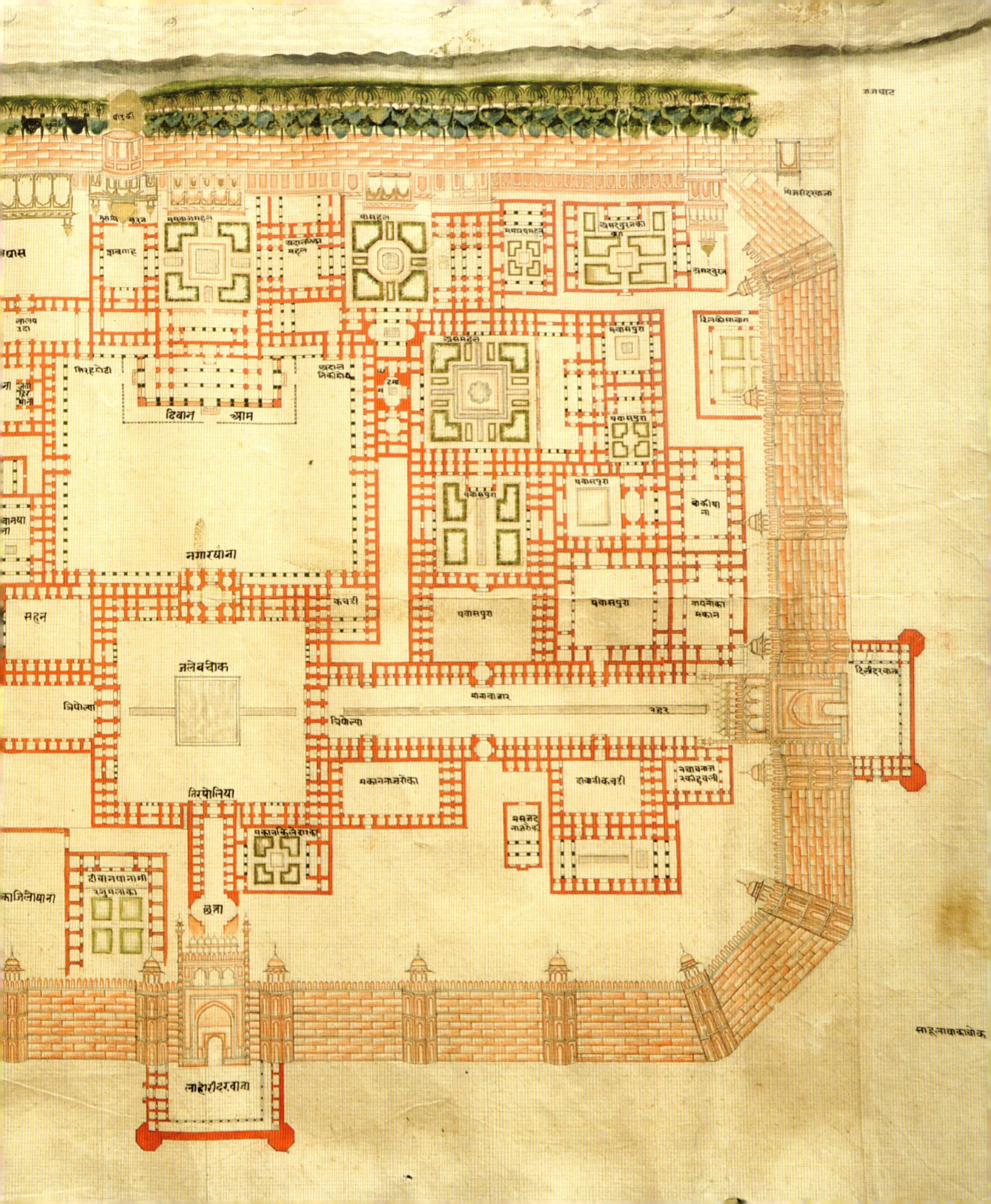
दिवान
आम
नगारखाना
सहन
जलेबचौक
त्रिपोल्या
त्रिपोल्या
तिरपोलिया
कचहरी
नहर
छत्रा
लाहोरीदरवाजा

the version ascribed to Ghulam Ali Khan in 1822 that it is based on actual observation and is not simply replicating pre-existent models such as the panoramic views (fig. 20). Above the palace walls can be seen structures that were built in Shahjahan's courtyards by the male relatives of the emperors Akbar II and Bahadur Shah II (1838-58).

Although it has been asserted that the Mughal emperors and princes did not behave like those in Lucknow in imitating European ways, these paintings disprove this contention.[54] At least three new palaces based on European architectural models were built within Shahjahan's courtyards and Shahjahan's buildings were altered to include European classical features.[55] One in the courtyard of the Rang Mahal was built by Mirza Babar, Bahadur Shah's eldest surviving brother, who 'built a European-style house whose Corinthian columns and stucco walls horrified admirers of Shahjahan's architecture. He wore European clothes, or rather, uniforms and drove about the city in a coach with six horses.'[56] Syed Ahmed Khan wrote in 1847: 'It [the Rang Mahal] is the largest palace (of this complex). It has a spacious court, with a garden, water-canals and fountains, which all have now vanished and unshapely houses have sprung up in their place.'[57] Various views show its upper stories poking over the roof of the Diwan-i Am (fig. 30), while it can be seen as the one on the left of the two towers to the left of the Rang Mahal in the view from across the river (fig. 29). The other tower belongs to the palace of the heir-apparent that was begun by Mirza Jahangir, Akbar's favourite son. Syed Ahmed Khan wrote again: 'This building is situated on the south of the Imtiaz-Mahal [the Rang Mahal] .... It is an extremely beautiful building but due to its alterations by Mirza Jehangir Bahadur it has lost much of its original charm.'[58] Other such palaces were also built later in this area as we shall see.

Other Delhi artists too now took up this new 'picturesque' style, as found in watercolours of the tombs of Humayun and of Safdar Jang datable to c. 1820 (fig. 33).[59] These two drawings are appended to a set of mostly Agra views by the Agra artist Latif, although it does include his two Delhi views of the Jama Masjid and the Qutb Minar noted above (figs 19, 21). Delhi artists were now abandoning the bilateral symmetry favoured by artists such as Latif for a more picturesque handling of the subject. Although Humayun's tomb is viewed centrally, the viewpoint is off-centre, thereby creating interesting angles

Preceding Pages: Fig. 22: PLAN OF THE RED FORT, Jaipur, late-18th century. This map constitutes the best available evidence of the layout of the Red Fort in the 18th century and the first to show its true plan. Unexpected inscriptions include swapping the names for the Khas Mahal (now called the Rang Mahal) and the Mumtaz Mahal (now the Museum), presumably by mistake. The central courtyard, the Jilau Khana is labelled Jalebi Chauk. The residences north of the Chatta were allotted to the titled officials Mir Atash (the Master of the Ordnance) and Mir Jumla, while the Fort Commandant lived just to the south of it. The road south to the Delhi Gate was then the Mina Bazaar, while a large part of the zenana area to its east is labelled Khawaspura, the area occupied by servants. In Salimgarh, the buildings are labelled Salatin ki haveli, i.e. the prisons where surplus Mughal princes were kept.
© *The Trustees of the Maharaja Sawai Man Sigh II Museum, City Palace, Jaipur, Kapad Dvara collection, no. 122, 113 x 176 cm.*

for the view of the barber's tomb to the side (fig. 33). Safdar Jang's tomb, on the other hand, is drawn from an off-centre viewpoint focussing on the side elevation, so that the rest of the tomb and the garden are viewed at an angle. It is clear that Sita Ram's view of the same tomb done in 1815 must have had some effect on the Delhi artists since these two views borrow various elements from it (fig. 32).

While this new 'picturesque' style appealed to Delhi artists in particular, Agra artists continued in their more clinical approach. A set dating from the early 1820s with watermarks of 1817 is the first such set not only consistently to place the monuments in an appropriate setting, but also to contain mostly Delhi views.[60] This set remained the standard for future subjects. Although a few of the views were based on earlier models, most of them had to be begun on the basis of actual observation. The view from the south-east of the Red Fort across the river Yamuna we have already looked at (fig. 29). The Diwan-i Khas, based on Ghulam Ali Khan's view of 1817, is the only internal view within the palace. The Jama Masjid is included of course, this time a slightly angled view of the *iwan* of the mosque that is based on the view in Daniell's *Oriental Scenery* and copying the splayed effect caused by the use of the *camera obscura*.[61] Also based on one of Daniell's views is the Qudsiya Bagh, the palace of the Qudsiya Begum, the favourite wife of the Emperor Muhammad Shah (1719-148), on the river north of the Red Fort.[62] For such a sharp recession in space some artists still needed the prop of a pre-existent view.

Other later Mughal mosques in Shahjahanabad are now included, such as the Zinat al-Masajid and the Sonehri mosque of Bahadur Ali Khan both in Daryaganj south of the Red Fort. The great Mughal tombs of Humayun and of Safdar Jang are of course present, based on earlier models. A more distant view of Safdar Jang's tomb in its garden is new. Two Muslim shrines also appear: that of Bu Ali Qalandar at Panipat, after Ghulam Ali Khan's view of 1822, and the Qadam Sharif at Paharganj (fig. 58). The Kotla of Firoz Shah and the Qutb Minar complex represent the earlier cities of Delhi, while the shrine and mosque of Nizamuddin Auliya also sometimes appears in these sets.

All of these paintings are slightly off-centre or angled views in keeping with the ideas of the picturesque. A painting from a small set with a watermark of 1834 takes this idea even further, and shows us the Jama Masjid in its urban setting (fig. 35).[63] The mosque's great *iwan* and domes and its east gateway are dramatically foreshortened in this view from the rooftops of the bazaar to the north. This painting marks the debut of the artist Mazhar Ali Khan, the first purely topographical artist known by name from late Mughal Delhi. He is an artist for whom difficult viewpoints held no terrors and who was obviously prepared to visit actual sites to make sketches rather than rely on works of earlier artists. His major work is the great 360° panorama of Delhi viewed from the Lahore Gate of the Red Fort done in 1846 which similarly makes use of dramatic foreshortening (fig. 99).

The cultural renaissance which the city of Delhi experienced after 1803 produced by the 1830s a lively interest in the antiquities of Delhi. Their leading investigator was

Fig. 23: DIWAN-I KHAS, RED FORT, perhaps by an eastern Indian artist, c. 1810-15. The drawing forms part of the collection of James Chichely Hyde (1789-1867) which was made in India from 1806 to 1837. It seems to be the earliest known rendering of the Diwan-i Khas. On the right can be seen Shahjahan's private apartments behind the one qanat the artist has decided to include and the beginning of the now vanished arcades that continued them round the courtyard in front of the Diwan-i Khas. Stylistically, it bears no resemblance to contemporary Delhi work and may be a version of a drawing done by one of Col. Mackenzie's draughtsmen.
Watercolour, 49 x 61 cm. on paper watermarked 1809. British Library, London, Add. Or.3245.

the young Syed Ahmed Khan (1817-98).[64] In 1847 there appeared the first edition of his *Asar al-Sanadid*, an account in Urdu of the history of Delhi and of its monuments, illustrated with nearly 130 woodcuts by the artists Faiz Ali Khan and Mirza Shah Rukh Beg, the latter the nephew of Ghulam Ali Khan (figs 30, 31, 94).[65] Some of the views are based on the earlier sets discussed above, but the majority of Delhi's monuments had never been drawn before. Syed Ahmed Khan's taste was catholic, and includes Hindu and Jain temples as well as Skinner's church of St. James and the houses of local

Fig. 24: THE RED FORT, DELHI, SEEN FROM THE OPPOSITE BANK OF THE YAMUNA, perhaps by an eastern Indian artist, c. 1810-15. This is another early view of Delhi from the Hyde collection. The artist here has simply taken a panoramic view of the Red Fort such as in fig. 27 and placed it across the drawing and tried to adapt the landscape to fit the ostensible viewpoint. Only Salimgarh and the Delhi Gate show any hint of the recession resulting from this chosen viewpoint. Visible are the new jharokhas added to the Musamman Burj, Khwabgah, and Rang Mahal and the tall palace of Mirza Babar erected in the Rang Mahal courtyard (seen here in front of the Lahore Gate). While the Shah Burj tower to the extreme right is in good condition, the Asad Burj to the left has collapsed. *Watercolour, 48.5 x 60 cm. on paper watermarked 1809. British Library, London, Add. Or.3244.*

notables. In his views of the Delhi palace and fort can be seen the new additions by the imperial relations: some of his adverse comments have already been noted above.[66]

Syed Ahmed Khan dedicated his book to a fellow antiquarian, Sir Thomas Theophilus Metcalfe.[67] Metcalfe had lived in Delhi since 1813, as assistant to the various Residents and Agents, including his brother Charles Metcalfe, until in 1835 he himself became the Agent representing British power at Delhi. Soon after in 1837 he had to deal with

Fig. 25: KALAN MASJID WITH LADY HASTINGS VISITING, by Sita Ram, 1815. From the albums of drawings done by Sita Ram for Lord Hastings 1814-15. A view of the entrance courtyard and east facade to the Kalan Masjid with its flight of steps to the entrance gateway. Sita Ram exaggerates the vertiginous nature of the approach in accordance with picturesque conventions. The Kalan or Kali Masjid was built in 1387 by the son of Khan-i-Jahan Junan Shah, prime minister of Firoz Shah Tughluq (1351-88).
Watercolour, 38 x 53.7 cm. British Library, London, Add.Or.4817.

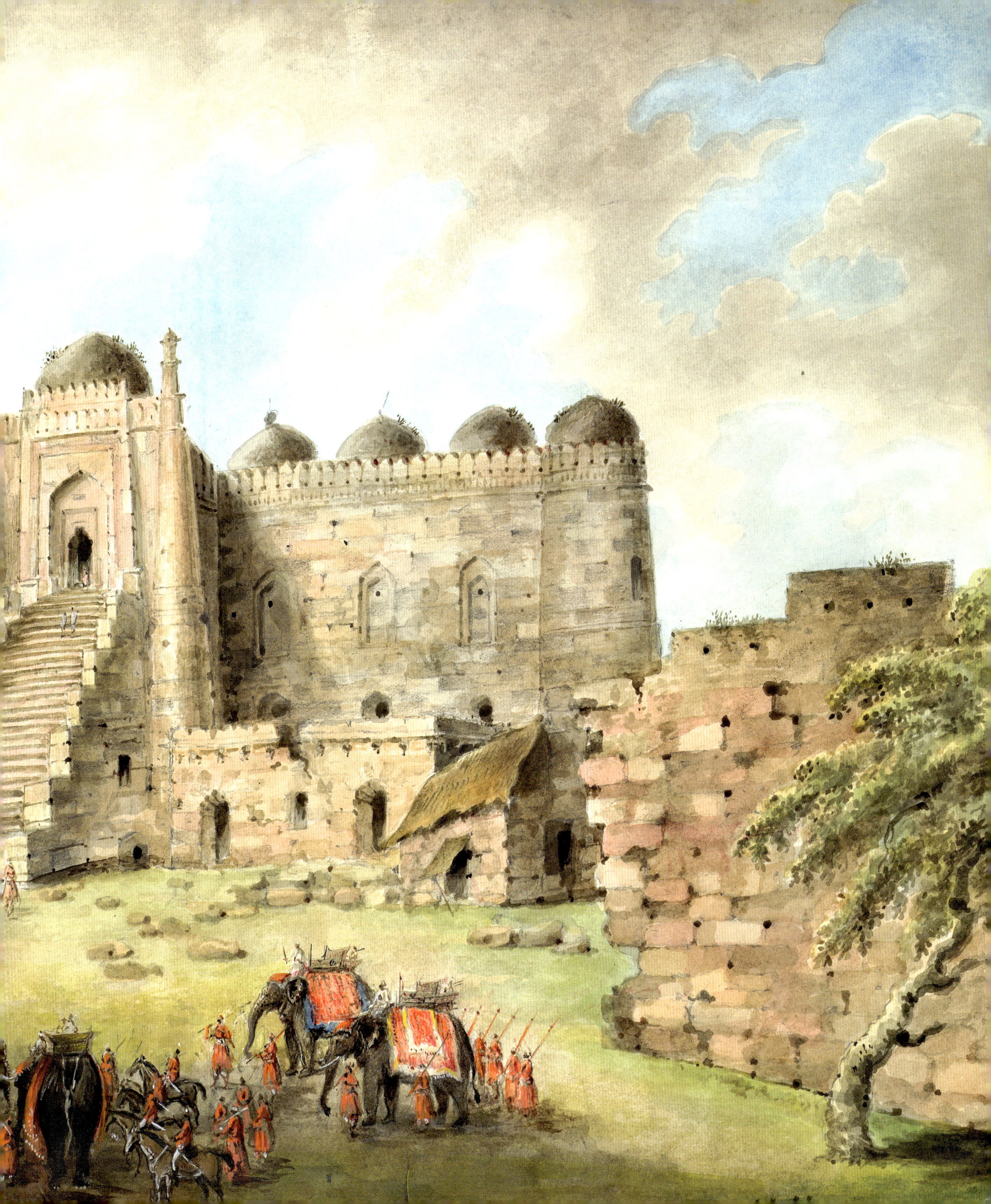

Fig. 26: GARDENS OF THE DELHI PALACE, by a Delhi artist, c. 1830. From a History of Shahjahan written by Muhammad Salih Kanbu, *'Amal-i Salih*, c. 1830. The artist has given us a charming picture of the Hayat Bakhsh garden in the Delhi palace focussed on the central pool of the Char Bagh garden over which Bahadur Shah was to erect his Zafar Mahal in 1842. On the terrace is the now vanished Moti Mahal with the Shah Burj to the left and a matching even if non-existent pavilion to the right against the back of the Hamman, linked by a serpentine Nahr-i Bihisht. Men dressed in short Shahjahani jamas stand around and even disport themselves in the pool, a lèse-majesté surely impossible in the 17th century but perhaps permissible in the 19th.
Opaque watercolour, size of folio 24.5 x 39.5 cm. British Library, London, Or. 2157, f.732.

the death of Akbar II and smooth handing over to the new emperor, Bahadur Shah II (1837-58) (fig. 47). In 1830 he had begun to build a mansion, Metcalfe House, by the river north of the city, where he housed his family's possessions brought from England (fig. 36). Metcalfe's interest in the history of Delhi was as intense as Syed Ahmed Khan's and between 1842 and 1844 he compiled a manuscript book, entitled *Reminiscences of Imperial Delhi*, in which he wrote about the history of the city and its monuments based on his researches. The book is centred around some 120 topographical paintings which he had obtained from Mazhar Ali Khan and his studio.[68] The work of assembling the illustrations for both Metcalfe's and Syed Ahmed Khan's works seems to have been undertaken simultaneously: sometimes there is coincidence of views and sometimes not.

Fig. 27: SHAHJAHAN RIDING PAST THE PALACE, by a Delhi artist, c. 1815.
Trying to resuscitate past Mughal glories in the Delhi of Akbar II, new illustrated manuscripts of the histories of Shahjahan was produced. This painting is from another manuscript and shows, immediately after the Diwan-i Am, Shahjahan riding on the opposite bank of the Yamuna past the imperial palace, all white marble and gilt on its red sandstone wall. Note the imperial pigeons flying above the palace. This is one of the earliest depictions of the palace in a picturesque landscape setting, predating Ghulam Ali Khan's further explorations of this theme.
Opaque watercolour, 14.5 x 30 cm. British Library, London, Add. 20735, f.371.

Where pre-existing images of the monuments existed, the artists of both books used them, so some of the images are the same as those from the set of the 1820s noticed above (for example fig. 58). The paintings in Metcalfe's book are laid down, so their watermarked dates cannot be ascertained, but they are very similar to another unascribed set with watermarked dates 1830-36 but obviously from the same studio.[69]

Other paintings in Metcalfe's book had to be begun from scratch. A number of images of the interior of the palace are all entirely new. These include the interior of the Diwan-i Khas and views of the Khwabgah and Shahjahan's screen as well as of the Diwan-i Am, the *jharokha* throne and its decoration. Also appearing for the first time are views of the Moti Masjid, the emperor's private mosque in the palace, and the Shah Burj, the tower at the north east of the palace marking the end of the terrace (fig. 95). Many of these palace views are ascribed to Mazhar Ali Khan and it is no doubt owing to Metcalfe's connection with the palace that he was able to gain access to the buildings. They do not appear in the similar set noticed above.

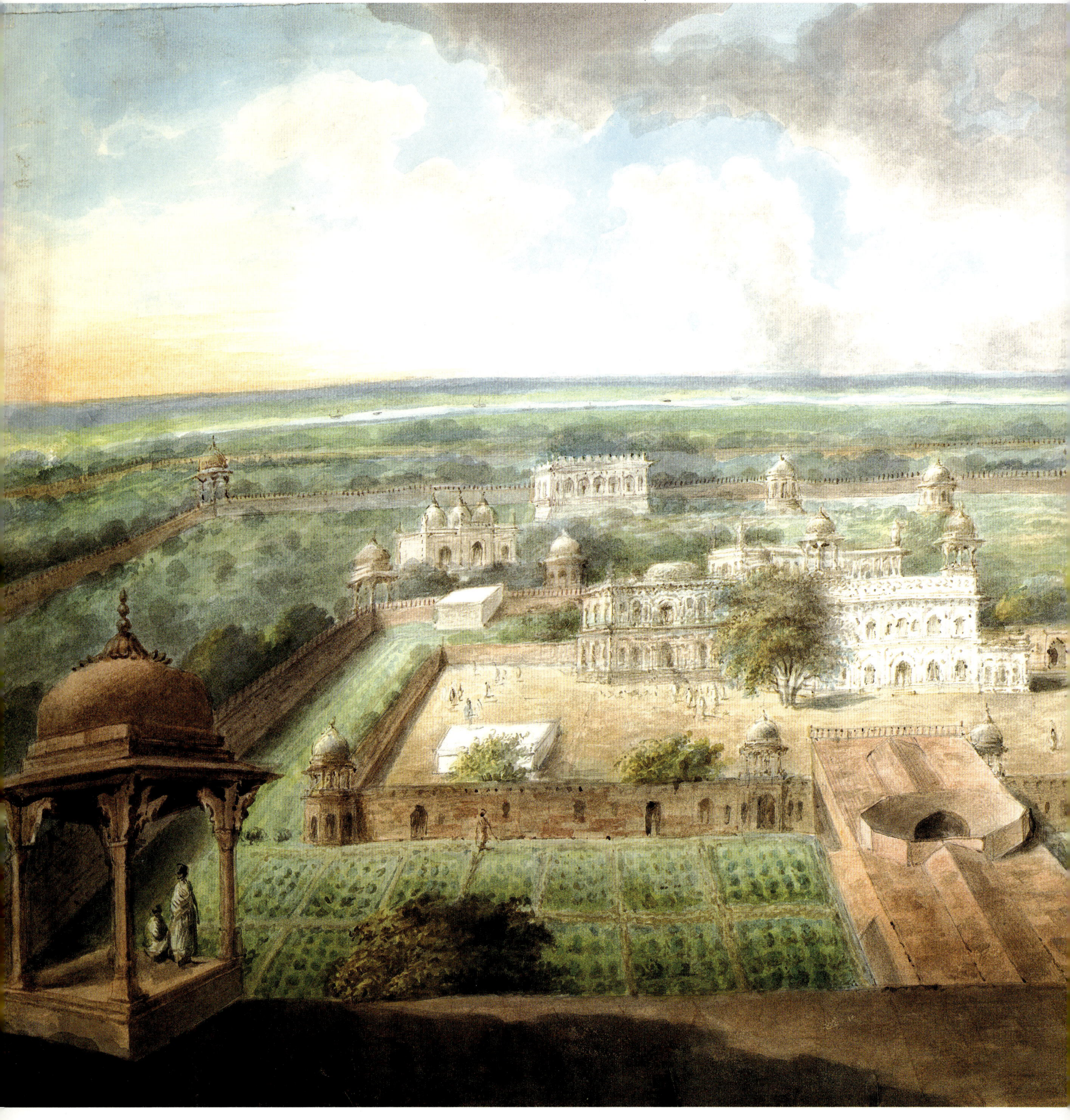

Fig. 28: VIEW OF THE PALACE FROM THE LAHORE GATE, by Sita Ram, 1815. Either the visit was very hurried or the awe and majesty which Sita Ram felt emanating from the *Qila-i Mubarik* was too much for him, since this view is hardly accurate except for the top of the great arcaded chatta in front of him and the gardens on either side of it.
Watercolour, 35 x 52.1 cm. British Library, London, Add. Or.4826

68

Fig. 29: S.E. VIEW OF THE RED FORT SEEN FROM THE OPPOSITE BANK OF THE YAMUNA, by a Delhi artist, c. 1820-25. This view of the Red Fort is from a set of topographical drawings that is the first to include mostly Delhi rather than Agra views and also to put the monuments into their landscape setting in a picturesque manner. In this picture the palace wall and the buildings thereon recede only slightly in perspective, the landscape is more skilfully manipulated particularly in order to make them appear to do so. It is a copy of one now in a private collection ascribed to Ghulam Ali Khan. It is a much more successful version of fig. 24 in its handling of the perspective. Here, the Asad Burj is in good condition unlike in fig. 24. The new palaces built by the Mughal princes are very obvious.
Watercolour, 23.5 x 33.5. British Library, London, Add. Or.3119.

Fig. 30: THE DIWAN-I AM, by Mirza Shah Rukh Beg, 1847. This is a woodcut print from Syed Ahmed Khan's *Asar al-Sanadid*, an account in Urdu of the history of Delhi and of its monuments, illustrated with nearly 130 woodcuts by the artists Faiz Ali Khan and Mirza Shah Rukh Beg, and published in Delhi in 1847. This view of the Diwan-i Am gives a very good idea of changes to Shahjahan's architecture. Looming over the back of the great hall is the palace built by Mirza Babar in the courtyard of the Rang Mahal. On the right is another palace built within the zenana, called the palace of the Heir Apparent (Mirza Vali Ahad). On the left can be seen another towered structure erected in the courtyard in front of the Diwan-i Khas. This can also be seen in Mazhar Ali Khan's panorama (fig. 99) and appears to be a pigeon-house for the emperor's favourite pigeons.
Woodcut print, 20 x 32 cm. British Library, London, 14109.c.1.

We catch glimpses of Metcalfe's life in his book as he goes about his duties and his leisure hours and we can explore his relationship with the Emperor Bahadur Shah (fig. 77). Mazhar Ali Khan and his studio were also busy out in the city and its ruinous suburbs. New buildings of British interest appear for the first time in the sets of views (figs 37-38). They made a thorough survey of the monuments in the shrine of Qutb Sahib and the complex around the Qutb Minar and then did the same to those in the shrine at Nizamuddin (fig. 55).

Metcalfe is almost certainly the patron of a large-scale panorama of Delhi, nearly five metres in length, painted by Mazhar Ali Khan in 1846 from a viewpoint on top of

Fig. 31: THE HIRA MAHAL, by Mirza Shah Rukh Beg, 1847. A woodcut print from Syed Ahmed Khan's *Asar al-Sanadid*. The Hira Mahal was a small pavilion added by Bahadur Shah II in 1842 to the palace terrace between the Hamman and the Moti Mahal overlooking the Hayat Bakhsh garden. It is a small square pavilion of three bays in late Mughal style. On either side are depicted buildings in a European classical style, while another now gone was according to Syed Ahmed Khan on the far side of the Moti Mahal. There seems to be what appears to be a permanent tiled shamiana round the Hira Mahal.
Woodcut print, 15 x 20 cm. British Library, London, 14109.c.1.

the Lahore Gate of the Red Fort (fig. 99).[70] The first of the five sheets into which the panorama is divided is dominated by the upper part of the Lahore Gate, soaring upwards under the frame of the paper. The eye is naturally led in the opening panel by the artist's orthogonals firstly along the lines of the gateway north towards Metcalfe House in the distance, and secondly along the axis of the Chattah towards the heart of the imperial palace. With an almost 360° panorama the artist had to choose to begin somewhere, but it is significant that he has chosen not to centre the Mughal palace, the *Qila-i Mubarik*, in the middle of the panorama, as had done Mihr Chand (fig. 13). On the contrary, Mazhar Ali Khan has adopted a stance which links the Briton and the Mughal together in a way very similar to pages in Metcalfe's own book.

Fig. 32: SAFDAR JUNG'S TOMB, by Sita Ram, 1815. From the albums of drawings done by Sita Ram for Lord Hastings 1814-15. Sita Ram's straightforward picturesque view placing the tomb within its garden complex was influential in later Delhi topographical views (such as fig. 33).
Watercolour, 38.5 x 51.2 cm. British Library, London, Add.Or.4824.

This panorama is of the greatest importance in establishing the appearance of the palace in the Red Fort and its surroundings in the 1840s ten years before the destruction of most of the connecting arcades and minor buildings of the palace in the fort, and almost all the buildings outside the palace to a radius of 450 yards, were blown up.[71] A contemporary large-scale map of Shajahanabad is a similar product of the intellectual climate within which Syed Ahmed Khan's and Metcalfe's work took place (fig. 86).[72]

This visually stunning piece of work, the first such 360° panorama by an Indian artist, is highly skilful in its marrying up of the various disparate viewpoints into a virtually seamless whole, and in its beautiful control of both linear and aerial perspective. The monuments outside the city are dissolving into a shimmering heat haze. The vista first looks north-east towards the Metcalfe House outside the city, then turns east to take in

Fig. 33: HUMAYUN'S TOMB, by a Delhi artist, c. 1820. The tomb of Humayun is set slightly off-centre in this drawing to accommodate also the small nearby tomb known conventionally as the Barber's Tomb. Departing from convention, here the monument is depicted in a landscape with figures and is typical of the new type of drawings which developed in Delhi under the influence of the picturesque style of English prints and watercolours, particularly as transmitted through the work of artists such as Sita Ram (see fig. 32) and the Fraser artist.
Watercolour and bodycolour, 52.3 x 73.1 cm. British Library, London, Add.Or.1809.

outer courtyards of the Red Fort with the palace structures in the distance on the east wall of the fort, including more of the new buildings of the Mughal princes discussed earlier, then turns south towards the Delhi Gate of the fort. Over the wall of the fort can be seen the Jama Masjid to the south-west. Next comes the great thoroughfare of Chandni Chowk leading westwards to the Lahori Gate of the city. On the other side of the road running past the fort wall are the mansions of the Mughal nobility, with the new Neo-Classical house of the Begum Samru at the beginning of Chandni Chowk prominent among them. Finally the view turns to the north again. Beyond the city walls can be seen the Kotla Firoz Shah, Humayun's tomb, the Purana Qila, Tughlaqabad, the Qutb Minar, Safdar Jang's tomb, and the Ridge.

Mazhar Ali Khan is supposed to have gone off to Arabia later in the nineteenth century to produce paintings of all the sacred monuments of Islam at the desire of the

Grand Sharif of Mecca. That Delhi artists did paint views of the shrines of the Middle East is quite certain. Muhammad Yusuf, for example, painted the shrine of Qutb Sahib at Mehrauli in the 1840s (fig. 53), but would seem later to have gone to the Middle East, since a view of the shrine at Karbala in Iraq dated 1875 is ascribed to Muhammad Yusuf Dihlavi.[73] Another member of the family, inscribed as *Muhammad-i 'Abdallah naqsha-i navis Dihli* (Abdallah son of Muhammad the cartographer of Delhi') is recorded as the artist of a large panoramic view of Mecca, very much in the style of Mazhar Ali Khan's panorama of Delhi.[74] Both artists may indeed have been taken to Arabia as assistants by Mazhar Ali Khan during a sojourn there, which would help to explain the absence of any datable work in Delhi after 1846. Richard Burton, who famously visited Mecca and Madina in 1853, wrote: 'At Mecca some Indians support themselves by depicting the holy shrines; their works are a truly oriental mixture of ground plan and elevation, drawn with pen and ink and brightened with the most vivid colours …'[75]

The panorama is the culmination of the Delhi topographical school but it is by no means the end of it. The studio continued to produce larger versions of some of these scenes noticed in the Metcalfe Album such as the Diwan-i Am and the shrine at Panipat. A new development is panoramic vistas in small. One appears in the Metcalfe Album while versions on ivory appear a little later (fig. 34).[76] Later in the century the major artist of topographical views is Ismail Khan, who is criticized for often working from photographs.[77] As Indian artists invariably worked from earlier drawings or sketches, this is hardly a damning criticism. His view of the Qutb Minar from the early 1860s on a large oval sheet of ivory is one of his best works. He and his studio and perhaps rivals continued to turn out topographical views of Delhi, and indeed of other monuments elsewhere, normally now painted on ivory. These were often mounted as brooches or other items of jewellery or inlaid into carved ebony frames or into boxes. The fashion came from Victorian Europe where plaques of painted or enamelled porcelain or of micro-mosaic showing views in Italy or elsewhere were inlaid into furniture and boxes or mounted as brooches.

We have been concentrating so far mostly on views of Delhi painted by Delhi artists. Sita Ram was the most important Indian artist from outside Delhi to have delineated its monuments, but there were others. An unknown Rajasthani artist perhaps from Kishangarh created a fascinating view of the Faiz Bazaar with a Mughal procession heading towards the Delhi Gate of the city (fig. 42).[78] The visit to Delhi of Maharao Ram Singh of Kotah in 1842 prompted the creation of a very large painting by Kotah artists showing the event in overhead bird's-eye viewpoint from outside the Lahori Gate of the city, so that the processional route along Chandni Chowk and the layout of the Red Fort itself are very clearly depicted (fig. 80).[79]

Of course there were other artists also at work in this period delineating the city. Thomas and William Daniell were the first of a series of British artists both amateur and

Fig. 34: PANORAMA OF DELHI SEEN FROM THE RIDGE, attributed to Mazhar Ali Khan, c. 1845. The view is taken from the Ridge, in the neighbourhood of Hindu Rao's house, and encompasses the northern and eastern walls with the Kashmiri, Mori, Kabuli, and Lahori gates. Within the city the Jama Masjid, the Red Fort and Salimgarh, and St. James's Church are prominent, as are the minarets of the Fatehpuri Masjid and the Akbarabadi Masjid. Outside the walls, the military camp is very prominent while on the left the Civil Lines with Ludlow Castle are seen with the river beyond. Perspective is most skilfully handled in the recession of the foreground dotted with trees, rocks and animals. The artist is still very Indian though in that he seems to have changed his viewpoint so that we see both the northern and western walls of the city, the eastern and western facades of the Jama Masjid and the whole of the Delhi Gate as well as the Lahore Gate of the Red Fort. Felice Beato took a photographic panorama from this same spot in 1858.
Watercolour on ivory, 10.5 x 21 cm. British Library, London, Add.Or.5476

Following pages: Fig. 35: THE JAMA MASJID FROM THE NORTH, Mazhar Ali Khan, c. 1835-40. This is the first drawing that can be associated with the topographical artist Mazhar Ali Khan, whose studio dominated the production of such views of Delhi in the mid-19th century. The scene is drawn from the rooftops of the bazaar to the north called the Bazar Kilhih in fig. 86 and is focussed on the north gate of the mosque. This results in two extremely difficult perspective viewpoints of the east gate and the main mass of the mosque proper, which the artist has mastered. Such a viewpoint had not been effected before and clearly Mazhar Ali Khan was an artist who believed in visiting and sketching buildings from new vistas. Even in the heart of Shahjahanabad where no Europeans lived, new buildings were being put up in a classical European style as can be seen here in front of the east gate of the mosque.
Watercolour, 13.5 x 19 cm. on paper with a watermark of 1836. Victoria and Albert Museum, London, IS 482-1950.

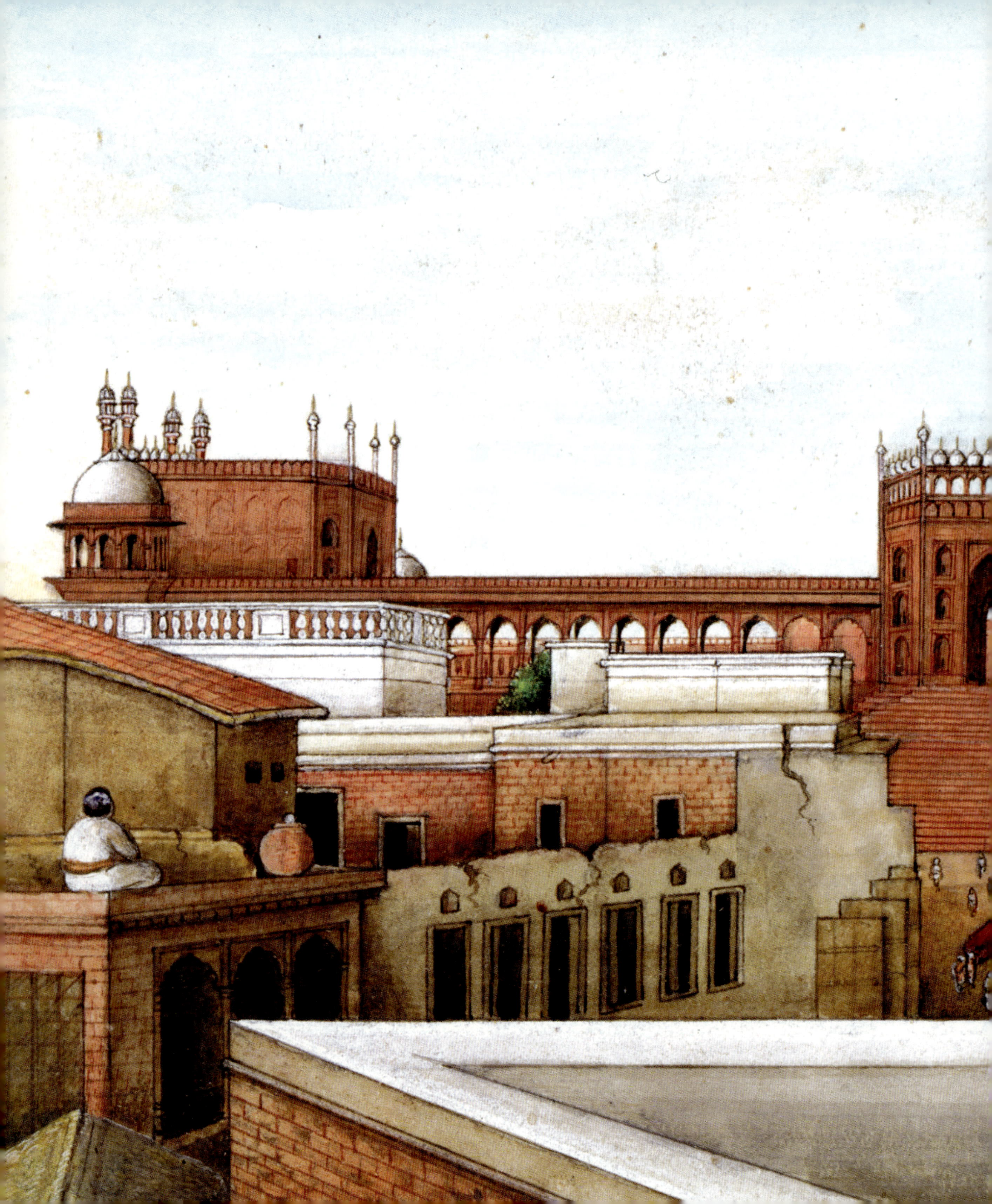

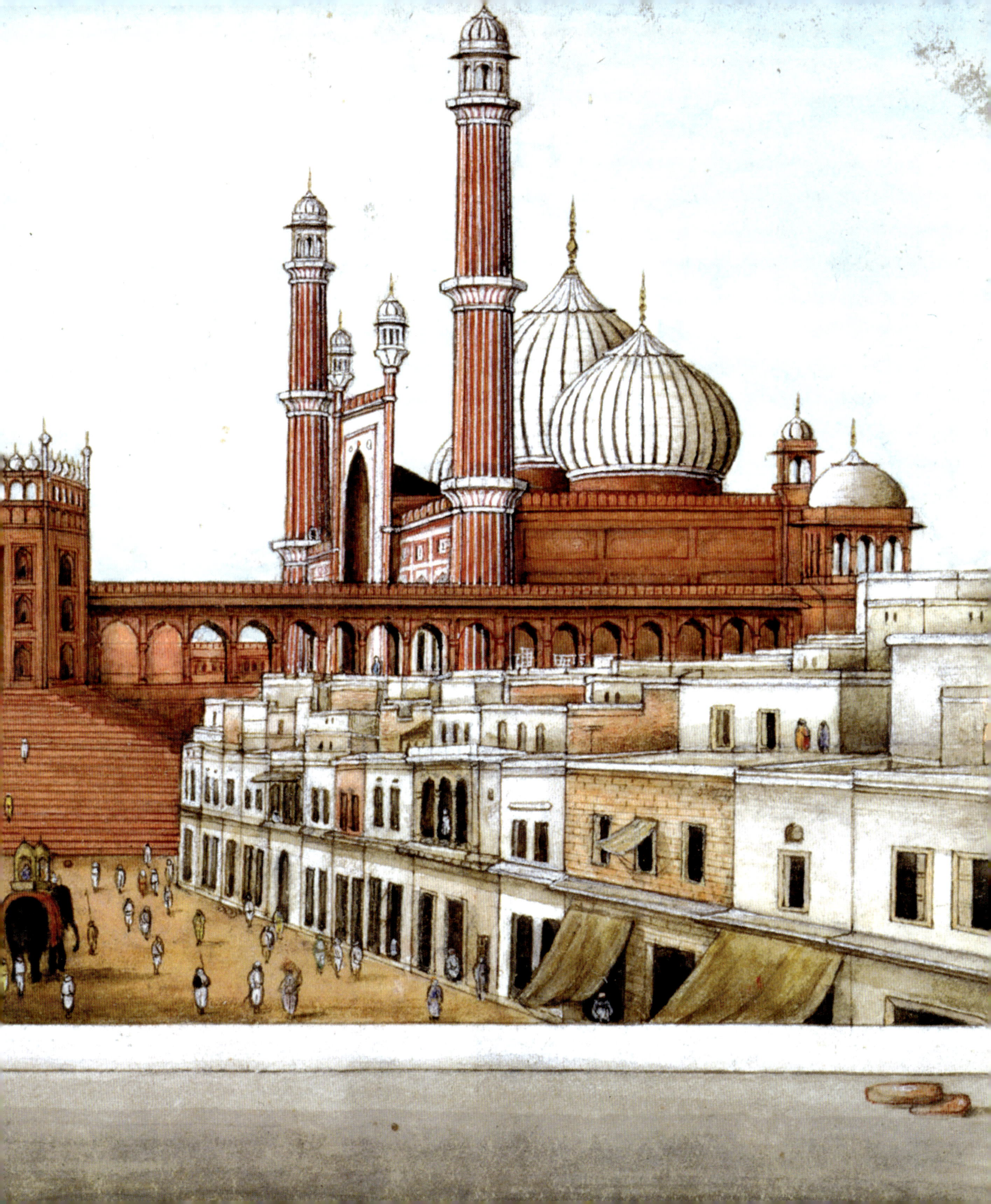

To you my very dear Children

Front View
West

These mementoes cannot fail to be of more common
Interest, — In this once happy Home you all passed
your Earliest Infancy — with Exception to Emy a
Charley all were born here. and all but Charley
here received the initiatory Right of Baptism
by which Ye were made members of Christ
Children of God. and Inheritors by Promise
of the Kingdom of Heaven — To your Father
it has been Endeared by many years of more

Back View
East

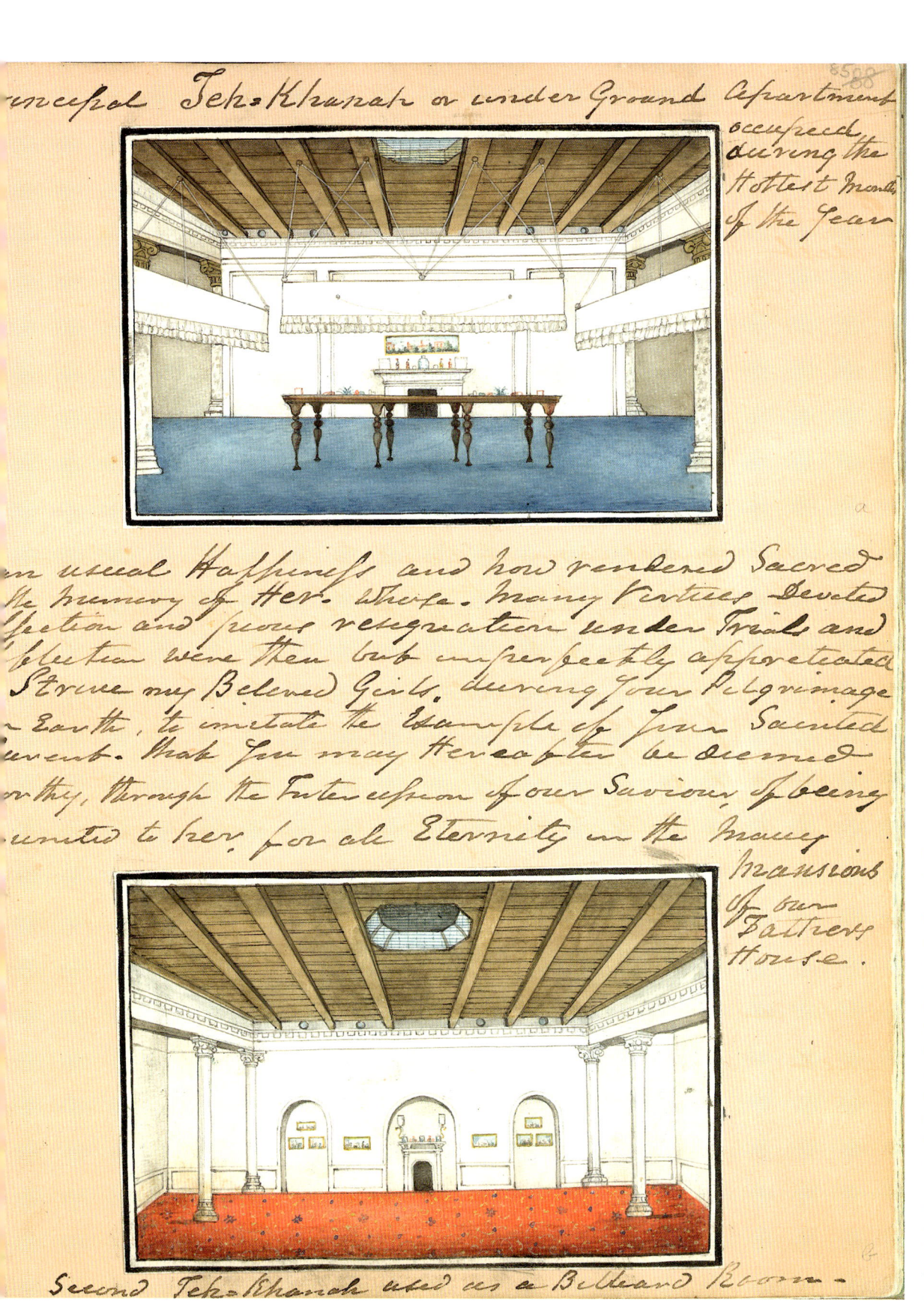

ncipal Tehkhanah or under Ground apartment occupied during the Hottest Months of the Year

an usual Happiness and how rendered Sacred the memory of Her. Whose Many Virtues Devoted Affection and pious resignation under Trials and Affliction were then but imperfectly appreciated. Strive my Beloved Girls, during your Pilgrimage on Earth, to imitate the Example of your Sainted Parent. That you may Hereafter be deemed worthy, through the Intercession of our Saviour, of being united to her, for all Eternity in the many Mansions of our Fathers House.

Second Tehkhanah used as a Billiard Room.

Fig. 36: METCALFE HOUSE, studio of Mazhar Ali Khan, c. 1840. From Metcalfe's Delhi Book. Metcalfe built his house from 1830 on in a colonial style to house his collections and possessions brought from England. The library had 25,000 books and a special room housed Metcalfe's Napoleonic relics. The house contained an ingenious series of underground rooms called taikhanas that were used during the hot season, arranged as a drawing room and a billiard room. It was greatly damaged in 1857 and the collections destroyed.
Watercolour, double folio size 25.8 x 42 cm. British Library, London, Add.Or.5475, ff.84v,85.

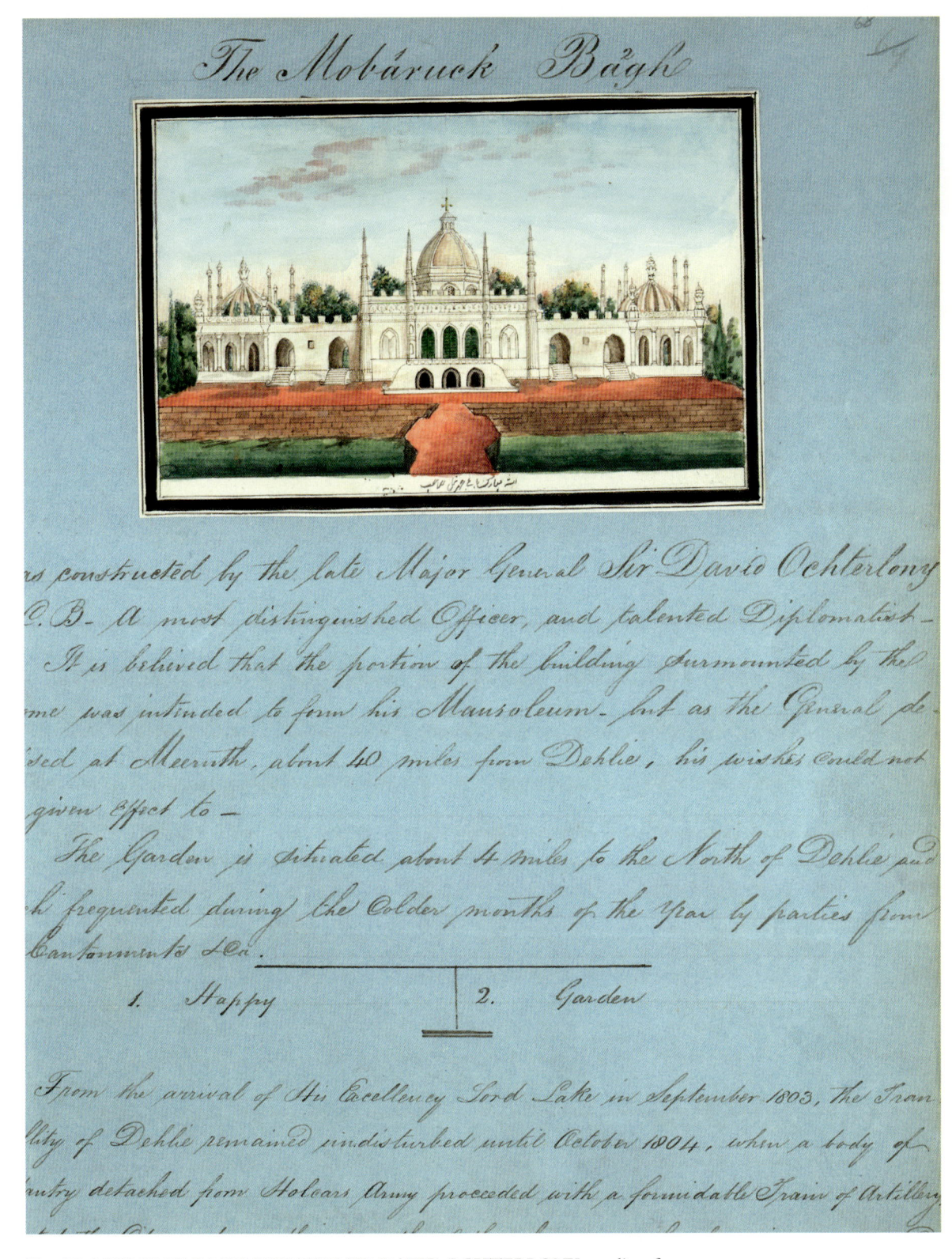

Fig. 37: MUBARAK BAGH BUILT BY SIR DAVID OCHTERLONY, studio of Mazhar Ali Khan, c. 1840. From Metcalfe's Delhi Book. The Mubarak Bagh of General Sir David Ochterlony (1758-1825) was built four miles to the north of Shahjahanabad and was named after Ochterlony's senior wife, Mubarak Begum, who inherited it after his death. The central portion under the dome is surmounted by a cross and seems to have served as a model for that of Skinner's St. James's church. Ochterlony intended it for his tomb, but in the event died at Meerut where he was buried.
Watercolour, folio size 25.8 x 19 cm. British Library, London, Add.Or.5475 f. 68.

As was ever Vouchsafed to Man
By His
Creator.
A Brother in Friendship
Has caused it to be erected
That when his own frame is dust

It may Remain
As a
Memorial
For those who can participate in lamenting
The sudden and melancholy loss
Of One
Dear to him as Life
William Fraser.

Fig. 38: WILLIAM FRASER'S TOMB IN THE CHURCHYARD OF ST. JAMES'S CHURCH, studio of Mazhar Ali Khan, c. 1840. From Metcalfe's Delhi Book. William Fraser (1784-1835) had served in Delhi for thirty years when he was murdered by Karim Khan, on the instigation of Shams al-Din, Nawab of Firozepur, the aggrieved son of his old friend Nawab Ahmad Bakhsh Khan. Fraser was buried first in the Christian cemetery north of the Red Fort (see fig. 106) before he was re-interred in the graveyard of St. James's Church in a marble tomb decorated with tree of life patterns in pietra dura provided by his old friend James Skinner.
Watercolour, folio size 25.8 x 19 cm. Brtish Library, London, Add.Or.5475 f.26.

Fig. 39: THE WATER GATE OF THE PALACE, photograph by John Murray, 1858.
The Water Gate, the south-eastern gate to the Red Fort was constructed by Emperor
Shahjahan (r. 1627-1658) for his new city Shahjahanabad. The Water Gate is sited
at the south-east corner of the Red Fort below the Asad Burj and leads into a small
triangular shaped barbican with a doorway into the palace near the baoli, which is all
that remains of the hamman marked on this site in fig. 86. Beyond the Asad Burj may
be seen indistinctly the changes wrought in the zenana area by the Mughal princes in
the 19th century.
British Library, London, Photo 52/(31).

professional who drew Delhi's monuments. The Daniells' views of Delhi taken in 1789 and published between 1795 and 1808 concentrate almost entirely on the picturesque ruins abounding in the area. The Jama Masjid is the only great Mughal building in Delhi that they included. In 1807 Charles Ramus Forrest, an officer in the Bengal Army visited Delhi as part of the delegation led by Charles Metcalfe to treat with Maharaja Ranjit Singh of the Punjab. His drawings were made into aquatints and published in 1824. His view of the Red Fort from the Jama Masjid is the earliest that people in Europe would

Fig. 40: EAST FACE OF THE PALACE FROM THE RIVER YAMUNA, photograph by John Murray, 1858. This view takes in the palace buildings from the Diwan-i Khas to the Asad Burj, including the Musamman Burj in the Khwabgah, the Rang Mahal, and the Mumtaz Mahal within the rest of the zenana with the River Palace of the heir-apparent with its triangular gable being particularly noticeable.
British Library, London, Photo 52/(28).

have seen. Many other British officers and officials drew views of Delhi on their visits and often had them published, normally as part of a large series of travel aquatints or lithographs.[80] So too did a series of European noblemen including Prince Waldemar of Prussia and Prince Alexei Saltuikov of Russia. All these views being by amateurs had to be worked up by professional artists. They were besides increasingly in the Orientalist manner then in vogue in Europe that adds little to topographical information. More informative is the work of Robert Smith, the executive engineer in Delhi (1822-30), who painted a series of canvases of Delhi monuments on the spot and after his retirement.[81] Two professional artists, William Carpenter and William Simpson, add more than most

Fig. 41: MUSAMMAN BURJ AND DIWAN-I KHAS, photograph by John Murray, 1858. The two jharokhas inserted by Akbar II into the Musamman Burj and the passage from the khwabgah to the Rang Mahal are particularly prominent in this photograph as is the high gabled tent over the Khwabgah in the courtyard of the Diwan-i Khas.
British Library, London, Photo 52/(30)

to the repertoire of monuments, since both were equally concerned to capture life on the street. Carpenter, who was in India from 1850 to 1857 visited Delhi twice (figs 44, 45). He was also a fine portraitist, as can be seen in his portrait of Mirza Fakhruddin, the heir-apparent to Bahadur Shah, taken in 1856 (fig. 49). Simpson visited India four times, the first time from 1859 to 1862 with the view to producing a set of chromolithographs of Indian life that would have rivalled the Daniells' *Oriental Scenery*. The project was aborted by the publisher's bankruptcy, but Simpson back in London worked up some fine watercolours from his Indian sketches.

The terrible events of 1857-58, which saw the destruction of much of the Mughal palace and all the Mughal residences around the walls of the Red Fort, coincided with the presence in Delhi of several talented photographers. The surgeon Dr John Murray, normally based in Agra, was in Delhi in 1858 and recorded many of its key monuments. His photographs include some of the buildings within the Red Fort as well as a view of the east face of the fort with the palace buildings before many of them were swept away (figs 39, 40, 41, 98). Other photographers also present in 1858 include Robert Tytler, an officer in the 34th Bengal Native Infantry regiment, who with his wife Harriet took photographs in Delhi in the immediate aftermath (figs 56, 57, 90, 91, 98, 105, 106); the professional photographer Felice Beato, fresh from the Crimean War (fig. 51); and Charles Shepherd, who along with Robert Tytler took the only known photograph of Bahadur Shah Zafar in 1858 (fig. 72). The Metcalfe family added to the Delhi Book a photograph of Begum Zinat Mahal taken in her exile in Burma (fig. 73).

Some of the most remarkable of Indian photographs are of the people of Delhi taken by Charles Shepherd in 1863. At the same time Samuel Bourne and Eugene Impey took many of the most memorable views of Delhi and its monuments. Some of their work echoes albeit unconsciously the work of the picturesque artist Sita Ram. Bourne's views became the standard ones of Delhi and were reprinted again and again from his negatives which remained in India with his firm of Bourne and Shepherd. Impey was an army officer in the Political Service, most notably at Alwar; his best views were published in 1865.[82] The Archaeological Survey began work in the 1870s and some of its earliest work was in Delhi with photographs taken by J.D. Beglar and W. Caney, continued by H.H. Cole in the 1880s (figs 88, 89). By the time of the transfer of the capital in 1911, the Archaeological Survey had taken many thousands of photographic records. Indian photographers such as Deen Dayal were now working in Delhi (fig. 83) as was S.C. Sen. The great events of Delhi's history under the Raj were all photographed: for the Prince of Wales's visit to Delhi in 1875-76 (fig. 109); the Imperial Assemblage in 1877 for the proclamation of Queen Victoria as Empress of India; Lord Curzon's Delhi Durbar of 1902-03 (fig. 109); the visit of the Prince of Wales in 1905; and the Delhi Durbar of 1911 where King George V (figs 4, 110) announced the transfer of the capital from Calcutta to Delhi and the building of a new city. But painters, both Indian and Western were still needed to bring these tumultuous scenes to colourful life (figs 107, 108).

MEN WHO RULED DELHI
FROM RED FORT TO RAISINA

SHAHJAHAN
1628-58

AURANGZEB (Alamgir I)
1658-1707

BAHADUR SHAH I
1707-12

JAHANDAR SHAH
1712-13

FARRUKHSIYYAR
1713-19

MUHAMMAD SHAH
1719-48

AHMAD SHAH
1748-54

ALAMGIR II
1754-59

SHAH ALAM
1759-1806

AKBAR II
1806-37

BAHADUR SHAH II
1837-1858

VICEROYS

EARL CANNING 1858-62
EARL OF ELGIN 1862-63
LORD LAWRENCE 1864-69
EARL OF MAYO 1869-72
LORD NORTHBROOK 1872-76
LORD LYTTON 1876-80
MARQUESS OF RIPON 1880-84
EARL OF DUFFERIN 1884-88
MARQUESS OF LANSDOWNE 1888-94
EARL ELGIN 1894-99

LORD CURZON 1899-1905
EARL OF MINTO 1905-10
LORD HARDINGE 1910-16
LORD CHELMSFORD 1916-21
MARQUESS OF READING 1921-26
LORD IRWIN 1926-31
EARL OF WILLINGDON 1931-36
MARQUESS OF LINLITHGOW 1936-41
LORD WAVELL 1941-47
EARL MOUNTBATTEN 1947

Life in Shahjahanabad

Salman Khurshid

Dehli or Dilli as it has popularly been known to its denizens over the centuries had seen metamorphosis at least six times, some believe ten, when Babur defeated Ibrahim Lodi in the First Battle of Panipat and marched victorious to occupy the imperial capital. Liberal historians make a point of underscoring the fact that the invading Mughal army overwhelmed the forces of the ruling Muslim dynasty and not a Hindu ruler. It is therefore a misreading of history to fix 1526 as the beginning of Muslim rule in India. Five dynasties that can be described as Muslim preceded the Mughals from 1206 to 1526, although blossoming of the Indo-Persian civilization may be said to have come with the arrival of the Mughals. Delhi over the ages has been believed to have surpassed the reputation of Samarqand, Bokhara and even Baghdad.

Traditionally, mediaeval invading armies from Central Asia simply gathered booty and returned home, sometimes handing over power to a local feudal regent. Babur sought to seek permanent roots in the soil of Hindustan, adding cultural nutrients of Persian and Turkish flavour, even as the later Mughals adapted to the ways of the conquered people. As Babur, a Chaghtai Turk from Fergana, sat by the river Yamuna and ruminated over his youthful and eventful life, the dramatic vicissitudes of Central Asia and now the vast land that included Agra, Gwalior, Kannauj, and Jaunpur that he now controlled beyond the river Sind, he was clearly being pulled from two directions – the deep yearning for verdant Kabul on one and the determination as well as foresight to hold on to an empire of great rivers and immense riches on the other. Although he chose to stay, he made his heir-apparent, Mirza Humayun promise to return him to a place of eternal peace in the land from where he came.

Babur occupied Delhi not with a hostile intent to erase all signs of the previous rulers but conscious of a sense of inheritance and continuity. Babur's account of his entry into

Delhi reads much like the diary of a modern-day tourist on a conducted tour of the historical sights of the city: 'I circumambulated the tomb of Khwaja Qutb Uddin (fig. 43) (a native of Osh in Fergana) and visited the tombs and residences of Sultan Ghiyas Uddin Balban and Sultan Ala Uddin Khilji and his minaret, the Qutub Minar (fig. 21), and his tanks called Hauz Shamsi and Hauz Khas, and the tombs and gardens of Sultan Bulhul Lodi and Sultan Sikander Lodi. Having done that we dismounted at the camp, and there drank araq.'

Despite Babur's evident cynicism about the poor quality of life in Hindustan, expressed in the *Baburnama*, he was not oblivious of the unimaginable riches of the land. He promptly ordered the laying out of beautiful gardens in Agra and Delhi, later to become a hallmark of the reign of successive Mughal emperors, dotting the subcontinent from Lahore to Kashmir, and from Delhi to the Deccan plateau. These gardens were geometrical in design, with square, rectangular and pentagonal shapes, with waterways and fountains using natural light and reflection of buildings in water bodies. Artificial waterfalls and strategically positioned pavilions or baradaris for recreation and rest for the sovereign, fruit and flowering trees and bushes lending a heavenly ambience. For Shahjahan architecture remained the most cherished pastime and culminated in the building of the Red Fort of Delhi (fig. 20) while it was the spectacular Taj Mahal that became the crowning glory of his vision. Marble was his favourite stone and before he dressed his grief for his beloved Mumtaz Mahal in the white stone of Makrana, he had already used it to enhance the beauty of Akbar's architectural structures in the Red Fort at Agra.

Almost five centuries after Shahjahan decided to resurrect and breathe new life into Delhi, strolling through the meandering *gullies* (alleys) and *kutchas* (lanes) of Shahjahanabad (figs 44, 45), the city conceived and built by the great-great-great grandson of Babur, now popularly referred to as Old Delhi or Purani Dilli, one is transported to days gone by. The aroma of inviting cuisine offered at local eateries with exotic names like 'Nematqada' reminiscent of the royal *dastarkhana* with parathas, sheermal, biryani, qorma, kebab, nahari and sweetmeats like jalebi and firni, as indeed the very smell (no longer matched by the fragrance of the perfumeries) of animals and humans living cheek by jowl may well come as an olfactory shock to the uninitiated but soon captures the heart of the visitor as does the legendary hospitality and distinct social charm of the local Dilliwallahs.

Once and repeatedly the heart yearns to return to Chandni Chowk, the mohallas in the vicinity of Jama Masjid, down Dariba, Urdu Bazaar, and Ballimaran. Similar were the sentiments expressed in the nineteenth century by the Poet Laureate of Bahadur Shah Zafar's court, Zauq:

'*Kaun Jaye Zauq*
Par Dilli ki galiyan chhor kar?'
[Which, roughly translated means, '*who would want to leave the streets of Delhi*']

90

Fig. 42: THE FAIZ BAZAAR, by a Rajasthani artist, c. 1840. The view is taken from the Chowk, the open square at the beginning of the Faiz Bazaar. Sadatallah Khan was one of Shahjahan's ministers and occupied the haveli adjacent to this chowk. The mosque is possibly the now vanished mosque of Roshanuddaula (see fig. 10). The large procession heading towards the Delhi Gate suggests that this is of the emperor on his way to his country palace at the Qutb Minar. We admire some of the lovely details in this fascinating painting: note the kite flying from the rooftops; the dancing girl with musicians in the foreground; the water channel running down the centre of the street.
Ink and watercolour, 27.6 x 43.3 cm.
Private collection, courtesy Francesca Galloway, London.

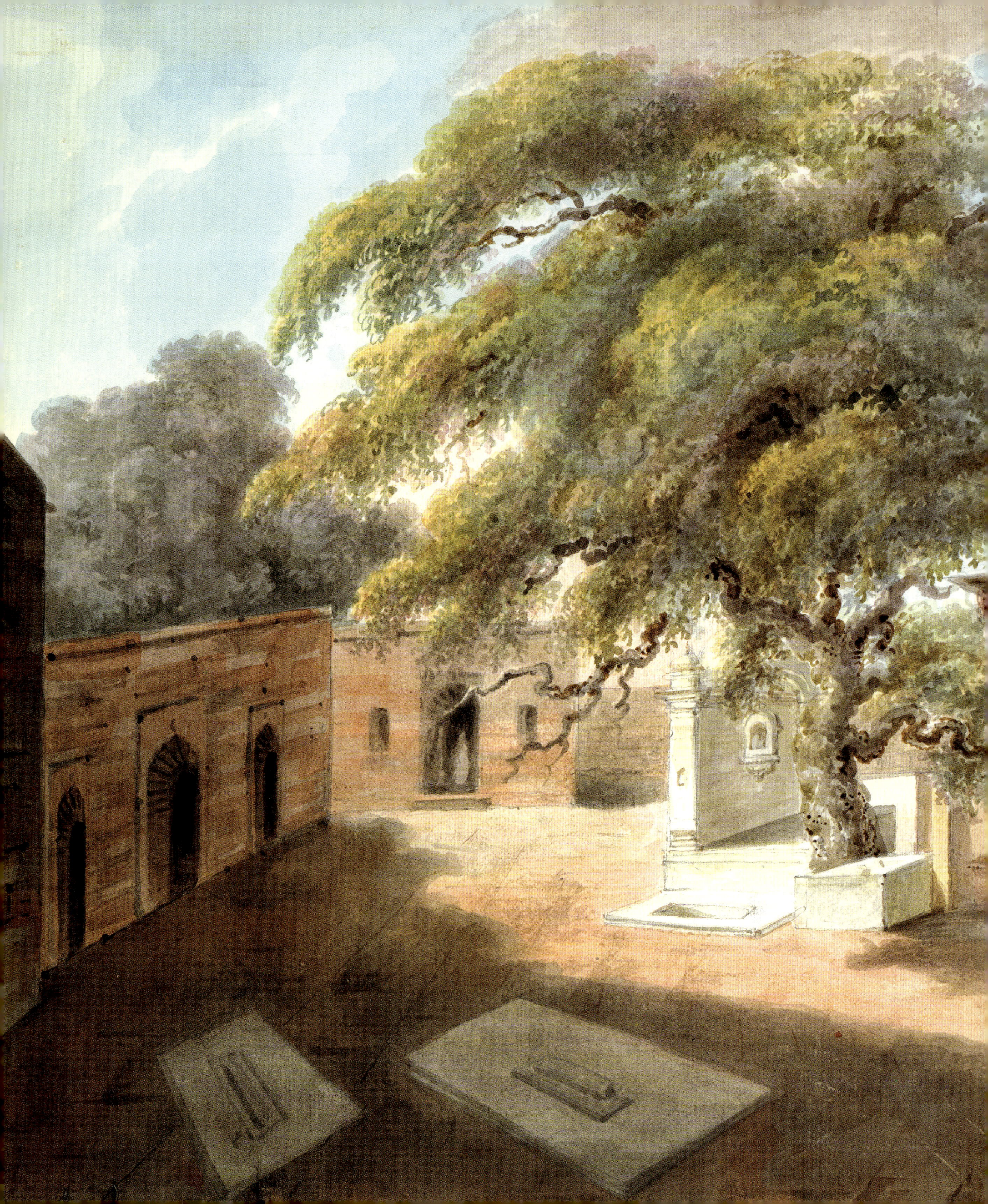

Fig. 43: THE SHRINE OF QUTB SAHIB AT MEHRAULI, by Sita Ram, 1815. From the albums of drawings done by Sita Ram for Lord Hastings 1814-15. Khvaja Qutbuddin Bakhtyar Kaki from Ush, who was known as Qutb-Sahib from his residence near the Qutb Minar near Mehrauli, went to India with the earliest Muslim invaders and became a disciple of Khvaja Moinuddin Chishti of Ajmer. He died in 1236 and was buried in a simple grave at Mehrauli. The beautification of the tomb did not apparently begin until the 16th century, but the tomb itself remained an open enclosure until 1944. To the left is part of the wall of coloured floral tiles traditionally associated with Aurangzeb. The gateway in the distance and surrounding walls were added by Farrukhsiyar in 1713. For a later drawing from the same viewpoint see fig. 53.
Watercolour, 36.5 x 51.5 cm. British Library, London, Add.Or.4815.

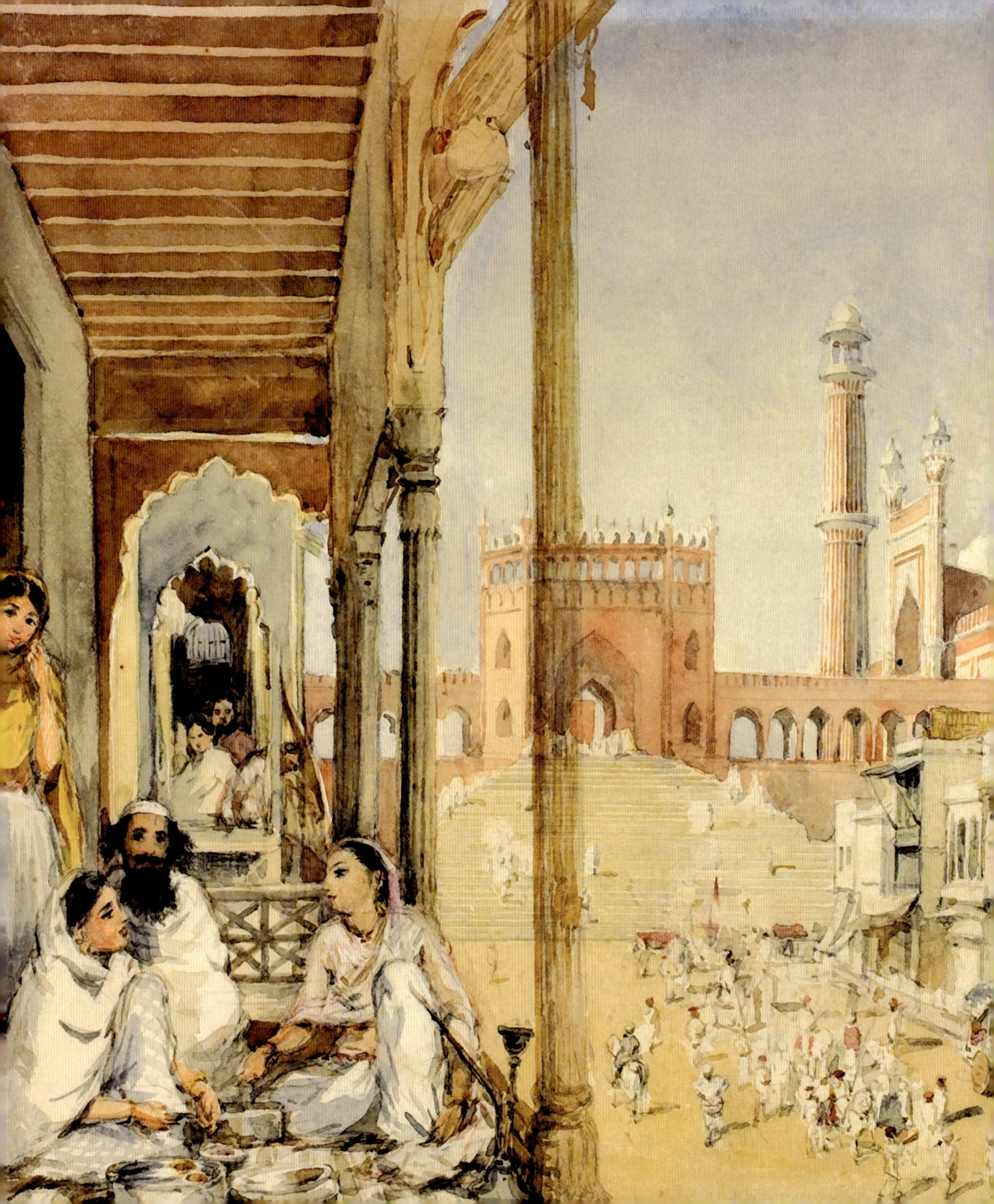

Fig. 44: JAMA MASJID FROM THE BALCONY OF A HOUSE TO THE NORTH, by William Carpenter, April 1853. The viewpoint from a house in the Dariba is very similar to that of Mazhar Ali Khan taken a decade or more earlier (see fig. 35). Carpenter was a professional artist who stayed in India from 1850 to 1857. Carpenter was a professional English artist who travelled extensively in India between 1850 and 1857 and produced hundreds of watercolours of its topography and its people.
Watercolour, 24 x 34.5 cm.
Victoria and Albert Museum, London, 189-1881.

Fig. 45: VIEW IN THE CHAORI BAZAAR BEHIND THE JAMA MASJID, by William Carpenter, April 1853. The Chaori Bazaar leads west from behind the Jama Masjid.
Watercolour, 24 x 34.5 cm.
Victoria and Albert Museum, London, 190-1881.

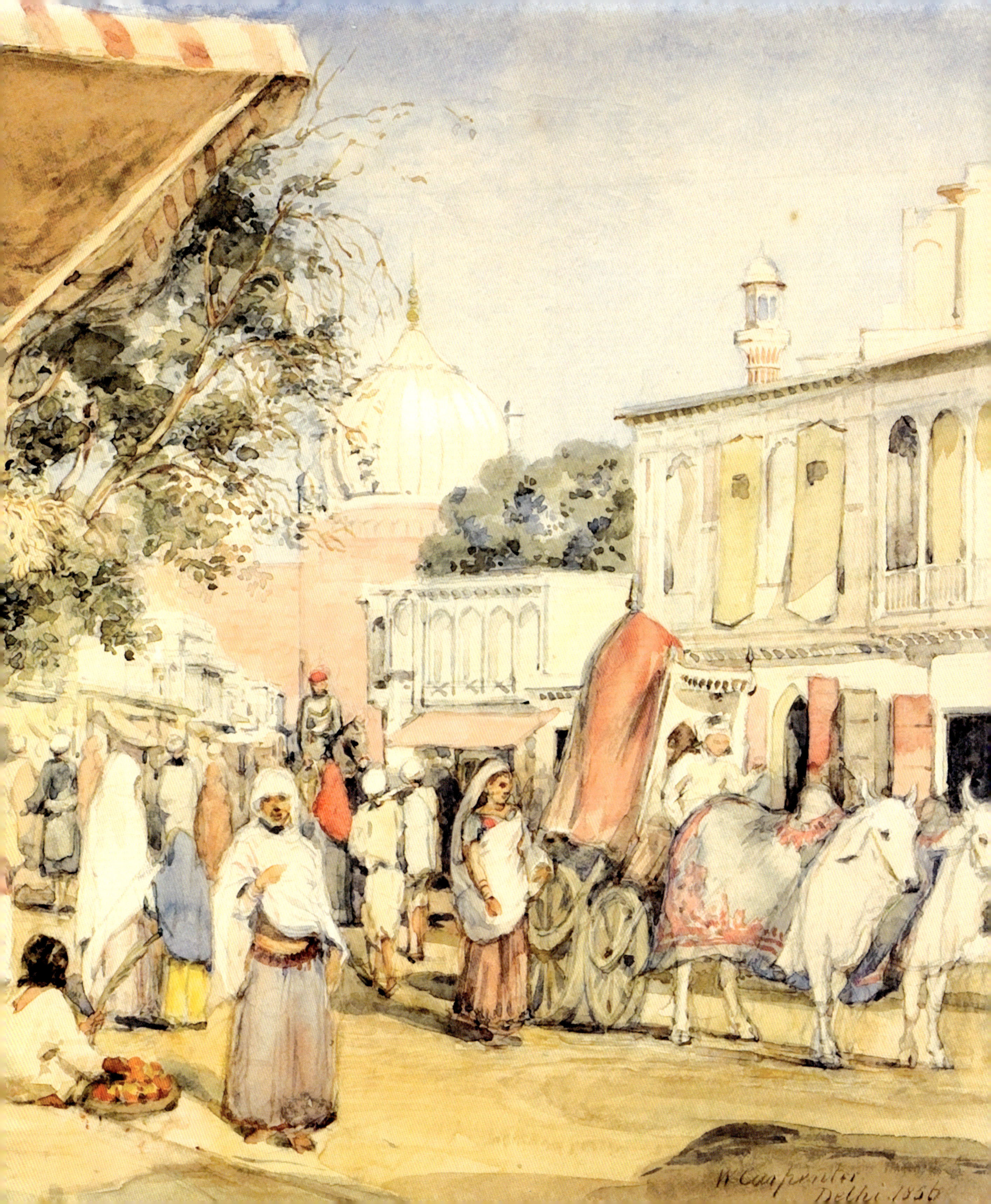
W Carpenter
Delhi 1856

Fig. 46: NAWAB AHMAD BAKHSH OF FIROZEPUR, Late Mughal style, c. 1810.
Inscribed on front in Persian: *shabih-i Nawab Ahmad Bakhsh Khan Firuzpurwala.*
Ahmad Bakhsh Khan was a distinguished chief who gave assistance to the British during the Maratha war and was rewarded with the districts of Loharu and Firozepur. He was the agent of the Maharaj Rao of Alwar in Delhi and was a great friend of Charles Metcalfe and of William Fraser, with whom he traded in horses bred on his friend James Skinner's estate (see Archer and Falk, p. 17).
Opaque watercolour, oval, 12.5 x 10.5 cm. Victoria and Albert Museum, London, 03552(IS).

Fig. 47: THE MUGHAL EMPEROR BAHADUR SHAH ZAFAR (1837-58), by a late Mughal artist, 1844. From Metcalfe's Delhi Book. Metcalfe writes in his Delhi Book: 'The Prince Aboo Zafr or the Victorious was the eldest son of the late Emperor Mohumud Ukbar Shah the 2nd, born in the year AD 1773, and ascended to the fallen Dignity of the once mighty House of Timour on the 29th September 1837.' This is the only painting specifically dated in the Delhi Book.
Watercolour, folio size 25.8 x 19.5 cm. British Library, London, Add.Or.5475 f. 17.

Fig. 48: MIRZA ASADULLAH KHAN GHALIB, by a late Mughal artist, c. 1855. The poet Ghalib (1797-1869) represented along with his great rival Zauq, the last literary flowering of Mughal Delhi. Appointed to a court position in 1854, this portrait shows him at the pinnacle of his success when he participated in the all-night *musahai'ras* or literary gatherings organized by the Emperor Bahadur Shah.
Opaque watercolour, 17.5 x 12.7 cm. Red Fort Museum, Delhi (286)

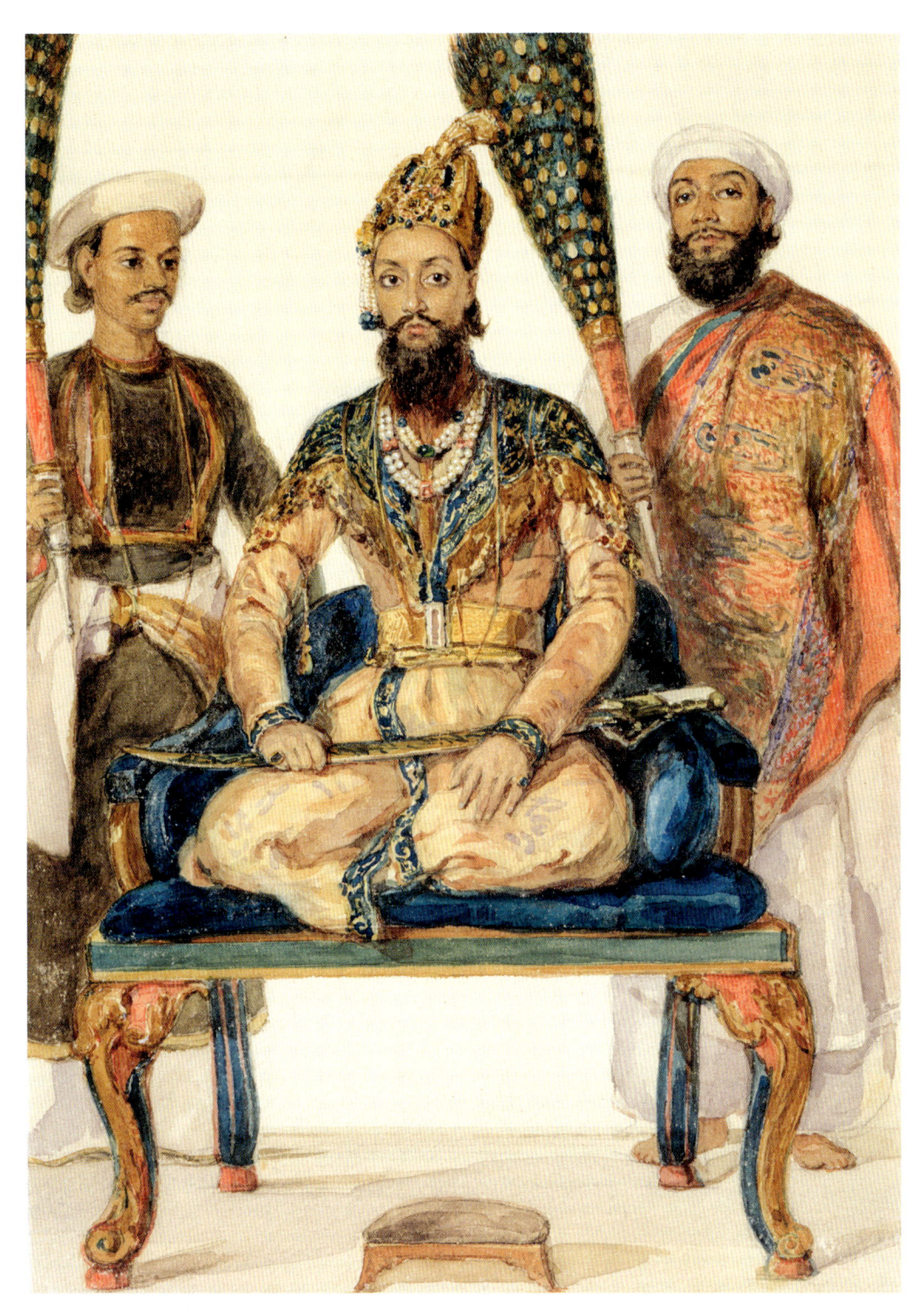

Fig. 49: MIRZA FAKHRUDDIN WITH HIS TREASURER AND PHYSICIAN, by William Carpenter, February 1856. Mirza Fakhruddin (1816-56) was a younger son of the Emperor Bahadur Shah II but the favourite of his father who wanted to make him his heir-apparent overriding the claims of his eldest son Mirza Dara Bakht. Sensitive like his father to literature, he appointed Ghalib (fig. 48) as his court poet in 1854, two years before his untimely death.
Watercolour, 35 x 24.7 cm. Victoria and Albert Museum, London, IS 193-1881.

Although a visit to Old Delhi soon shows up a considerable sense of decay and neglect and some attempt to bolster overloaded civic facilities, there is scant concern for aesthetics. However, with little effort the cul-de-sacs and crowded buildings unravel fascinating treasures of Delhi's rich past: artifacts, ornate furniture, coloured crystal chandeliers, enchanting brocade apparel, and tomes of scholarly treatises bound painstakingly in crafted leather. The visitor discovers the part of Delhi where its heart beats with the rhythm of the seventeenth century in the twenty-first century. Thus does. Old Delhi or Shahjahanabad captivate contemporary visitors as it once did the likes of the Mughal Emperor Bahadur Shah Zafar (fig. 47) and a legion of poets who surrounded him and his decaying Mughal court – Zauq, Mirza Ghalib (fig. 48) and many others.

The Chandni Chowk (fig. 8) that we see today bustling with wholesale traders and their eager customers has been a silent witness as many ages come and go, some resplendent, others gory and traumatic. Designed by Shahjahan's favourite daughter Jahanara, its havelis still valiantly resist the heartless sweep of contemporary, pragmatic architectural forms even as their owners gradually give up the fight of tradition against modern commerce, egged on by younger generations who prefer the charms of Lutyens' New Delhi and the more recently proliferating DDA habitations of south and west Delhi. The Chandni Chowk once had a canal flowing right through the middle along which the royal processions passed with rich and poor on both sides paying obeisance to the emperor who showered gold coins and precious stones on such as pleased him. During the years of decline of the Mughal Empire, widening of the road caused the loss of shade trees, which once lined the street as well as the covering up of the canal. Though the electric trams came much later, now they too have disappeared, their rails buried under layers of asphalt as though Chandni Chowk's historical personality asserted itself. The Chowk was silent witness to many dramatic developments. The public humiliation of Dara Shikoh; the ninth Guru of the Sikhs Guru Tegh Bahadur

Fig. 50: A DURBAR OF NAWAB ABDURRAHMAN KHAN OF JHAJJAR (1845-57), ascribed to Ghulam Ali Khan, 1852. Jhajjar was one of the small states carved out of the newly conquered territories round Delhi in 1803 and given to mercenary leaders who had helped the British against the Marathas. Abdurrahman Khan was a great builder in his little principality and also maintained a large mansion in Delhi south of the Red Fort, where he no doubt met Ghulam Ali Khan and engaged his services. In 1857, he made the mistake of hedging his bets and paid for it with his life, while his estates were confiscated.
Opaque watercolour, 29 x 42 cm. British Library, London, Add.Or.4680

103

being tortured to death; the massacre of thousands by Nadir Shah in 1739; widespread plunder and looting by Ahmad Shah Abdali and the attacks by Ghulam Qadir Rohilla, the Marathas and the Jats; the gradual return to prosperity and peace after the British takeover in 1803; the recapture of the city by the British after short-lived freedom during the first war of Independence; the slaughter of Mughal princes; the ruthless hanging of the Nawab of Jhajjar (fig. 50) and the Raja of Ballabhgarh along with hundreds of commoners.

The Faiz Nahar canal constructed by Ali Mardan Khan on the orders of the emperor, entered the city through the Kabuli Gate rushing through the Tis Hazari Bagh and Begum Jahanara's garden and stretched from the Fatehpuri Masjid at the other end of Chandni Chowk (fig. 8) to the Urdu Bazaar and was then taken inside the fort through a unique siphon called Shutr-gulu or the Camel's neck, as though kingship and divinity kept a decent distance but remained connected. Curiously, the flow of the canal implicitly indicated the order of nature and the world. Halfway down the great street the canal grew into a circular pool designed by Jahanara. The reflection of the moon in this pool is said to have given the street the name Chandni Chowk or the Moonlit Plaza. Not everyone appreciated the canal: there were people who thought its water would turn noxious and therefore advised the citizens to eat adequate amounts of spices to protect their health. Chandni Chowk is home to some legendary names and reputations like the Ghantewala Halwai established in 1790. Among the many famous mansions or havelis in the area were Begum Samru's Palace built in 1806, Naughara haveli in Kinari Bazaar, Mirza Ghalib's haveli in Ballimaran, Zinat Mahal's haveli in Lal Kuan Bazaar. The structure of the havelis broadly had two parts: the outer area was for official work, for receiving visitors, and meeting with staff, with a diwankhana; the inner area was the zenana where the family lived and that had verandas and rooms around a courtyard called *dalaan* or *sehan*. Inevitably, there was a *tehkhana* or a basement for retreating to in the hot weather.

The Chandni Chowk in various segments was known for the wares or services it provided: immediately near the fort and up to the Dariba was the Urdu Bazaar that provided for the daily needs of the fort; from Dariba to the Kotwali was the Phool ki Mandi or flower sellers' market; next came the Ashrafi or Jauhri Bazaar, the jewellers' market, and the final section was the Fatehpuri Bazaar known for the Fatehpuri Masjid. Dariba Kalan to this day retains the charm of offering exquisite gold and silver jewellery. Khari Baoli, although named after the hard-water step-well, offers spices of all kinds. Chawri Bazaar or the Wide market (fig. 45) was once the haunt of nautch girls and domnis (courtesans) whose lilting melodies drew many a noble to their distraction. Nai Sarak that once boasted of precious textiles is now a reader's delight. Churi Walan is the street of bangle sellers. The biggest wholesale market in Asia, Sadar Bazaar is for people who prefer to buy in bulk and at very reasonable prices.

Khas Bazaar, the street that connected the Jama Masjid with the Akbarabadi Gate of the fort was developed into a large square that was known as Sadatallah Chowk (fig.

Fig. 51: JAIN TEMPLE, photograph by Felice Beato, 1858. The Sri Digambar Jain Naya Mandir has been rebuilt many times, but this beautiful doorway to it is dated to 1807. It is situated between Chandni Chowk and the Jama Masjid. This piece of land in Delhi was given apparently to the Jain community by the Emperor Aurangzeb for their services as bankers to the Mughal courts.
Victoria and Albert Museum, London, 80-119.

10) having been the initiative of Sadatallah Khan, Shahjahan's minister. Here too could be found dancing girls, physician *hakims* and *vaids*, *dastango* story tellers, astrologers, traders, shops that sold flowers, fruits, cloth, medicine, hot food, weapons, birds, animals, incense, and perfumes. Traditional Persian-style coffee houses could be found in all the bazaars where the amirs gathered to converse, play chess or simply watch the passing traffic and people. For transport within the city the amirs used stately bullock carriages and doli or decorated palanquins carried by four sturdy men.

The bazaars and caravanserais were the emerging signs of gradual urbanization of society and natural congregation points of the city. The emerging economy of the land was at display as merchants, farmers, travellers from distant lands brought their wares and looked for good bargains. To this day the *pheriwalas* continue to provide mobile convenience started in the days of Shahjahan, offering a variety of wares including eatables and utility items. The Jama Masjid (fig. 11) was not part of the original plan of Shahjahan's Red Fort or city, but with a growing population was built upon a hillock south-west of the fort. Shahjahan and his principal wives had built other mosques (figs 85, 94) as well and for non-Muslim subjects there arose the Sri Digambar Jain Lal Mandir (fig. 51), Naya Mandir, and Gauri Shanker Temple built by the Marathas in 1761.

Historical researches show that like most mediaeval cities Delhi too grew around the qila (fort) and the court. For obvious reasons the ethno-religious background of the founder and the Mughal dynasty made its indelible mark on the city landscape. Strategically placed as a triangle between the Yamuna and two fingers of the Aravalli range, Delhi shared its spatial bearings with past inhabitants of the area. But although brought into existence in the seventeenth century as the capital of the Mughal Empire it potentially was fertile ground for organic growth of economic, commercial, and cultural manifestations of the society consciously conceived and developed by Shahjahan's ancestors. The Mughals had by the time of Akbar virtually ceased to be traditional Muslim rulers and morphed into an identity that reflected a unique syncretism and a Hindustani flavour. While the visible signs of a traditional Islamic city such as an imposing grand mosque and Islamic architecture were significant, a closer look at the pattern and lifestyle of the city would tell another tale.

The Mughal rulers supported military forces and patronized cultural doyens such as poets and writers. In turn they supported others who depended on their art and creations. The *domnis* or nautch girls, for instance, looked to rich nobles and court poets for appreciation and even affection. The tales of Mirza Ghalib's infatuation with a famous courtesan are etched in the literary history of the times. Shahjahanabad, from Shahjahan Abad or the place inhabited by Shahjahan, considered the axis mundi (the meeting of Earth and Sky) as well as Dar al mulk, reportedly owed its founding to several factors that made Agra unsuitable as the capital: unbearable summer weather conditions caused by hot desert winds blowing from Rajasthan where the sand dunes were thought to have

Fig. 52: DIWAN-I AM, by a Delhi artist, c. 1815. Trying to resuscitate past Mughal glories in the Delhi of Akbar II, new illustrated manuscripts of the histories of Shahjahan were produced. In them for the first time are found images of his buildings as isolated architectural monuments. A particularly revealing sequence of paintings in this manuscript of the *Amal-i Salih*, a history of Shahjahan by Muhammad Salih Kanbu, shows the major buildings on the processional way from the Fatehpuri Masjid at the end of Chandni Chowk, via the Lahore Gate and the Naqqar Khana to the Diwan-i Am itself as here, with prominence given to the jharokha at the back of the hall.
Opaque watercolour, 14.5 x 26.5 cm. British Library, London, Add. 20735, f.370.

been shifting towards Agra; the constant erosion of the river banks and severe shortage of water in Fatehpur Sikri. The latter, despite being the hallowed site of Shaikh Salim Chishti's dargah, had been deserted during Akbar's reign itself. The site of Delhi was familiar with the seat of power having been the Court city seven times before Shahjahan opted to move the Dar al-Khilafat or the Capital of the Kingdom from Agra to Delhi in 1638 and ordered the building of the Red Fort on the western bank of the Yamuna. Ustad Ahmad and Ustad Hamid were entrusted with the onerous responsibility under the overall direction of Sadatallah Khan (fig. 22).

Construction of the Red Fort at the site adjacent to the older and smaller Salimgarh Fort began in May 1639 and took all but a decade before Shahjahan arrived to take

Fig. 53: DARGAH OF QUTB SAHIB AT MEHRAULI, Muhammad Yusuf, 1840-50.
For the dargah of Qutb Sahib at Mehrauli, see fig. 43. ascribed to Muhammad Yusuf is a rare artist, obviously not from Mazhar Ali Khan's studio since his style is so radically different, much more linear and less picturesque. He is an artist who appears to have gone to the Middle East to earn a living after 1858, since he is recorded as the artist of a drawing of the shrine at Karbala in Iraq dated 1875.
Watercolour, 45 x 59 cm. British Library, London, Add.Or.4308.

residence, at the head of a magnificent retinue that included the popular eclectic Prince Dara Shikoh, who is said to have showered gold and silver coins over his royal father's head. The royal court was held for the first time in the Diwan-i Am and upon Dara Shikoh was conferred a ceremonial khilat or gown. Immediately the city adjoining the fort was attended to. The great wall surrounding the city that provided protection to it was made of sun-baked mud and stones but due to damage by rain had to be subsequently replaced by a sturdier stone wall of 6,664 yards in circumference with 27 bastions and 14 gates. It was 27 feet high, 12 feet thick and enclosed 1500 acres (fig. 86). A similar restored mud wall can still be seen at the Bagh-e Babur in Kabul where Babur lies buried. The city walls had several gates generally coinciding with the main avenues, such as Kashmiri Gate, Mori Gate, Kabuli Gate, Lahori Gate, Ajmeri Gate, Turkamani Gate, and Akbarabadi Gate.

Fig. 54: THE ENCLOSURE CONTAINING IMPERIAL TOMBS AT THE QUTB SAHIB SHRINE, by Sita Ram, 1815. The drawing shows the marble enclosure containing imperial Mughal tombs and beyond it the Moti Masjid (Pearl Mosque) built by Bahadur Shah I (1707-12) around 1709, at the dargah of Qutb Sahib at Mehrauli. Qutb Sahib's fame and sanctity (see figs 43 and 53) attracted many of the Mughal emperors and nobility to be buried near him, including Bahadur Shah I, Shah Alam II, and Akbar II, while a grave was also prepared for Bahadur Shah II, who still lies in exile in Rangoon.
Watercolour, 36 x 50.7 cm. British Library, London, Add.Or.4811.

During Shahjahan's reign the fort was called the Urdu-i Mu'alla but towards the end of the dynasty was known as *Qila-i Mubarik* or the Fort of Exalted Dignity. The fort was a complete city in itself. There were resplendent halls of audience, the Diwan-i Khas for private audiences and the Diwan-i Am (figs 52, 87) for general audiences of the nobles of the empire. A red railing within the great courtyard divided the nobles from the common people. An embroidered velvet canopy was put up from four silver pillars that covered the elect. In addition there were palaces with ethereal gardens and running streams; a grand hammam or baths as well as accommodation for regalia, horses, elephant stables, quarters for retinue and somewhat modest homes for the extended royal family members or salatin. Well-organized factories for manufacturing articles for royal service too were situated within the fort complex. The piece de resistance was the fabled Peacock Throne later to be looted along with the Koh-i-noor and transported by Nadir Shah to Persia. A moat surrounded the fort wall and beyond that were gardens.

The fort was designed to provide all nature of comforts for the emperor and the royal family. In addition it was to be equipped for all necessary court functions and military operations. The red sandstone used for construction was brought from a quarry near Fatehpur Sikri. Much of the heavy material was carried by boats and barges on the river that flowed throughout the year. The Nahar-i-Bahisht flowed through the fort, feeding running water in channels and cascades through the various well-laid gardens, baths, and palatial residences later known as Khas Mahal or Rang Mahal, Aramgah or Khwabgah, and Mumtaz Mahal (fig. 20).

On the river front of the city near the fort were at least three gates, Raj Ghat, Qila Ghat, and Nigambodh Ghat for Hindu subjects of the emperor to reach the river for bathing and worship. The sandy beach between the eastern wall of the fort and the river known as the Mahabat Khan ki Reti was where the subjects gathered to obtain an audience of the emperor every morning and elephant jousts were conducted in the evenings for the amusement and entertainment of the sovereign and his family. Additions were made to the palace during the reign of later emperors, such as the addition of a *jharoka* to the Musamman Burj overlooking the river by Akbar II, gardens outside the palace walls by Bahadur Shah Zafar, and houses for the heir-apparent and other princes in the English style within the zenana.

The words of Amir Khusrau first spoken for the beauty of Kashmir were appropriately inscribed on the white-marble walls of Diwan-i Khas:

'Gar Firdaus bar-ru-e-zameeast,
Hameen asto, hamee asto, hameen ast.'
(If on Earth, there is a Heaven of Bliss'
It is this, it is this, it is this.)

Mosques are an intrinsic part of the landscape of Muslim cities and so was it in Delhi. The skyline had conspicuous minarets and domes from where the muezzins' call was heard. Between 1639 and 1857 almost five dozen large mosques were constructed and at the top of the hierarchy and the largest not just in Delhi but in India, was the Jama Masjid. The foundation of this majestic mosque was laid on 6 October 1650, well after the court had been established. Sadatallah Khan, who developed the nearby chowk of his name, was given this added responsibility (fig. 35). Red sandstone and marble as well as the imposing but delicate structure make it a befitting architectural companion of the Red Fort. On the stairs on each side leading up to the second-storey level where the congregational prayer was held, could be bought kebabs, sherbats, chickens, as well as find story tellers, magicians, and jugglers who entertained visitors.

Fig. 55: THE SHRINE AND MOSQUE OF NIZAMUDDIN, studio of Mazhar Ali Khan, c. 1840. From Metcalfe's Delhi Book. Shaikh Nizamuddin Auliya (1236-1325) of the Chishti order was Delhi's most revered Muslim saint and his tomb or dargah is still a site of pilgrimage. The tomb was originally erected in 1325 and was last rebuilt in white marble with a dome and perforated screens (jalis) in 1652-53 by the Governor of Delhi Nawab Khalilallah Khan. The mosque which is built of red sandstone stylistically resembles the Alai Darwaza near the Qutb Minar. From the 14th century the area around the dargah of Nizamuddin became a burial ground for Muslim nobility.
Watercolour, folio size 25.8 x 19 cm. British Library, London, Add.Or.5475 f.44.

112

Fig. 57: THE ENCLOSURE CONTAINING IMPERIAL TOMBS AT THE QUTB SAHIB SHRINE WITH THE ADJACENT MOSQUE, photograph by Robert and Harriet Tytler, 1858. The marble screen with its beautiful jalis contains imperial Mughal tombs, including Bahadur Shah I, Shah Alam II, and Akbar II, while a grave was also prepared for Bahadur Shah II who still lies in exile in Rangoon. Beyond is the Moti Masjid built by Bahadur Shah I (1707-12) around 1709, at the dargah of Qutb Sahib at Mehrauli. The viewpoint echoes that of Sita Ram in 1815 (see fig. 54).
British Library, London, Photo 193/(15).

Facing page: Fig. 56: THE DIVING WELL AT THE QUTB, photograph by Robert and Harriet Tytler, 1858. The Gandhak ki Baoli or step-well in Mehrauli was built by Iltutmish (1211-36). It is supposedly named after the strong presence of sulphur (gandhak) in the water which was said to have tremendous healing properties. It is six storeys deep into the centre of the earth and was used to provide fresh water to the area.
British Library, London, Photo 53/(13).

Fig. 58: DARGAH QADAM SHARIF, by a Delhi artist, 1820-25. The drawing is of the Dargah Qadam Rasul or Qadam Sharif, the Court of the Print of the Prophet's Foot, showing figures seated in the courtyard. Originally, Firoz Shah Tughluq constructed the monument as a tomb for himself and then his son Fateh Khan who died in 1376, and added a stone with a footprint of the Prophet Muhammad, which Firoz Shah had brought in from Mecca. It is enclosed by massive walls in typical Tughluq style. A mosque and a madrassa round out the inner tomb complex.
Watercolour, 26 x 36.5 cm. British Library, London, Add.Or.547.

Although the city of Shahjahanabad was centred upon the palace complex, it was far from being confined within the high walls of the fort. Suburbs were both important as well as intrinsic parts of the urban landscape. They extended on all sides of the fort for several miles and on the eastern bank of the river as well. Almost half the population actually lived in the suburbs with bustling wholesale bazaars, vast gardens and grand tombs. At its peak, Shahjahanabad could boast of 52 bazaars and 36 mandis, mostly outside the walled city and in the suburbs. Apart from the extensive economic activity that the suburbs supported, several sought-after Sufi saints and preachers founded their quarters there as well. Many of these traced their origins to the times of earlier rulers of Delhi. The tomb of the Sufi Saint Qutb-ud-din at Mehrauli (fig. 53) became a special place for Bahadur Shah Zafar who visited it during the rainy season for a unique celebration of religious harmony.

Fig. 59: THE DELHI MADRASSA OF GHAZIUDDIN KHAN, by Sita Ram, 1815.
From the albums of drawings done by Sita Ram for Lord Hastings 1814-15. Ghaziuddin Khan (d. 1710) was an important noble during the reigns of Aurangzeb (1658-1707) and his successor Bahadur Shah I (1707-12). He founded a madrassa just outside the Ajmeri Gate of the city. The double-storeyed buildings are constructed on two sides of a large courtyard with a central fountain which is entered through an imposing red sandstone gateway, while a mosque and the founder's tomb closes off the western side.
Watercolour, 36.8 x 54 cm. British Library, London, Add.Or.4819

Beautifully decorated pankhas (fans) were carried in procession to the dargah of the saint as well as to the nearby Jogmaya Temple as part of the Phool Walon ki Sair, a tradition that continues to present times since its revival at the behest of Pandit Jawaharlal Nehru.

The walled city had careful layout zoning following that of the palace, dividing it into quarters for distinct social groups such as physicians, barbers, washermen, and gardeners etc. There were quarters such as Kucha Chini Wala, Kagzi Bazaar, and Neel Katra. Over time many of the saints who had lived in the suburbs moved into the city and took residence in the madrassas or seminaries. The katras were intimate living spaces for homes of different classes of tradesmen and guilds. Contemporary maps (fig. 86) of the city show innumerable madrassas, mosques, temples, sarais, reservoirs, and bazaars interspersed. The walled city had a variety of residential buildings; the elite had large mansions, sometimes of several storeys, surrounded by great walls and furnished with gardens that had beautiful water courses. Lesser mortals lived in smaller residences with walls of stone, bricks or even clay.

In the eighteenth century, of the various approximations that are available, the suburbs possibly extended to about 2000 acres beyond the fort walls. Paharganj outside Ajmeri Gate was the principal grain market while other suburbs such as Patparganj as well as Shahadra collected grain from the Doab region in Punjab and supplied it to Paharganj. Beyond the Kabuli Gate was Mughalpura, believed to have been the favoured area of immigrants from Central Asia, and even further was the Sabzi Mandi. Amongst the innumerable other popular spots in the suburbs and the countryside were tombs of saints where annual urs were celebrated. The area being replete with religious spots the walled city was appropriately called Hazrat Dehli. The tomb of Shaikh Nizamuddin Auliya was considered most auspicious (fig. 55) whilst other places like Humayun's Tomb nearby as indeed the tombs of Abd al-Rahim Khan-i-Khanan and Amir Khusrau drew a large number of visitors to pay respect, make offerings or simply for rest and recreation. Other places of pilgrimage included the Qadam Sharif (fig. 58) (the sacred footprint), the tomb of Ghaziuddin Khan (fig. 59) at his madrassa outside the Ajmeri Gate, the tomb of Khaja Baqi Bilal who introduced the Naqshbandi silsila in India, and Nasir al-Din Muhammad of the Chishtiya silsila, entitled Raushan Chiragh-i-Dilli.

FOOD CITY

Food was central to the life of nobility. Being an accomplished gourmet came next only to appreciation of music and dance. It formed an integral virtue of hospitality or the traditional *mehman nawazi* associated with Muslim society. Even ordinary meals had not less than half a dozen main dishes such as cooked flat and lean mutton pieces known as pasandas and several kinds of kebabs: shammi, tikka, and sheikh, as well as the gourmet's delight, the roasted leg of lamb. Korma and yakhni were gravy dishes relished with different types of bread – rumali roti, tandoori naan, sheermal, etc. Amongst the elite, serving barbecued entire dumba (Hill goat) was inevitable. Biryani and pullow, the delectable rice dishes came after one had ones fill of mutton; fish was served as kebab or with gravy; karhi, bhagare baigan (brinjal), stuffed karela (bitter gourd) called dulma and a variety of pulses such as lal masoor, chana or yellow moong were also served. Nahari and payas or trotters were cooked all night to be served at breakfast. Bread came in many forms: chapattis or phulkas, rumali roti, earth-oven baked naans, paranthas (both plain and stuffed with mashed potato or chopped vegetables), sweet bread called sheermal. Parantha were popular enough to have a dedicated Paranthewali Gali for a variety of breads. Cooking was done on slow burning *choolas* or the process known as *dum pukht* in which the cooking vessel was sealed with dough and the ingredients allowed to cook in their own steam and juices. Soaked and ground wheat was cooked with mutton and lentils to a paste-like consistency called haleem. Dessert included various kinds of halwas, rice kheer, firni, and shahi tukra. The meal was usually topped with a cup of tea, traditional paan (betel leaf and nut) and finally hookah. Since the beginning of the nineteenth century, Ghantewala Halwai's sweet shop has been a landmark for those with a sweet tooth. Some favourite sweets included pista launj, qalaqand, imarti, jalebi, balushahi, badam barfi, rasgullah, gulabjamun, rasmalai, revri, gajak, rabri, halwason, habshi halwa, and kulfi. During summer, residents of the city generously enjoyed various varieties of mango... Mirza Ghalib is reported to have been particularly partial to mangoes and both he and the emperor often ate to the limits of good health. Once when a cynical man indifferent to mangoes pointing to a donkey who sniffed at mango peels and moved on, remarked that even donkeys do not eat mangoes, Ghalib, never at a loss in repartee, retorted, 'Yes indeed, it is donkeys who do not eat mangoes!' Besides mealtime a variety of snacks livened up the evenings of Dilliwallahs: dahi ki gujiya, papri chat, alu chat, and the incredible daulat ki chat.

GAMES THAT PEOPLE PLAYED

Great social events and celebrations as indeed vignettes of rich cultural life and togetherness were of the greatest importance. During the eighteenth century the nobility took great interest in mehfils or musical gatherings and dances (figs 46, 50, 60, 61, 63). During Muharram *Marsiyakhawans* were in great demand. Testing each other's skills at Shatrunj and Chaupar were pastime for the elite whilst others settled for kushti (wrestling), panja kasha (arm wrestling), kabaddi, and swimming competitions. At other times there were other forms of entertainment such as wrestling bouts and ram fights as well as cock and partridge fights (fig. 62). Special days were set aside for kite flying from roof tops as well as the sandy slopes of the Yamuna bank known as Mahabat Khan ki Reti, as well as pigeon flying competitions. Animal and bird fights were no less popular. Cock fights and partridge fights called for considerable effort to train and fortify the birds for battle. Bahadur Shah Zafar's father Emperor Akbar II's consort started the uniquely syncretic festival of Sair-e-Gulfaroshan (Phoolwalon ki Sair) during which beautifully embroidered *pankhas* and flowers were taken in a procession of faithful from the dargah of Qutbuddin Bakhtiyar Kaki to the Jogmaya Temple in Mehrauli.

There were other processions too as they were part of rituals amongst Hindus and Muslims alike (fig. 1), like the hoisting of chariyan or flags in memory of Ghazi Mian, Madar Sahib, and Goga. The emperor's processions, beginning with Shahjahan were of course extraordinarily impressive and awe inspiring. The animals were richly decorated in gold ornaments and embroidered velvet and silk. Freshly made flower garlands added to the glory. At the head of the procession were several hundred mounted soldiers followed by chobdars or mace-carriers. Elephant-riding standard-bearers came next followed by more soldiers on foot and on horse-back, some elephants with men carrying royal insignia and then more horses. Close on their heels came the infantry with a variety of weapons, groups

Fig. 60: NAUTCH AT HINDU RAO'S HOUSE, by a Delhi artist, c. 1840. Hindu Rao was the brother of the Baiza Bai of Gwalior, the widow of Daulat Rao Sindhia. From 1835, he lived in the house on the Ridge named after him.
Watercolour, 17.8 x 28.6 cm. British Library, London, Add.Or.4684.

Nautches were part of the Mughal way of life in Upper India and those from the dancing girls of Lucknow and Delhi were the most famous. Nautches were given to entertain guests both by Indian and British inhabitants of Delhi. The Fraser brothers were

of musicians and drummers, *raths* and carts pulled by bullocks, followed by servants and coolies who sprinkled water to settle the dust before the emperor. There were then legions of more servants with different services to offer including water, perfume, and handkerchiefs. A palanquin was carried just in case the emperor needed to rest. Finally it was the emperor who came on a large elephant and more men on horses, royal princes, princesses behind veils, with ladies in waiting and eunuchs, with the rear being watched by the cavalry, camel corps, and more infantry. The procession extended for several miles and took considerable time to pass. Common folk cheered and paid obeisance from rooftops and the sides of the road.

Hindus worshipped deities at their numerous temples with special kathas and jagran at Navratri. Dipawali, the festival of lights was celebrated with great gusto with each festival

Fig. 61: NAUTCH AT COL. SKINNER'S HOUSE, by a Delhi artist, dated 1838.
For Skinner, see fig. 78.
Gouache, 13.5 x 21 cm. British Library, London, Add.Or.2598

particularly struck by the nautch girl Malaguire or Malliyagir and had portraits painted of her in which almost for the first time in Indian painting the subject looks boldly out at the viewer, as well as of other famous dancing girls of Delhi (Archer and Falk, figs 15, 124-28).

being the opportunity for special fairs and gatherings. Nine days after Holi the festival of Nau Roz was celebrated. This was when the unique egg-fights took place using the rare eggs of sabzwar hens that laid six to seven eggs in about three months. There was also the Akhiri Chahar Shamba when young men were presented with finger rings (*anguthi* and *challey*) and women given dupattas.

Education had already been given high priority during the reign of Akbar, described also as the age of renaissance. Tulsi Das was a contemporary of Akbar and had actually been to the court through the good offices of his disciples Raja Man Singh and Mirza Abdur Rahim Khan-i-Khanan. From the time of Shahjahan's reign not only did the existing institutions flourish in Delhi but some new ones were established including Delhi

Fig. 62: PIGEONS AND PIGEON COOP, Mughal, c. 1650. Pigeon racing and flying was a traditional favourite pastime in Mughal India and especially in Delhi. The later Mughal emperors were especially fond of it. Akbar II and Bahadur Shah II in their durbar processions regularly took with them a big wicker basket of pigeons mounted on an elephant (fig. 1) and pigeons can be seen flying above the palace in a miniature of c. 1815 (fig. 27) while raised lattices for them to perch on are visible in Mazhar Ali Khan's panorama of the palace (fig. 99) along with a pigeon house beside the Diwan-i Khas.

Opaque watercolour, 18.8 x 11.3 cm. Private collection, courtesy Brendan Lynch and Oliver Forge, London.

Fig. 63: MIAN HIMMAT KHAN KALAVANT THE BLIND SINGER, Delhi style, c. 1825. This portrait of a famous Delhi singer is from James Skinner's *Tasrih al-Aqvam*, an account of the different castes, tribes and occupations of people in Delhi and its neighbourhood, written in Persian and illustrated with 110 miniatures. This particular manuscript was dedicated by Skinner to Sir John Malcolm, Governor of Bombay. While Ghulam Ali Khan's earliest work for Skinner is dated 1827, he may have worked on some of the many fine portraits present in this manuscript.
Opaque watercolour, 20 x 13.6 cm. British Library, London, Add. 27255, f.134v.

Fig. 64: JUGAL KISHORE GOSAIN AND HIS ENTOURAGE, Late Mughal, Delhi, c. 1820. Jugal Kishore Gosain, a senior Vaisnava cleric, is sitting within a group of his disciples and attendants. All the figures are meticulously labelled and all bear Hindu names. Despite Delhi's Muslim appearance with its domes and minarets, throughout its Mughal history a large proportion of its inhabitants were Hindus. The Gosain impresses with his massive physical authority, a trait associated with the paintings done for William and James Baillie Fraser in Delhi 1816-20. Two of the disciples here appear in a similar painting in the Fraser Albums (Archer and Falk, no. 84).
Watercolour and bodycolour, 29.9 x 40.7 cm. British Museum, London, 1966.10-10.0.7.

Fig. 65: A PERFUMERY SHOP, Delhi style, c. 1825. Like fig. 63, this picture is from James Skinner's *Tasrih al-Aqvam*, an account of the different castes, tribes and occupations of people in Delhi and its neighbourhood. This picture immediately conjures up images of the little shops that used to line Chandni Chowk and its neighbouring streets. Skinner retained several artists to illustrate his manuscripts and also to produce individual studies for his albums.
Opaque watercolour, 20 x 13.6 cm. British Library, London, Add. 27255, f.340v

124

College which was first established in the madrassa of Ghaziuddin Khan (fig. 59). The English Institute was set up in the library of the palace of Dara Shikoh and at one time boasted eminent intellectuals like Syed Ahmed Khan, Ramchandra, the mathematician, Dr Mukund Lal, Nazir Ahmed, Aftab Husain Hali, Maulvi Zakaullah and many others.

Shahjahan continued his father's patronage of the fine arts although his principal interest was in architecture. He inherited some of his father's finest artists including Balchand, Govardhan, Bichitr, Payag, and Abid, who all contributed to the great manuscript of the events of his reign, the *Padshahnama*, while other artists such as Chitarman and Hashim were renowned for their portraiture. The imperial court was also the focal point of performing arts with musicians like Jagan Nath and Janardhan Bhatt, Sur Sen, Sukh Sen making their contribution to the great age of art. Under Akbar II and Bahadur Shah Zafar, Ghulam Murtaza Khan, Ghulam Ali Khan, and Raja Jivan Ram became the leading artists of the Delhi school of painting.

THE SETTING SUN: 1857

Aurangzeb (fig. 66) imprisoned his ailing father Shahjahan inside the Agra Fort in 1658 and occupied the Red Fort as his capital only to leave for Deccan in 1679 to wage war against the Marathas for the rest of his life. He passed away twenty-eight years later in 1707 at the age of ninety-one and was buried at Khuladabad near Ahmadnagar in a modest open-to-the-sky grave. He was succeeded by Bahadur Shah I (fig. 51) at the age of sixty-three, who travelled through Delhi several times but did not venture throughout his five-year reign to enter the fort. From 1679 to 1712, Delhi did not have a king in residence. The succeeding emperors, Farrukhsiyyar and Muhammad Shah were puppets in the hands of their ministers (figs 67, 69). In 1738, Nadir Shah swept into the capital having met with little real resistance at Karnal and thereafter. During the occupation of the city an altercation between Nadir Shah's soldiers and locals, either over demand of grain or as the romantics would have us believe, refusal of a local to sell pigeons, led to an unparallel mayhem of brutality and destruction. Less than twenty years later devastation returned with Ahmad Shah Abdali in the reign of Ahmad Shah. The only silver lining was the response of two of the finest poets of Urdu, Mirza Muhammad Rafi with the pen name of Sauda and Muhammad Taqi Mir, pen name Mir. The *Shahr ashob* (ruined city) genre of poetry reflected the mood of despondency and defeat felt by the poets and common folk alike.

Fig. 66: THE MUGHAL EMPEROR AURANGZEB (1658-1707) ON HORSEBACK,
Mughal, c. 1670. Having dethroned his father, executed his eldest brother and caused
the deaths of the remaining two, Aurangzeb ascended the throne in Delhi in 1658. In
this triumphal equestrian portrait, Aurangzeb is depicted as a mail-clad warrior as he
no doubt would have wished to be remembered, as a *ghazi* or warrior for the orthodox
faith. He left Delhi for the Deccan in 1679 never to return.
Opaque watercolour and silver, 30 x 24 cm. British Library, London, Johnson Album.3, no. 4.

Fig. 67: THE MUGHAL EMPEROR FARRUKHSIYYAR (1713-19), Mughal, c. 1715.
Two wars of succession followed the death of Aurangzeb, one in 1707 which brought Bahadur Shah I to the throne, and another on his death in 1712, when Jahandar Shah was temporarily victorious. Farrukhsiyyar was the son of Azam ush-Shan, one of the brothers defeated and killed by Jahandar in 1712. He raised an army in the east and marched victoriously on Delhi, having his defeated uncle strangled and his body left outside the Red Fort to rot.
Opaque watercolour and gold, 19.6 x 11.7 cm. British Library, London, Johnson Album 2, no. 3.

Fig. 68: THE MUGHAL EMPEROR SHAH ALAM II (1759-1806), after Dip Chand, Murshidabad or Patna c. 1760. Shah Alam was the son of Alamgir II. He had fared no better than his predecessors in ruling the disintegrating empire and the actions of his reckless vizier Ghaziuddin led to another major sacking of Delhi and looting of the palace by the Afghans under Ahmad Shah Abdali. The emperor was murdered by his vizier in 1759. In the meantime his eldest son Mirza Ali Gauhar fled Delhi hoping to raise support in the east from Avadh and Bengal and also the East India Company's forces. Enthroned at Allahabad in 1759 under the name Shah Alam II, he became a pensioner of the Company.
Opaque watercolour and gold, 19.5 x 14.7 cm. British Library, London, Add.Or.5694.

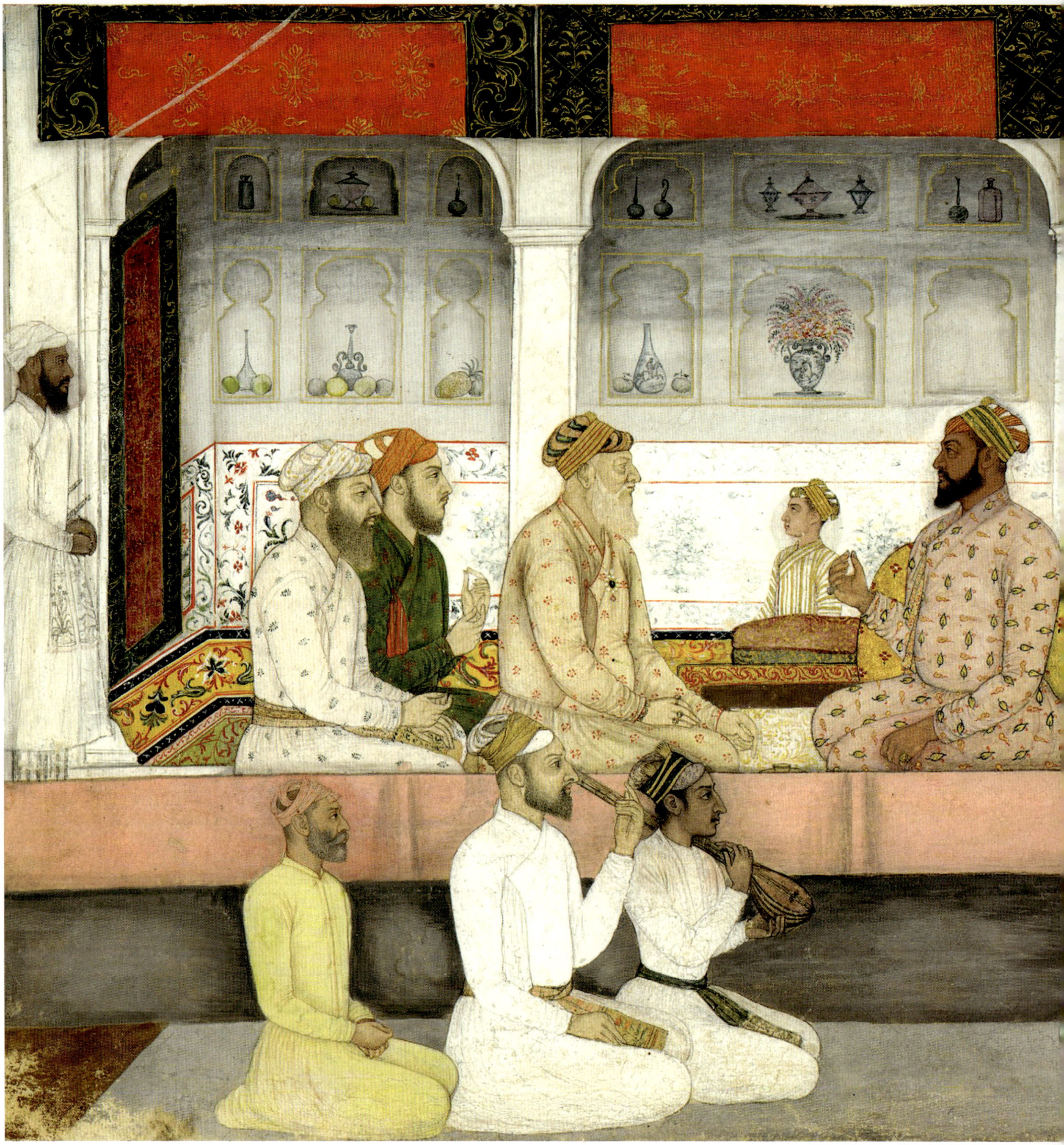

Fig. 69: FARRUKHSIYYAR'S VIZIER SAYYID ABDALLAH KHAN IN COUNCIL, Mughal, c. 1720. Farrukhsiyyar was assisted in his claim to the throne by the Barha Sayyid brothers Abdallah Khan and Husain Ali Khan, the governors of Allahabad and Bihar, whom he rewarded by making them his two chief ministers, the wazir or chief minister and mir bakhshi or paymaster. The Iranian and Turkish elements at court worked continuously to detach Farrukhsiyyar from the Sayyid brothers, who were Indian Muslims, and eventually fearing for their lives they had Farrukhsiyyar dethroned and blinded. They then put Muhammad Shah, son of Jahan Shah and grandson of Bahadur Shah I, on the throne (1719-48). Under him, the great provinces became independent and Delhi was sacked and looted by Nadir Shah of Iran in 1739.
Opaque watercolour and gold, 21.4 x 41.5 cm. British Museum, London, 1921,10-11,0.4.

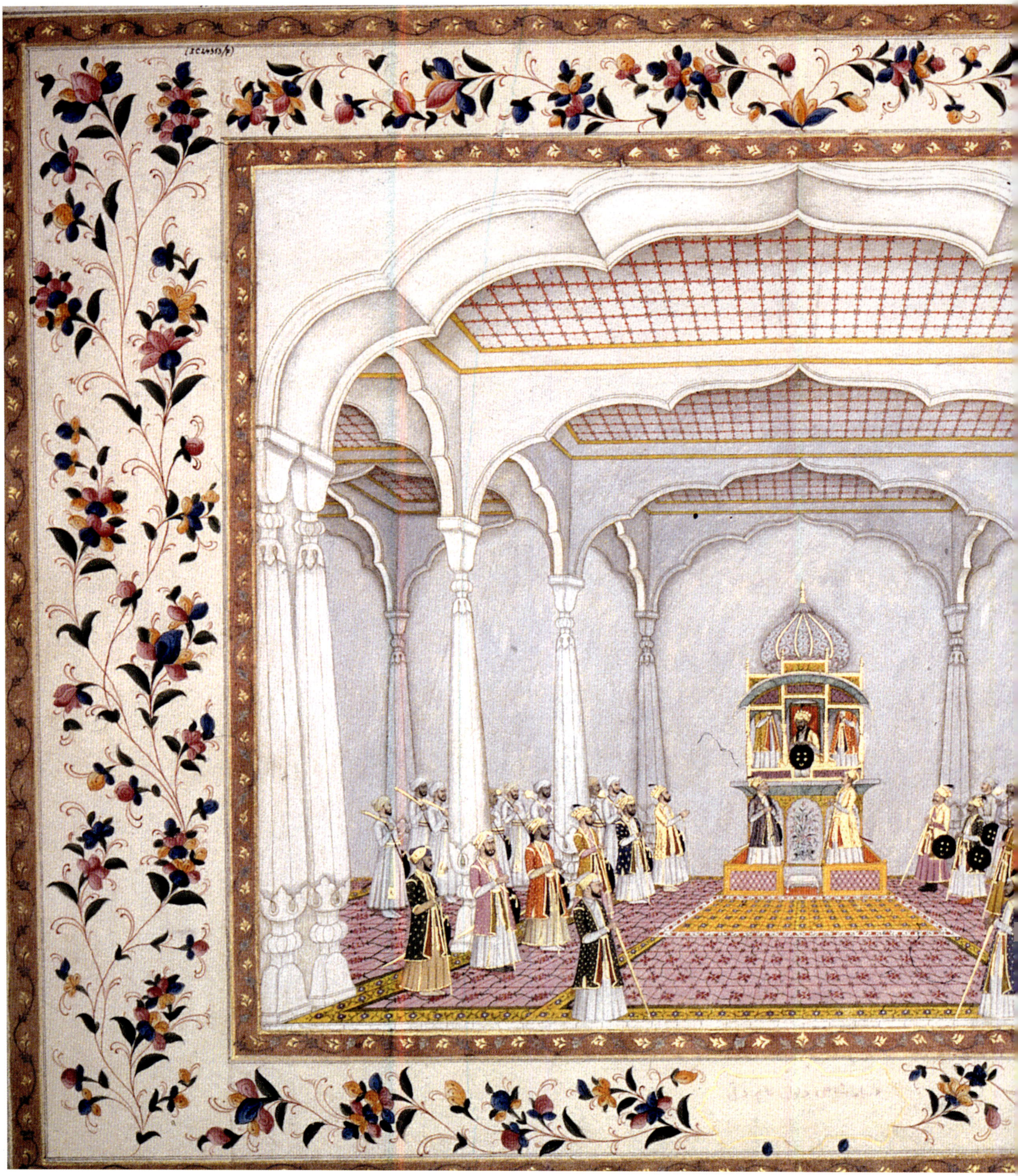

Fig. 70: SHAH ALAM IN DURBAR IN THE DIWAN-I AM, attributed to Mihr Chand, Lucknow, c. 1780. In 1771, with the aid of the Marathas, Shah Alam returned to Delhi from his self-imposed exile in Allahabad where he had resided under the Company's protection. A temporary reversal for the Marathas in Rajasthan in 1787 enabled the Rohilla Afghan Ghulam Qadir to take and sack the capital and once again loot the palace, assault the women in the harem and blind the emperor. Order was restored in Delhi by the Marathas again until their defeat in 1803 by the British under Lord Lake, when Shah Alam became a British pensioner and Delhi all but the palace passed into British control.

Opaque watercolour and gold, miniature 32.5 x 41.4 cm. page 45.5 x 62.25 cm. Museum für Asiatische Kunst, Berlin, I 5005, fol. 7.

The reigns of emperors saw the beginning of the rot by the middle of the eighteenth century with the saddest moment being the blinding of Emperor Shah Alam (figs 68, 70) by the Rohilla chieftain Ghulam Qadir in 1788. Nawab Dargah Quli Khan, who came to Delhi from Deccan in June 1738 has recorded in his memoirs, *Marqa-e-Dehli*, how life in the imperial capital had taken to singing, dancing and promiscuity. Although he witnessed the massacre of Nadir Shah, there is only a passing reference to the tragedy. Shah Alam's misery came to an end with his death in 1806. The British ruled Delhi between 1803 and 1857. The old order began to give way to the new. No longer did the court provide the impetus for prosperity of the city and instead the Company's army and new cash crops became the base for an emerging economy and Hindu merchants and professional class. Bahadur Shah Zafar came to the throne upon the death of his father, Akbar Shah II in 1837 (fig. 71). During their reigns a short-lived renaissance revived the fortunes of Delhi that had been ravaged by Nadir Shah, Marathas, and the Jats. Delhi had survived the onslaughts but lost most of its prized possessions including the famed Peacock Throne, carried away to Persia. By the second half of the eighteenth century the Mughal grandeur that had fascinated the Occident had sadly faded. While Nadir Shah carried off the Peacock Throne, three decades later the Jats had removed the silver ceiling of the Rang Mahal and gorged out the semi-precious stones from the walls of the halls of audience.

In 1806 Shah Alam's death was the beginning of the final decline of the Mughal Empire over the next half century. The *Qila-i Mualla* had lost its power and wealth but retained the pretension to be the literary and intellectual centre. A semblance of the faded glory continued with the emperor riding out to Jama Masjid on a decorated elephant for festive occasion and holding darbar (figs 1, 71). The 2000 or so Salatins or royal princes of varying stature remained confined to modest quarters within the fort. The old gardens and many palaces were in ruins and the population considerably reduced. Outside Kashmiri Gate modern bunglows came up for the British as the Civil Lines came into their own. Commercial quarters and residences for lesser European employees were built within the city at Darya Ganj. Chaises and buggies, picnics and summer balls, the playing of European music by military bands were the harbinger of the times to come, causing much curiosity and disquiet amongst the populace of Delhi.

Bahadur Shah Zafar was resigned to the dominance of the Company Bahadur and the abolition of the sovereign title upon his demise, when early on a Monday

Fig. 71: AKBAR II IN DURBAR IN THE DIWAN-I KHAS, Late Mughal style, c. 1820. Near the emperor stand the princes of the royal blood; on his left Mirza Jahangir Bahadur, Mirza Babar Sahib, Mirza Hussain Bahadur and Mirza Kai Qubad, on his right Mirza Salim Bahadur and Mirza Abu Zafar, his eldest son and the future Bahadur Shah II. Nearby is the British Resident at Delhi, Sir David Ochterlony, in his second period in office 1818-22. Nearly everyone is identified by tiny inscriptions.
Opaque watercolour and bodycolour, 48.5 x 41 cm. British Library, London, Add.Or.3079.

133

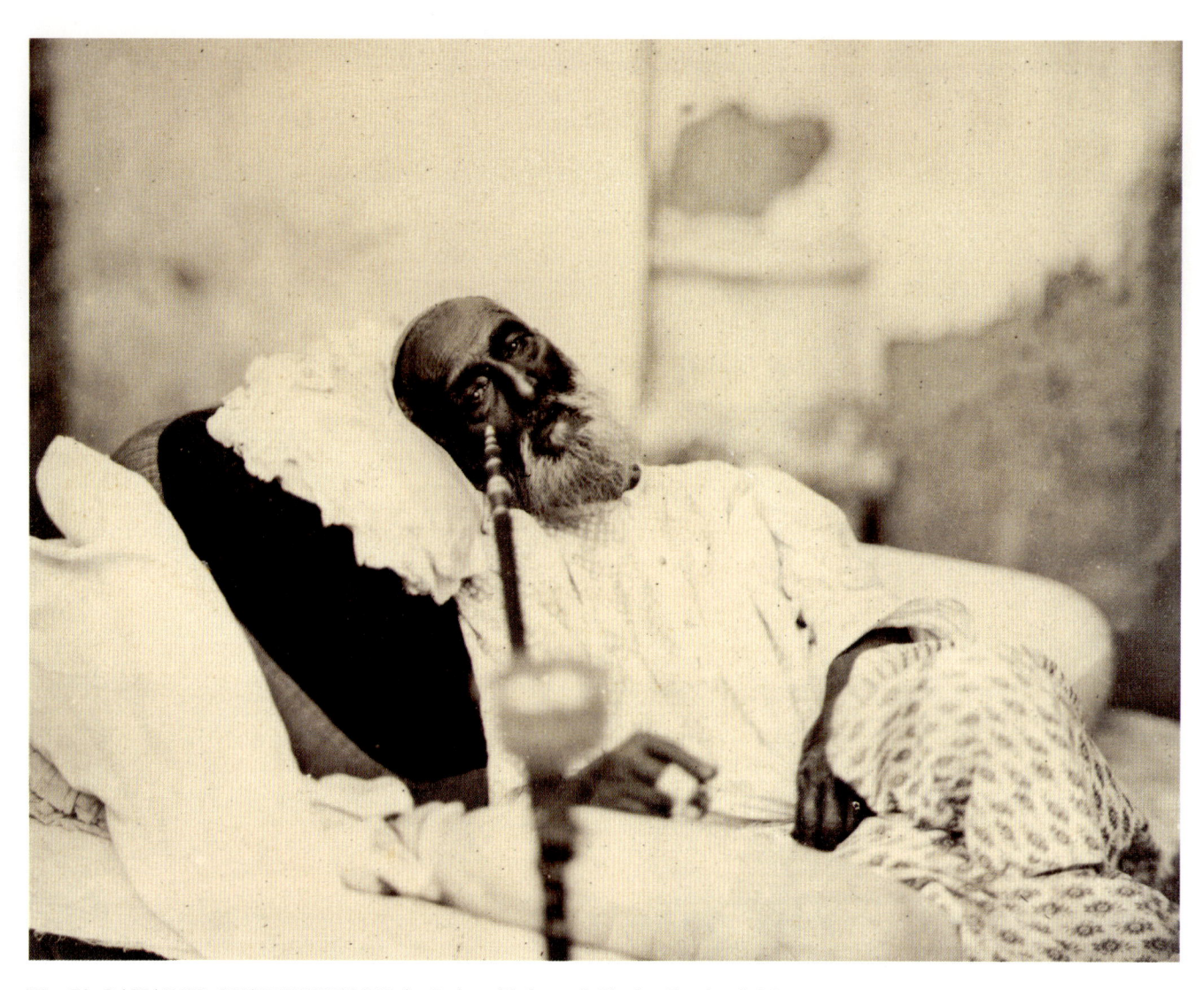

Fig. 72: BAHADUR SHAH IN PRISON, by Robert Tytler and Charles Shepherd, May 1858. This portrait of Bahadur Shah II, the last Mughal emperor (1837-58), shows him in captivity awaiting trial by the British for his support of the Uprising of 1857-58. It was, apparently, common practice for Europeans to visit the ex-king in his captivity. He was kept in the house of Mirza Nili in the Bazaar Naumahal in the Red Fort. Shortly afterwards he was sentenced to permanent exile in Rangoon with his favourite wife Zinat Mahal and their son Jawan Bakt. He died in Rangoon in 1862 where he lies buried.
British Library, London, Photo 797/(37).

morning of 11 May 1857 the rebel sepoys from Meerut arrived under his window seeking his leadership to lead them into battle described variously as the Mutiny, the First War of Independence and even a *jehad* against *kafirs* who wanted to defile the religions of Muslims and Hindus by insisting that the sepoys bite bullets greased with the fat of cows and pigs. He was, however, acutely conscious of his limitations and condition.

Bahadur Shah Zafar may not have succeeded in throwing out the British but he certainly was central to the foundation of modern India. Hindu and Muslim sepoys and

Fig. 73: ZINAT MAHAL IN EXILE IN RANGOON, c. 1870. From Metcalfe's Delhi Book. Zinat Mahal Begum (1823-82) was Bahadur Shah's youngest and favourite queen whom he had married in 1840. She worked tirelessly to have her own son Mirza Jawan Bakht declared heir-apparent but this was resisted by Sir Thomas Metcalfe and the government in Calcutta who saw no reason to overturn the rights of Bahadur Shah's eldest surviving son who had already agreed to vacate the Red Fort and live in retirement at Mehrauli. Metcalfe died mysteriously in 1853 and it was rumoured that she had had him poisoned. This photograph was presumably acquired later by Metcalfe's family and pasted into the album.
Photographic print, folio size 25.8 x 19 cm. British Library, London, Add.Or.5475 f. 17v.

peasants joined together in the name of 'deen' to rally behind their emperor against foreign rule. It was truly a peoples' movement for a king.

The defeat and surrender of Bahadur Shah Zafar on 21 September at Humayun's Tomb was the end of an era but also the beginning of a campaign to destroy the last vestiges of Mughal rule. By October 1857 the British were once again in control of Delhi. The emperor was put on trial (fig. 72) and finally deported to Rangoon on 7 October

136

Fig. 74: DAVID OCHTERLONY BEING ENTERTAINED BY A NAUTCH AT HIS HOUSE, Delhi style, c. 1820. A European, probably Sir David Ochterlony (1758-1825), in Indian dress and smoking a hookah, is watching a nautch in his house at Delhi. Ochterlony became a famous Delhi character for he was in and around the city from 1803 to 1825. He had a house there as well as a garden-house called Mubarik Bagh on the road to Azadpur and lived in Indian style. He was twice the British Resident at Delhi, 1803-06 and 1818-22. The lined face and white hair would suggest that this portrait was made in his later years. The family portraits on the wall are indicative of the way many European artistic conventions were translated into the Late Mughal art of Delhi. See fig. 71 for Ochterlony in his official capacity.
Opaque watercolour and gouache, 22 x 32 cm. British Library, London, Add.Or.2.

Fig. 75: DIWAN BABU RAM AND HIS ADOPTED SON, 1820-30. Diwan Babu Ram is seated on the ground with papers, books, pen-cases and spectacles; beside him is his adopted son and a chuprassy stands behind. The painting is from an album compiled from drawings done by Col. James Skinner's artists at Hansi and Delhi. Skinner (see fig. 78) employed Ghulam Ali Khan to work on three large paintings done for him at Hansi in 1827 and the elongated figure of the chuprassy here is also found standing to the side in Ghulam Ali Khan's regimental durbar picture in the National Army Museum, London. He is wearing a chapra or badge on his sash ornamented with a mounted cavalryman, clearly indicating his connection with Skinner's regiment and hence Babu Ram as Skinner's diwan or man who looked after his finances.
Watercolour and bodycolour, British Library, London, Add.Or.1264.

1858. Retribution was swift and ruthless. Despite protestations and resistance by some level-headed persons amongst the British, considerable parts of Delhi were flattened by large scale demolitions or properties confiscated and sold. Sadatallah Chowk, once the throbbing centre of city life was demolished to provide an uninterrupted line of fire between the Red Fort and the Jama Masjid. Muslims were expelled from the city they loved and not permitted to return for a long time. The fort was occupied by the British and in order to defend the fort walls the habitations between the Jama Masjid and the fort were cleared, even the Akbarabadi mosque reduced to rubble and debris. The Fatehpuri Masjid was sold to a trader whilst the Zinat al-Masajid made a bakery! For half a decade Delhi was an occupied city of defeated and rudderless people. Their emperor tried for treason in his own realm and banished to Rangoon.

Fig. 76: SAYYID MIRZA AZIM BEG OF HANSI WITH HIS HOUSEHOLD, 1820-30. The painting is from an album compiled from drawings done by Col. James Skinner's artists at Hansi and Delhi with the involvement of Ghulam Ali Khan. Saiyid Mirza Azim Beg of Hansi is seated on a cane-stool with his vakil Dai Lal, his munshi Kisan Lal, and his kitmutgar or servant Pir Bakhsh. Mirza Azam Beg according to the inscription was a Jagirdar at Hansi and was then 108 years old; in his youth he had been a great champion.
Watercolour and bodycolour, British Library, London, Add.Or.1265.

When the plunder and destruction inside and beyond the fort was finally over Mirza Ghalib wrote 'four things kept Delhi alive: the fort, the daily crowds at the Jama Masjid, the weekly walk to the Yamuna bridge, and the annual fair of the flower people. None of these survives, so how does Delhi survive? Yes, there once was a city of the name of Delhi in this land of India'. In another letter he wrote: 'the light has gone out of Hindustan. The land is lampless.'

Farhatullah Baig has described the final days of the empire in his 'Dilli ka Yadgar Mushaira'. The mood was summed up by Mirza Ghalib thus:

Zulmat kade mein mere shab-e-gham ka josh hai,
Ik shama hai daleel-e-sahas so khamosh hai.
Daag-e-firaaq-e-shobat-e-shab kee jalee hoee,
Ik shama reh gaee hai wo bhee khamosh hai.

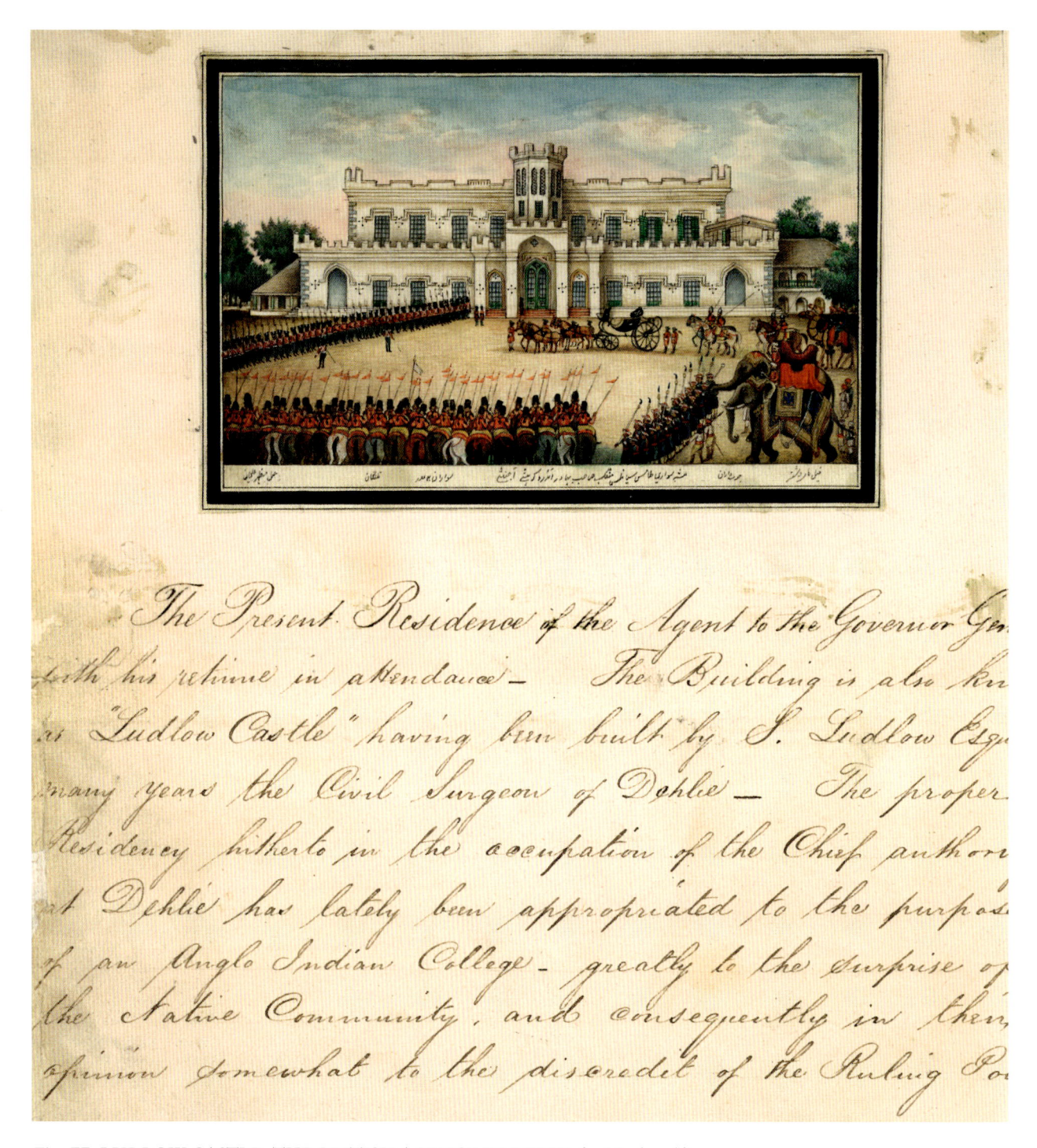

Fig. 77: LUDLOW CASTLE, THE BRITISH AGENCY IN DELHI, by Mazhar Ali Khan, c. 1840. From Metcalfe's Delhi Book. Outside the Agency, Ludlow Castle, there is a carriage waiting for Metcalfe's appearance, the Agent's sowarry of camels and elephants, and an escort of a troop of Skinner's Horse and a company from a Bengal Native Infantry. The house was built in the Civil Lines north of the Kashmiri Gate by Samuel Ludlow (d.1853), a surgeon with the Bengal establishment of the East India Company, who was stationed with the Delhi residency from 1813-31.
Watercolour, folio size 25.8 x 19 cm. British Library, London, Add.Or.5475 f.60v.

In the world of darkness, there is spirit of my night of sadness...
One candle which is proof of morning, is silent too...
Stain of separation of company of night is burnt...
One candle is left and that too is silent...

BIRDS AND ANIMALS

Pigeon keeping was and remains till today a special passion with the Dilliwallahs (figs 27, 62). Although homing pigeons and fancy breeds like fan-tails, pouters, homing, racing and tumblers had their own following, the skies were dominated by flocks (golas) in flights of widening gyres, in pursuit of other flocks to poach. Such was the sentiment associated with pigeons that reportedly an altercation over pigeons between a pigeon seller and soldiers of Nadir Shah actually led to the great massacre of the city.

ARTISTS AND PAINTERS

The Delhi school of painting was patronized by the emperors with Ghulam Murtaza Khan, Ghulam Ali Khan, and Raja Jivan Ram keeping alive a valuable tradition that could trace its roots to Akbar and Jahangir. But as the hold of the British grew, the artists found new patrons for their talent and their style and subjects were quickly adapted to accommodate the British taste. Although some attempt was made to emulate European conventions and perspectives, using pen-and-ink with pastel shades and soft tones, the traditional emphasis on detail of construction and refinery remained evident. Watercolour paintings of monuments and landscape became popular with the British. Qadam Rasul, Qudsiya Bagh, Zinat al-Masajid and Firoz Shah Kotla were the most popular subjects even as the Red Fort, Diwan-i Am, Diwan-i Khas, Jama Masjid, the tombs of Humayun and Safdar Jung had been earlier.

William Fraser (1784-1835) left behind a voluminous collection by several unknown artists, the best of whom captures with finesse and meticulous attention to detail scenes from the life of his patron as well as costumes and customs of local people. Fraser was succeeded by Sir Thomas Theophilus Metcalfe who commissioned the Delhi artist Mazhar Ali Khan to make paintings that were bound in a family album entitled *Reminiscences of Imperial Delhi* (figs 36, 37, 38, 55, 77, 82, 95). Colonel James Skinner (1778-1841) added to the repertoire by commissioning artists like Ghulam Murtaza Khan and Ghulam Ali Khan to do paintings of himself, his friends and the 'Yellow Boys' of his regiment (figs 75, 76, 78, 102, 103).

Music was an important dimension of the ambience of Mughal society except for the years during which Aurangzeb frowned upon it. Yet, his long absence from Delhi diluted the rigour of prohibition. The Delhi Gharana, traced back to the reign of Shamsuddin Iluatmish lays claim to Mir Hasan Sawant and Mir Bula Kalawant, the former being the first of Sufi singers influenced by Khwaja Muinuddin Chishti. Amir Khusrau, the beloved disciple of Hazrat Nizamuddin Auliya, gave the present-day repertoire of the popular qawwali form in addition to khayal and thumri. These were adopted by Miya Saamti and followed by his descendants. The two traditions, darbari and sufiana, were combined by Ustad Mamman Khan in the eighteenth century. Many of the traditions that were developed have probably been lost now, such as naqsh-o-gul, hawa, basit and savela. Amongst many legends associated with the Delhi gharana are the musical exploits of brothers Sadarang and Adarang, Haddu Khan and Hassu Khan who founded the Gwalior gharana, Ustad Tanras Khan and his disciple Ustad Zahoor Khan who used the pen name of 'Ramdas' for Braj compositions and 'Mumkin' for Urdu compositions. Apart from the rich repertoire of music the Delhi gharana is also credited with the invention of instruments like the sursagar and sarangi.

Ustad Zauq, Mirza Ghalib, Mir, Momin, Sauda, Dard, Dagh, Mushafi, Insha, Bahadur Shah Zafar himself, as well as Sir Syed Ahmed Khan, Nazeer Ahmad, Zaka Ullah, Altaf Husain Hali, Shibli Naumani, and Meer Amman Dehlavi amongst others became the torch bearers of the renaissance. Long before the last lamp of the Mughal Empire began to flicker, Mir Taqi Mir had witnessed the pillage and destruction caused by Ahmad Shah Durrani's armies and the growing pressure of Marathas and Afghans. His famous verse sums up his distress:

Delhi, which was the city select of the world where the elite of the times lived;
Has been robbed and destroyed by circumstance
I belong to that very desolate city

The cradle of a language: Urdu Persian was the language of the Mughal court and thus spoken by the elite. Ordinary people including the peasants of the region around Delhi spoke Khariboli and Brajbhasha. Sufi saints like Nizamuddin Aulia and their followers such as the remarkably talented Amir Khusrau used the dialect to promote what got to be known as Hindvi, weaving Persian into the local vocabulary. From that and the need to communicate with camp (urdu) soldiers became the cradle for Hindvi, Rekhta, or Urdu as it was variously called. Wali Daccani (1667-1744) arrived in Delhi and provided impetus to the growth of the language. He made the ghazal form easily accessible to the streets and homes. Soon the outstanding poets of Persian language, Arzu Abru, Hatim and Bedil began to acknowledge the dominance of Urdu. It became the language of the 1857 War of Independence and in a sense the most enduring symbol of the contribution of Mughals to the making of modern India's composite culture that despite the rude shock of Partition in 1947 remains the corner-stone of the nation. The last mushaira of Delhi, exquisitely portrayed by the author and the silent shamma of Mirza Ghalib were to become the epitaph of Mughals but were far from an accurate prophecy of an age to come.

In 1874 even as the horror of the post-uprising vengeance had begun to recede, the devastation of Delhi continued to haunt the minds of sensitive people like Khwaja Altaf Husain 'Hali':

Do not grieve for the glories of the past.
Ghalib, Shefta, Nayyar, Azurda and Zauq will never come again,
After Momin, Aalavi, and Shehbai, who is left to speak of the art of poetry?
The light of their greatness also shone on us who were not great.
Listen to the poetry of Dagh and Majruh, for after them
No nightingale will warble in this rose garden.
Those musha'aras of the past are no more.
And it is unseemly that I should grieve others with my own lament.

Although in about four or five years the exiled Muslim citizens were allowed to come back to the walled city from the neighbouring areas such as Mehrauli where they had taken refuge and gradually normalcy returned to Delhi, it was never going to be the same ever again. For a whole generation Delhi became a city of distant nostalgia mixed with bitter and sad memories, shattered monuments and ruins of its imperial days. As time went by and the British began to think of a capital to be called New Delhi, Shahjahanabad was reduced to being the transit route between the Civil Lines, the Cantonment and Raisina Hill, waiting to be rediscovered. On 15 August 1948 as India's first prime minister unfurled the tricolour from the ramparts of the Red Fort the soul of Shahjahanabad stirred once again as new India was born through a peaceful, non-violent revolution.

Following page: Fig. 78: LT. COL. JAMES SKINNER (1778-1841), by Ghulam Husayn Khan, Delhi style, c. 1835. Skinner was an Anglo-Indian military adventurer in his youth working for the Marathas before going over to the British in 1803 when he founded his first regiment of irregular cavalrymen, Skinner's Horse. He founded a second regiment in 1814 to assist the British in the Anglo-Nepal war. His legitimate feelings of being largely mistreated by the British on account of his mixed birth were assuaged when in 1814 the Governor General Lord Moira (afterwards Hastings) promoted him to a Lieutenant Colonelcy and made him a CB (Companion of the Order of the Bath). He maintained a large house in Delhi near the Kashmiri Gate and nearby built the church of St. James, consecrated in 1836, where he lies buried (figs 102-103). *Oil on canvas, 83 x 78.5 cm. British Library, London, F9.*

144

Fig. 79: RECRUITS TO SKINNER'S HORSE, c. 1815-20. From the Skinner Album. The uniforms and weapons indicate that the young men have come in from the countryside to be recruited for the second regiment of Skinner's Horse which James Skinner founded in 1814 to assist the British in the war with Nepal. The painting is a second version of one in the Fraser albums, which gives us all their names (Archer and Falk 1989, no. 57). They are all either Jats or Gujjars, the peasant castes of south and west of Delhi. One of the men here seems to be in undress uniform, while another is dressed in the full uniform of tall shako and yellow surcoat or kurta (which gave the regiment its name of 'The Yellow Boys') worn over a black jacket with red frogging.
Watercolour and bodycolour, 25 x 37.6 cm. British Library, London, Add.Or.1261.

Following Pages: Fig. 80: THE VISIT OF MAHARAO RAM SINGH OF KOTAH TO DELHI IN 1842. Maharao Ram Singh of Kotah (1827-66) is making a visit to Delhi, only he seems to have come on pilgrimage rather than to see the Emperor Bahadur Shah. We see him heading on his elephant past the fort towards the Nigambodh Ghat and again, dismounted, crouching by the river between Salimgarh and the Red Fort. Bahadur Shah is in the Shah Burj spying on him through a telescope. At the bottom of the picture he is depicted leaving heading past the Fatehpur Masjid towards the Lahori Gate. The Kotah artist gives a remarkably accurate view of the Red Fort and the city, save only for what was left of the zenana area of the palace. The city is depicted as composed of large and elegant havelis.
Opaque watercolour and gold on cloth. 445 x 259 cm. Rao Madho Singh Trust Museum, Fort, Kotah, no. 1003. Image courtesy of the Metropolitan Museum, New York

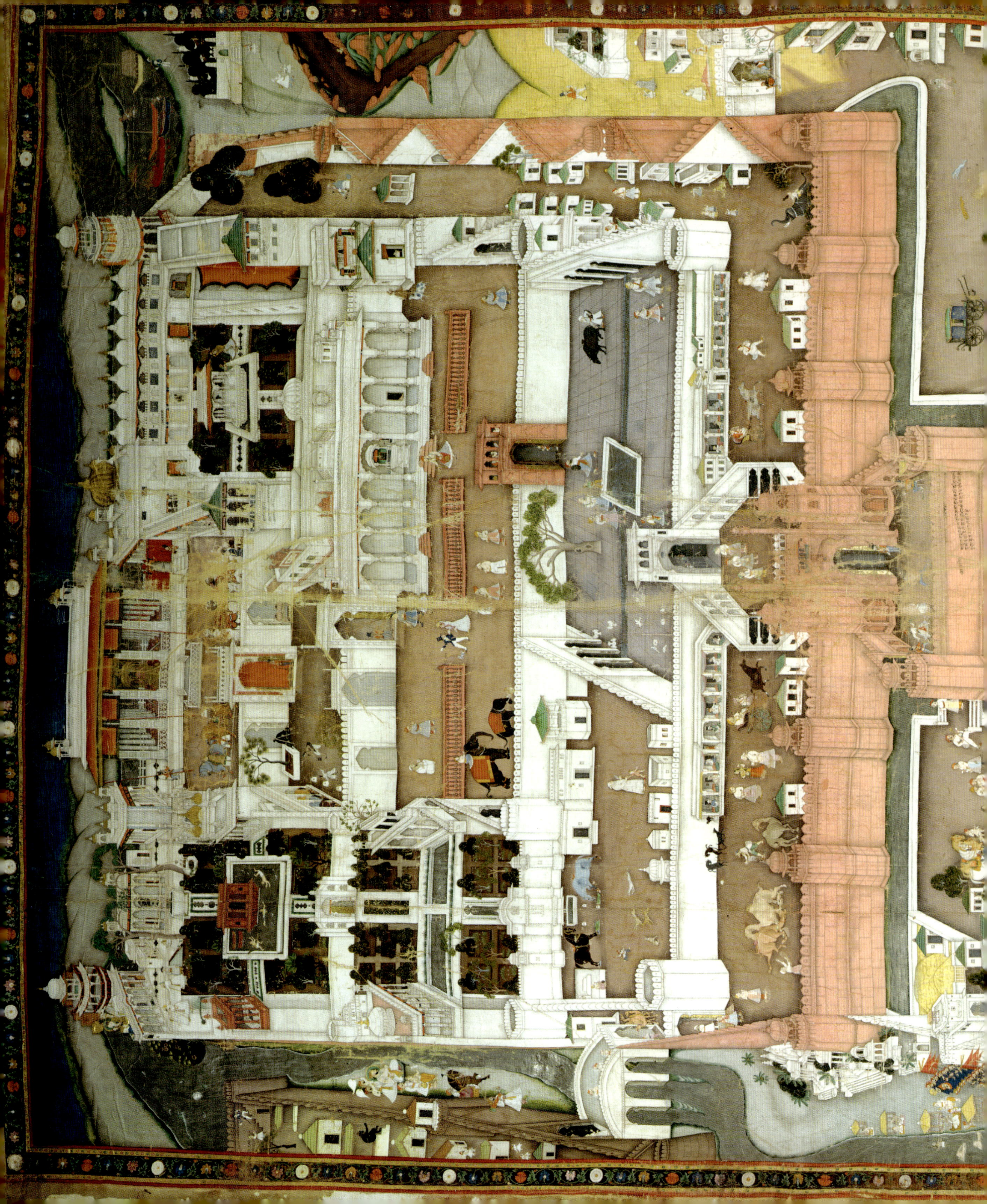

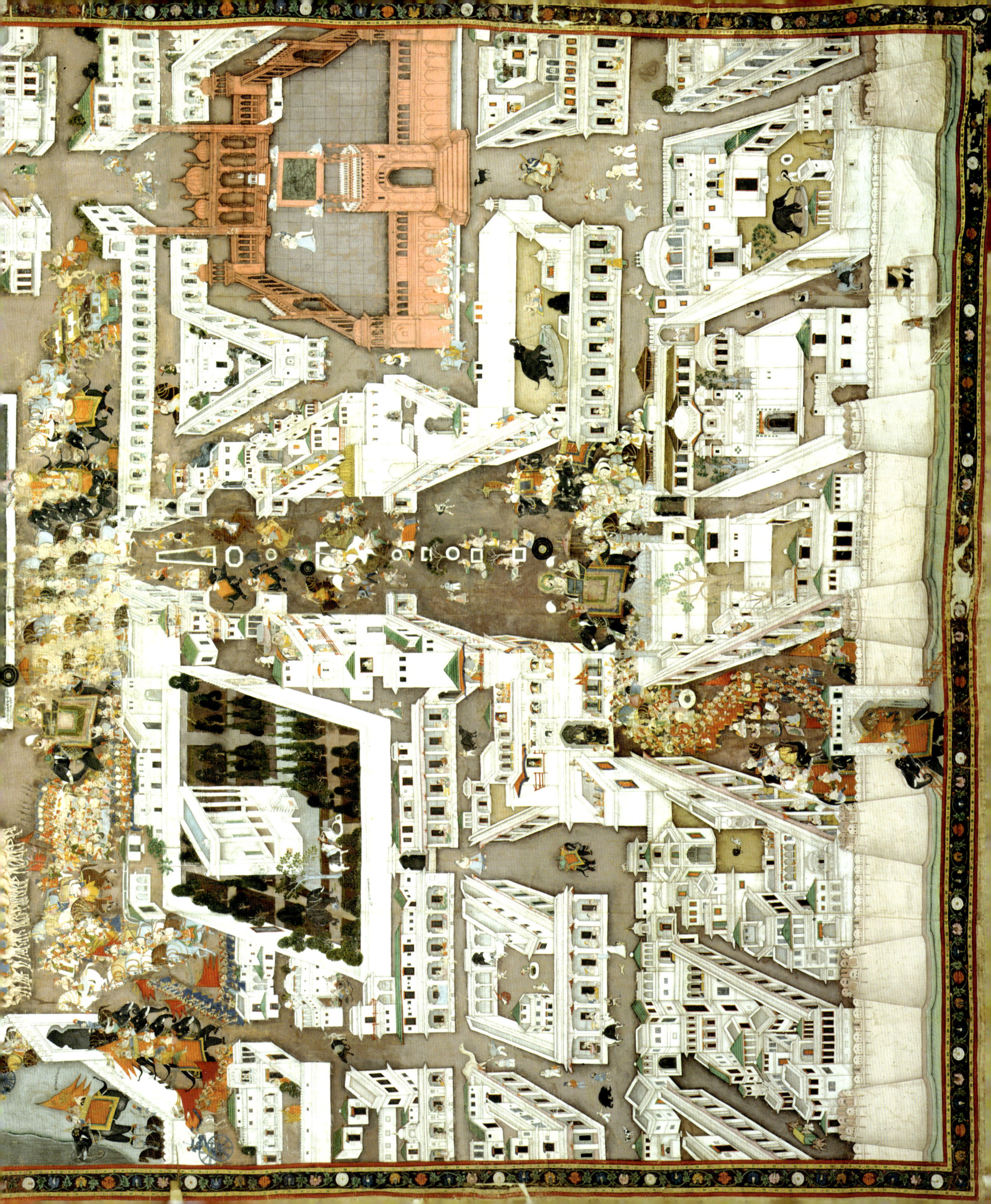

Architecture of Shahjahanabad

Ratish Nanda

A HISTORICAL BACKGROUND

The urban landscape of Shahjahanabad, marked by narrow lanes and houses jostling for space, neighbourhoods by a domed mosque or the intricately carved façade of a Jain temple, shops below and houses above, today seems alien to some and fascinating to others. For 'New Delhi' residents there is no affinity between the 'garden city' of New Delhi that the architect Sir Edwin Lutyens designed in the early twentieth century and the seventeenth-century 'Old Delhi'; yet, when one looks deeper, Shahjahan's city and the British New Delhi were both the result of a passion for building, both imperial in scale and designed to awe, and both were built when the respective imperial power was at its zenith. Most significantly, both were planned as 'garden cities' with the layout being determined by the open spaces; both had ceremonial axes – Chandni Chowk and Kingsway (later renamed Rajpath) respectively – and major streets in both Shahjahanabad and New Delhi culminated in monumental buildings.

Delhi had been in continuous existence as an imperial capital for almost 600 years when the Emperor Shahjahan, in the twelfth year of his reign, decided to build a complete new capital city on the bank of river Yamuna. The Tomar Rajputs and the Chauhans had ruled in the eleventh-twelfth centuries from Lal Kot and Qila Rai Pithora on the southern edge of present Delhi, where Mehrauli now stands, as did the Ilbari Turks or the Slave dynasty. Siri Fort, the second city of Delhi, was built by the Khalji king, Alauddin Khalji in the fourteenth century. The Tughluqs who ruled Delhi from AD 1320 to AD 1414 were great builders and built the cities of Tughluqabad (fig. 96) at the south-eastern edge of present-day Delhi; Jahanpanah bridging Qila Rai Pithora and Siri; and the city of Firozabad, Delhi's largest medieval city, the exact boundaries of which remain uncertain but which would have included parts of later Shahjahanabad.

The Tughluqs were succeeded by the Sayyid and Lodi dynasties that are not known to have built any new city in Delhi but their regime was marked with a profusion of tomb and mosque building stretching from the very northern edge of Delhi to the southern where a baoli (Shamilat Deb) still survives in Sultanpur.

The Mughal Emperor Humayun commenced the construction of Dinpanah before he was ousted by Sher Shah, but Humayun, on his recapture of the throne of Delhi, was able to complete Dinpanah, together with its citadel, now known as Purana Qila. The Mughal-era buildings in Delhi built during the reigns of the emperors Humayun, Akbar, and Jahangir, are all clustered around the shrine of Hazrat Nizamuddin Auliya, though several have been lost in the post-independence era with the building of new neighbourhoods. Buildings such as Humayun's Tomb (fig. 14) with its contrasting red sandstone and white marble facades and its grand scale being the predominant features; Ataga Khan's Tomb with intricate decorative patterns in inlay; and Chaunsath Khamba built entirely of marble, all in the Nizamuddin area, were important early Mughal-era buildings that influenced the architecture during Shahjahan's reign and in turn Shahjahanabad.

Several buildings from earlier dynasties became a part of the walled city of Shahjahanabad, the construction for which commenced in AD 1639. The grave of Shah Turkman and his disciple, the Ilbari Turk ruler, Razia Sultana Begum – the first woman to rule Delhi – are on the southern edge as is the lofty Tughluq-era Kalan Masjid (fig. 25). A fourteenth-century Lodi-era baoli of a unique 'L' shaped plan is found within the Red Fort. It is also believed that the city walls of Humayun's Dinpanah and Firoz Shah Tughluq's Firozabad were quarried for stone to build the city walls of Shahjahanabad.

THE MUGHALS

Just as the Tughluqs in the fifteenth century and the British in the twentieth century, the Mughals too used architecture to reaffirm their supremacy and legitimize their right to rule in an alien land. Shahjahan seemed to be aware that by building on the grandest scale he was ensuring a deep respect for him amongst his subjects and, as we now know, for a worldwide population for whom his name is synonymous with the Taj Mahal. That seven buildings of the Mughal era – Fatehpur Sikri, Lahore Fort, Taj Mahal, Humayun's Tomb, Red Fort Delhi, Red Fort Agra, Shalimar Bagh in Lahore – are today World Heritage Sites while more are on the tentative World Heritage List – Bagh-i Babur in Kabul, the Mughal Gardens of Srinagar – is an acknowledgment of the contribution of the Mughals to architecture.

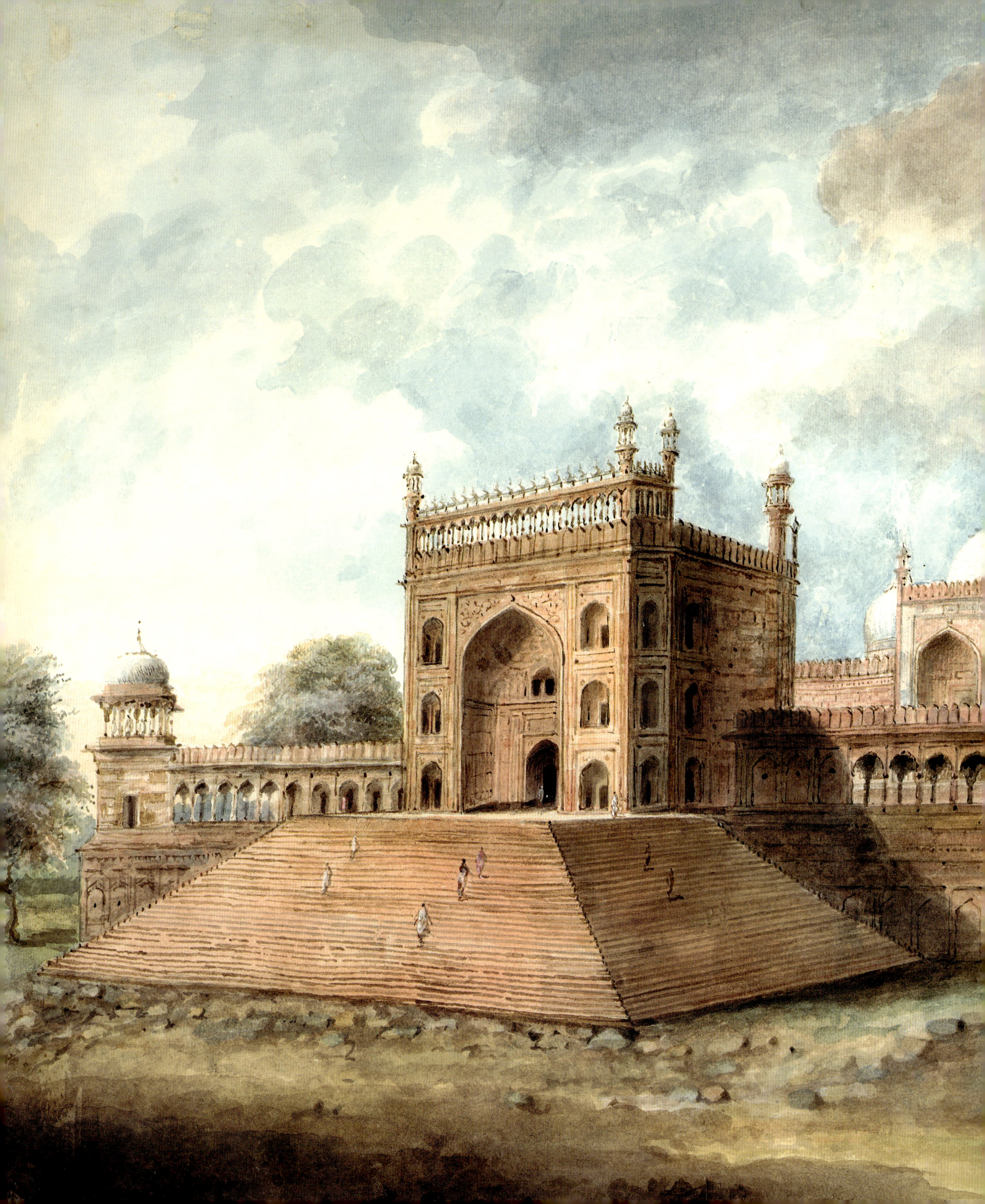

Fig. 81: JAMA MASJID, by Sita Ram, 1815. From the albums of drawings done by Sita Ram for Lord Hastings 1814-15. In this view of the Jama Masjid, Sita Ram clears away the clutter of buildings that surrounded the mosque in the early 19th century and presents a monument isolated in its magnificence, very much in accordance with picturesque conventions.
Watercolour, 38.5 x 52 cm. British Library, London, Add. Or.4809.

Emperor Babur, the first of the Mughal rulers of India (1526-30), lamented the lack of enclosed gardens and flowing water in the towns of Hindustan and on securing his new kingdom set about building gardens along the river Yamuna in Agra, thus setting the precedent for siting major buildings such as Humayun's Tomb, the Red Fort of Agra, the Taj Mahal, and the city of Shahjanabad on the banks of the river. Humayun (1530-40, 1555-56) succeeded his father Babur but was soon ousted and though he regained the throne, no significant building was built under his patronage. The architecture of Persia and what is now Afghanistan, where he spent over fifteen years in exile, symbolized by symmetry and the significance given to garden spaces, forever influenced Mughal architecture and court etiquette.

It was the great Emperor Akbar (1556-1605), ascending the throne at the age of thirteen, who defined Mughal architecture and whose buildings continue to influence architects even today – ironically since architecture as understood in the West is itself a discipline the British introduced to India. The Mughal emperors seemed to have relied on master craftsmen, who ranked high in status at the Mughal court. The court bureau of architects conferred with the emperor on the basis of three-dimensional models, as form and symmetry preceded functionality in Mughal-era structures. It is assumed that once the 'model' for the structure had been approved, no doubt by the emperor for imperial projects, the craftsmen had freedom to work on the details – the stone patterns, the decorations, the internal layout – but within well-established norms that ensured conformity with the emperor's aesthetic preferences. Though it may seem unbelievable that the perfection in architecture and planning of the great Mughal-era buildings were achieved without minute drawings such as the 1500 or so that Sir Edwin Lutyens prepared for Viceroy's House (now Rashtrapati Bhavan), no architectural drawings survive from the pre-British era and even today our craftsmen – though no longer enjoying the status of their predecessors – work with the same tools, techniques and with models as they remain illiterate and continue to lack any understanding of architectural drawings.

For the monumental Mughal buildings such as Humayun's Tomb, 'form' was of much greater significance than 'function' in the modern sense of the term. It was the splendour of Humayun's Tomb that established the key principles of Mughal architecture for the generations to come. These included: building to a never-before-seen monumental scale; siting buildings in prominent locations, often along a river and within a garden, symmetrical along a central axis, with flowing water brought into the enclosure; the use of red sandstone and white marble in great quantities and to great contrasting effect with the ceramic tiles extensively used in Persia now used only symbolically; and extensive use of textiles as floor and wall coverings to mitigate the effect of climate and to ensure greater privacy.

Akbar replaced the mud walls of the Lodi-era fort at Agra with stone walls clad with red sandstone (1565-73) giving the structure the name, Red Fort. Within the Red Fort some of Akbar's buildings survived Shahjahan's reconstruction and can be seen as a

Fig. 82: THE KOTWAL'S CHABUTRA IN THE CHANDNI CHOWK, studio of
Mazhar Ali Khan, c. 1840. From Metcalfe's Delhi Book. The Kotwal's Chabutra, or the
easternmost of the two principal squares in Chandni Chowk. The Kotwal was the chief
native magistrate of the city, who controlled the police and guards in Delhi.
Watercolour, folio size 25.8 x 19 cm. British Library, London, Add.Or.5475, f.16.

series of courtyard units placed along the riverfront. Thus the architectural principles for Mughal buildings, whether funerary, palatial or secular, remained unchanged.

Several sixteenth-century buildings in the Nizamuddin area of Delhi, especially Ataga Khan's tomb, built adjoining the Dargah of Hazrat Nizamuddin Auliya (fig. 55) by Akbar and finished in 1567, were profusely ornamented with decorated sandstone on the façade coupled with inlay with ceramic tiles and marble, starting a trend that became the hallmark of the buildings built during Jahangir's reign (1605-27). The gateway to the tomb of Akbar, in Sikandra near Agra, built 1605-13, is breathtaking with its ornamentation, grandeur, lofty arches, and the white marble minarets, the tops of which were reconstructed under orders of Lord Curzon in the early twentieth century.

It is, however, the tomb of Itimaduddaula (completed in 1626), Jahangir's father-in-law and prime minister, built in white marble that is profusely inlaid with coloured and semi-precious stones that influenced Shahjahan's Taj Mahal. In fact several Agra residents and guidebooks refer to the tomb as the '*chota* Taj'.

Chaunsath Khambha, the tomb of Akbar's foster brother Mirza Aziz Koka, which as the name suggests has sixty-four pillars supporting the twenty-five domed bays, was also built of white marble in 1624. Today, hemmed-in within Hazrat Nizamuddin Basti, the tomb is a 'pillared/arcaded hall' and clearly inspired the Shahjahani palace buildings in the Red Fort of Delhi, both essentially being 'garden tents in stone'.

Thus, Shahjahan's reign (1628-58) was preceded by a hundred years of Mughal rule where architectural styles had rapidly evolved with new territories being included within the empire. Mughal rule itself had been preceded by over 1500 years of stone building traditions in India. Shahjahan's architecture is defined as the classical phase of the Islamic architecture of India. The Taj Mahal is probably the only building in the world that inspires similar awe both when seen by astronauts from the moon and by visitors standing only a few inches away from the gracefully decorated surfaces.

SHAHJAHANABAD

Even before he became emperor, Shahjahan had established a reputation for architecture and was responsible for some of the imperial projects such as the Shalimar Bagh in Srinagar. However, he spent the first ten years of his reign altering significantly the buildings erected by Jahangir in the palace forts at Agra and Lahore and in the process establishing a vocabulary of architectural elements and material of preference – marble.

The stability of the empire coupled with economic prosperity gave Shahjahan an opportunity to undertake building projects on an unprecedented scale. It was in 1638 that Shahjahan, with a known passion for building, decided to build a new city. Thus along the banks of river Yamuna, in the historic city of Delhi, like a modern planner, he acquired a large tract of land to build his city between 1639 and 1648. Like his predecessors, the palace-fort was built along the river with streams of water channelled through the fort and the city – both to create a genial micro-climate and confirm a Mughal aesthetic that Babur longed for in Hindustan. Shahjahanabad was thus built on the western bank of the Yamuna, north of Humayun's city Dinpanah and extending up to Salimgarh on the north – a small island fort built in AD 1546.

Shahjahanabad was well planned under the direct, creative influence of Shahjahan who invited reputed and successful craftsmen/artisans to Delhi to oversee the building of his new city. Access and circulation for the royal household, the ministers, the officers and the general public determined the layout of the city, the palace-fort, and the mohallas. This division of the city into several homogeneous units with the public, semi-private, and private space clearly defined at every level was in keeping with Islamic practice, as with almost 500 years of Islamic rule in Delhi before the building of Shahjahanabad, Islam had become a second cornerstone of city culture in Mughal-ruled India.

The principal built elements of the city, enclosed within the stone masonry walls interspersed with gateways, were the luxurious palace-fort, the lofty Jama Masjid and several other grand mosques that were mostly sited at the culmination of important axes, the north-south axis of Faiz Bazaar and the east-west axis of Chandni Chowk, the elaborate system of aqueducts/water channels, and significant gardens that extended beyond the surrounding city walls. The rest of the city was built by in-fill with the mohallas, developed as mini cities and replicating the processional segregation of spaces of the palace-fort.

The Red Fort (fig. 20) was the principal focus and the first complex of buildings to be constructed, while the monumental Jama Masjid, erected between 1650 and 1656 on a hilly outcrop south-west of the fort, provided the second focus of the new city as it was being built. The Jama Masjid (fig. 19) was one of the largest mosques to have ever been built in India and designed to inspire awe and establish Shahjahan's position as a reviver of Islam in India.

The public could access the Red Fort from the west gate and up till the Diwan-i Am (fig. 52) or the 'hall of public audience'. This east-west axis of the fort was extended into the city via the Chandni Chowk – a forty-yard-wide bazaar street with a canal running along its centre and being bounded by a colonnade of over 1500 shops of similar design and culminating in the grand Fatehpuri Masjid (fig. 85). Chandni Chowk, in historical accounts is known more for its way of life than its architectural grandeur; the heart of Shahjahanabad, lined with tea houses and fine goods, was in many ways a combination of Connaught Place and the Kingsway of British New Delhi.

The main north-south axis for Shahjahanabad was laid out from the Delhi Gate of the city walls through Faiz Bazaar (fig. 42) to the Akbarabadi or Delhi Gate of the palace-fort with an extension stretching past the Red Fort to the Kashmiri Gate of the city.

With the Red Fort placed along the river Yamuna, the Jama Masjid on the highest land, the principal boulevards established, the nobility were allotted lands and, on occasion, funds to encourage the building of their mansions in the new city. Several centuries later, Sir Edwin Lutyens, the architect for British New Delhi, was to do the same by allocating space for the palaces of the Indian princes centered at the culmination of the Kingsway – a ceremonial boulevard like Chandni Chowk.

Together with the completion of the principal buildings, one of the key first steps undertaken by Shahjahan's engineers was to divert the Yamuna many miles north of Delhi into a system of canals (fig. 86) to bring in a year-round supply of water into the new city, to mitigate the hot dry climate of Delhi. The principal canal entered the city in the north-western section, near the Kabuli Gate, and its branches flowed down the Chandni Chowk and through the over 50 acres of enclosed gardens, the Shiba Abad, built by Shahjahan's daughter, Jahanara Begum, north of Chandni Chowk, and then entered the fort-palace on the north.

Jahanara Begum's expansive gardens made way for the railway tracks and station in the nineteenth century and some of the other gardens of the Mughal era that were a significant urban element and used for a variety of royal functions, suffered similar fate. Most of the gardens of Shahjahanabad lay outside the city walls though within

156

Fig. 84: THE SHRINE OF NIZAMUDDIN AULIYA, photograph by G.W. Lawrie & Co., 1890s. The hangings make for a most striking pattern round the shrine.
British Library, London, Photo 752/15(16).

Facing page: Fig. 83: CARVED DECORATION IN THE INTERIOR OF THE TOMB OF ILTUTMISH (1211-35), photograph by Lala Deen Dayal, 1890-1900. Built in 1235, this tomb illustrates the development of Indo-Islamic architecture. The entrance is intricately carved with geometrical and arabesque patterns along with some Hindu motifs like wheels, the lotus, and diamonds.
British Library, London, Photo 430/21(60).

the vicinity of the city. The most significant of these seventeenth-century gardens were Shahjahan's own 'Tis Hazari Bagh' (Tis: 30; hazari: 1000) just outside the northern Kabuli Gate of the city; Roshanara Begum's garden near the western Lahori Gate; and Nawab Akbarabadi Begum's Shalimar Bagh six miles beyond Lahori Gate, where the coronation of Emperor Aurangzeb (1658-1707) was held. Most of the large courtyard mansions built by the nobility in the city also contained gardens and orchards.

Shahjahanabad thus had an intense, even if organic relationship with its gardens – where much time was spent both at work and leisure. While many of the gardens mentioned here were exclusively for the Mughal royalty and nobility, the vast open spaces did give Shahjahanabad, until the nineteenth century, an atmosphere of a garden city, which the builders of New Delhi replicated centuries later. However, what was the 'private' for the Mughals became the 'public' for British. In fact, the Viceroy House, now Rashtrapati Bhavan, had an expansive 'Mughal garden' attached to it which even today is a major attraction – as would have been the gardens at the Red Fort if they had survived destruction following the 1857 war of independence or will be if the political will can be mustered to restore the Hayat Bakhsh Bagh – designed to imitate a Quranic paradise.

RED FORT

The Red Fort was the zenith of Mughal palace-fort building, symbolizing the enormous power of the emperor. The overbearing sandstone walls, with canopied watch towers at regular intervals, concealed an enchanting 'paradise' centred on the emperor.

The buildings within the Red Fort were extravagant garden pavilions set within formal gardens, which covered more than half of the palace-fort. The pavilions were more 'tents in stone' than 'palace buildings' as understood in today's context. Even during the stable Shahjahani era, the Mughal court was on the move more often than not and in that sense the nomadic lifestyle of Babur continued. The series of gardens, enclosed within arcades or colonnades were intricately linked to one another and served as forecourts defining the spaces attached to important buildings.

The Delhi palace was probably the only instance of an urban Mughal palace to be built as a complete entity quite like the British city of New Delhi being the only complete city built during the British rule in India.

The Red Fort was a mini-city in itself, with administrative palaces, striking residential quarters, ceremonial courtyards, and housed a retinue of thousands. Shahjahan introduced harmony, symmetry along a central axis, and several formal elements with an architectural vocabulary purposely limited to a few elements to ensure consistency of design. The stone buildings are today incomplete, seen today without the essential textiles and tent awnings (fig. 87). Each of the buildings – the Diwan-i Am, Naubat Khana, Diwan-i Khas – had grooves in their parapet wall to tie the ropes that would support the large tent awnings

The Futtehpooree Mosque

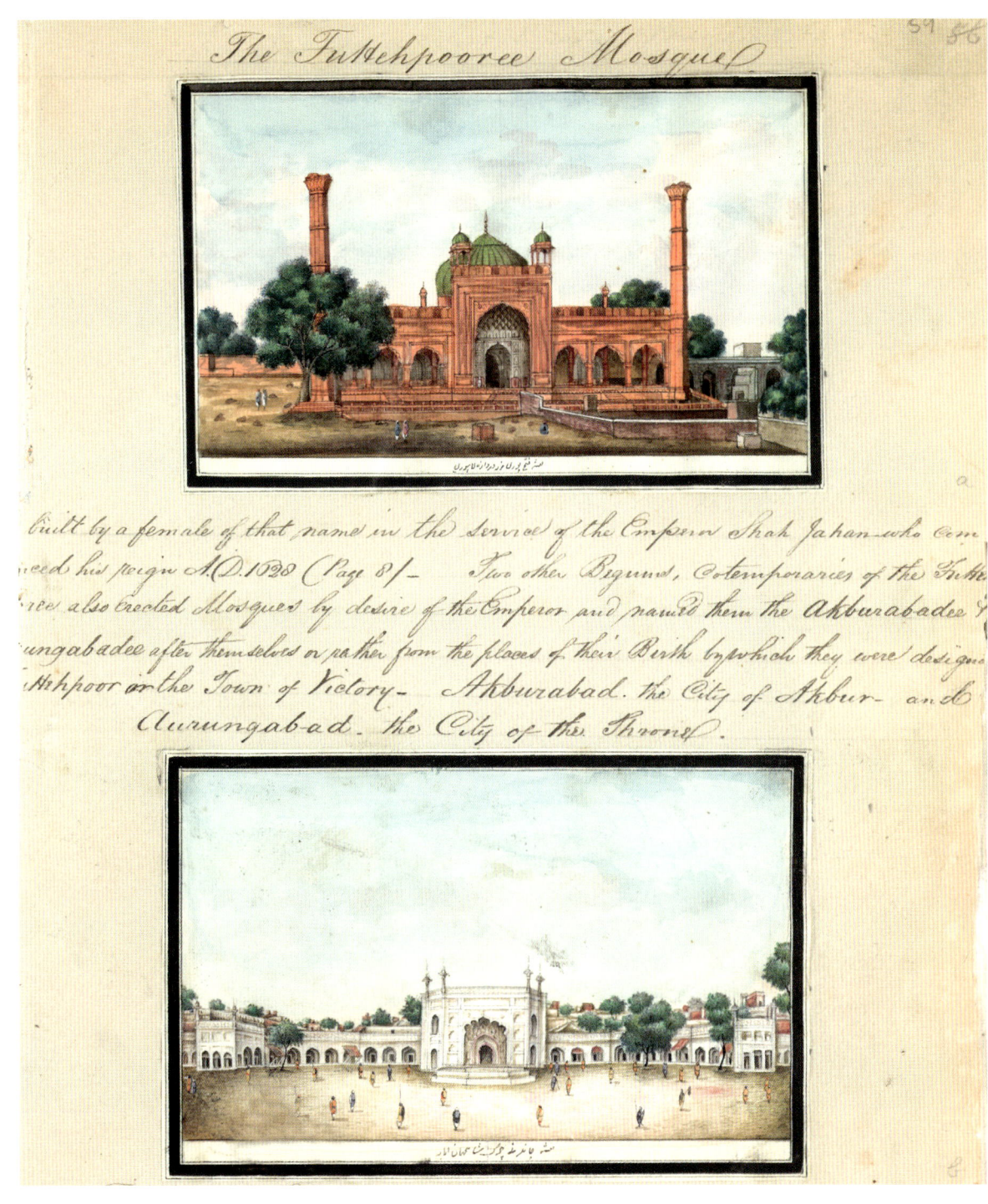

Built by a female of that name in the service of the Emperor Shah Jahan who com[men]ced his reign A.D. 1628 (Page 8/— Two other Begums, Cotemporaries of the Futteh[poo]ree also erected Mosques by desire of the Emperor and named them the Akburabadee & [A]urungabadee after themselves or rather from the places of their Birth by which they were design[ated] [Fut]tehpoor or the Town of Victory — Akburabad. the City of Akbur — and Aurungabad. the City of the Throne.

Fig. 85: FATEHPUR MASJID AND CHANDNI CHOWK, studio of Mazhar Ali Khan, c. 1840. From Metcalfe's Delhi Book. The Fatehpuri Masjid was built in 1650 at the end of the Chandni Chowk thoroughfare by one of Shahjahan's queens Fatehpuri Begum. The lower view is of the octagonal piazza Chandni Chowk, two thirds of the way along the street that took its name, itself with gateways to the Queen's Gardens (Bagh-i Begum) to the north and a baths (hamman) to the south. It was the reflection of the moonlight in the central tank that gave the piazza and then the street its name.
Watercolour, folio size 25.8 x 19 cm. British Library, London, Add.Or.5475 f.59.

such as the one that would have covered the entire Diwan-i Am courtyard to shelter the assembled nobles and public during the summer months. Privacy and thermal comfort in the pavilions were achieved in much the same manner as it would have been in the elaborate Mughal tents, with brightly coloured curtains of wool in the winter and moist grass mats in the summer hanging from the iron rings that can still be seen in place. Magnificent carpets and embroidered curtains adorned the 'stone tents' while gilding on the ceiling, covered with star patterns in the Diwan-i Khas, resembled the heavens. Each of the surviving buildings is today out of context without the arcaded corridors enclosing the garden courts in which the 'tent-like' royal pavilions originally stood.

The pavilions were built in a manner that allowed the outdoors to permeate within and in turn allowing external open space to function virtually like a building. This concept of space was very different from that seen in the bungalows of New Delhi and their surrounding gardens, where the division between the outside and inside is definite.

Shahjahan formalized the hierarchy of spaces, clearly derived from the layout of imperial camps, with the 'most private' royal pavilions – both for the emperor and the zenana – placed at the far end from the public entrance, on terraces along the river to benefit from the cool breezes of the north-east and in turn connected by the stream of paradise, the Nahr-i Bihisht lined with gracefully fine hand-carved stone fit for the emperor. The stream on the terrace with the 'sea like' river below would have achieved the 'Infinity pool' effect that the best modern hotels aim for but never quite achieve – such was the refined sense of aesthetic of Shahjahan. No doubt, Babur – with his longing for flowing water in the heat of Hindustan – would have been proud.

In plan the Red Fort is roughly like an irregular octagon with its two long sides on the east and west, and six smaller ones on the north and south. The fort was bounded by the river on the east and on the north by the ramparts of the sixteenth-century Salimgarh citadel. Visitors to the city – especially coming by river – would be stunned by the grandeur of the Red Fort; the gleaming white marble palace buildings along the river also gave the royal household privacy and views over relatively uninhabited fields across the river with the river-bank used in the dry months as a gathering place for crowds to view the emperor in the daily 'darshan' ceremony and as a staging ground for entertainment such as elephant fights.

Visiting nobles and public to the Red Fort would have entered at the western or 'Lahore Gate' of the Red Fort, from the ramparts of which the Indian prime minister addresses the nation each year on Independence Day.

Just beyond the Lahore Gate stands the vaulted bazaar the Chatta, the inspiration for which lay in the covered bazaars of Persia: Shahjahan had visited one such covered bazaar in Peshawar. The Chatta was almost an extension of the Chandni Chowk, as the shops in the palace sold the highest quality products catering not only to the thousands who inhabited the Red Fort but by virtue of the location at the periphery of the fort and also to the nobility and the public en-route to the Diwan-i Am. The walls and ceilings of

Map of Shahjahanabad 1846-47

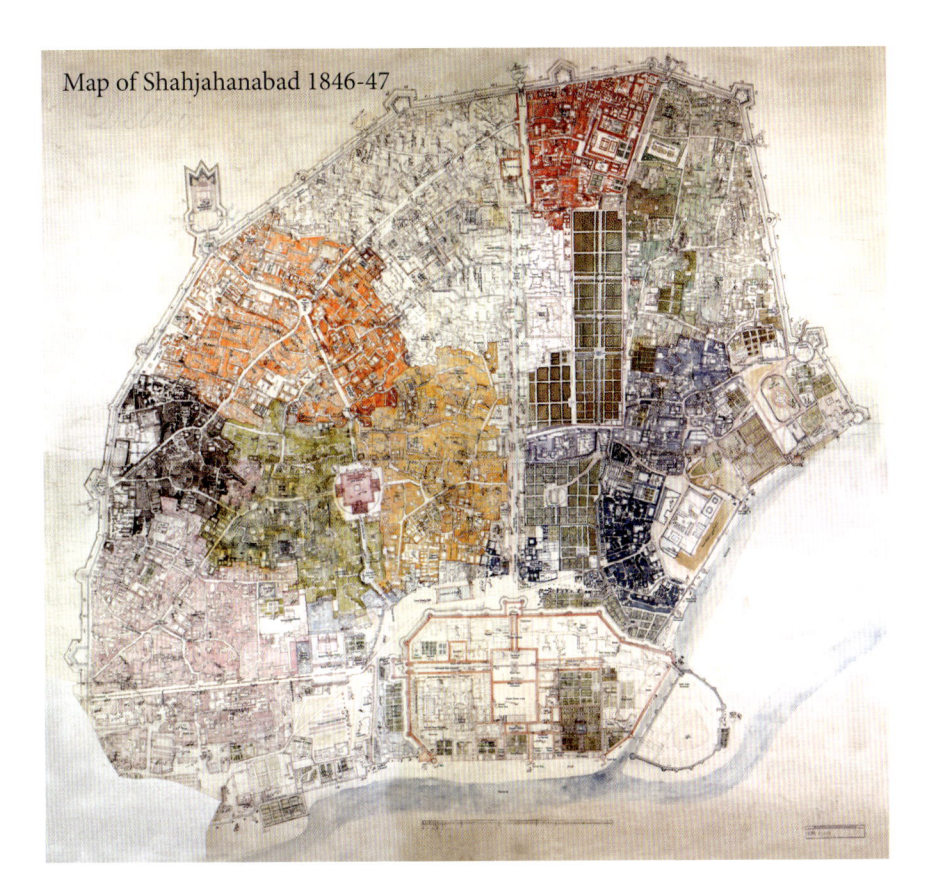

Fig. 86: MAP OF SHAHJAHANABAD by a Delhi cartographer, 1846-47.
The map is obviously drawn by an Indian cartographer, in that it includes little vignettes of important buildings seen in elevation and plan, and is covered with Urdu inscriptions identifying mosques and other religious buildings, havelis and other mansions, as well as the buildings in the Red Fort. In its precision, however, with regard to the overall shape of the city and the Red Fort, the layout of roads, moahallas etc., it is clearly under European inspiration. It can be precisely dated through its recording the Lal Diggi tank in front of the Red Fort replacing the Gulabi Bagh, finished in 1846, and likewise the Delhi Bank's presence still in a little classical building opposite Red Fort prior to its move to the Begum Samru's house in 1847. At this date the only likely patron is Thomas Metcalfe, who had already commissioned the panorama (fig. 99) the previous year. The map is of the greatest importance in recording the appearance of the city before the destruction of 1858.
Pen-and-ink and watercolour, 108 x 98.5 cm.
British Library, London, IO Maps X/1659

Map of Shahjahanabad (Delhi) with labels including:

- Zinā Khāss Bazār
- Hawelī Khān Daurān Khān
- Kūchah Bulāqī Begum
- Darwāzah Khān Daurān Khān
- Kūchah Mirza Ḥajqīr Beg
- Sarmast Khān Katra
- Tahakair Darwāzah
- Hawelī Ṣafātjan
- Kūchah Bulāqī Begum
- Hawelī Badr ad-Dīn
- Garem Sahib
- Darwāzah Hawelī Ram Rattan
- Kūchah Mīr Jahān
- Koṭhī Bank
- Koṭhī ʿAlī Khān
- Rastah Begum Bud
- Sayid Bhore Shāh
- Chashmah Lāl Diggi
- Khāss Bazār
- Masjid Kashmīrī Katra
- Bazār Kashmīrī Katra
- Sunahri Masjid
- Girjāghar
- Chaunī Safarmīna Daryā Ganj
- Ṭīlla Qabristān
- Koṭhī Kewīn Sahib
- Chaplain's House
- Rāj Ghāṭ Darwāzah
- Bāghīchah Mirza Gawhar
- Dihlī Darwāza
- Rāstha Bakht Burj
- Buland Bāgh Bādshāh
- Rath Khānah
- Nazārat
- Bārahdārī
- Masjid
- Lāhawrī Darwāzah
- Bāghīchah
- Zīnat Mahall
- Chawk Chattah
- Darwāzah Chattah
- Ḥawḍ Nahr
- Rastah Salīm Garh
- Bazār Dihlī Darwāzah
- Darwāzah Naw Mahallah
- Mīna Bazār
- Naqqār Khānah Darwāzah
- Mahtāb Bāgh
- Chhotī Masjid
- Kūchah Naw Mahallah
- Hammām
- Bāghīchah
- Jahān Kharu
- Chandni Mahal
- Chawk Dīwān-e-ʿĀm
- Dewari Hawā Sīra
- Dewari Afghāni
- Jawahir Khānah
- Motī Masjid
- Zafar Mahall
- Chhota Rang Mahall
- Daryā Mahall
- Rang Mahall
- Naqqār Khānah
- Darwāzah Lāl Burdāh
- Khānah-e Qaṣabī
- Dīwān-e Khāss
- Ḥammām Aqab
- Motī Mahall
- Burj
- Suman Burj
- Yamuna

the bazaar were ornately decorated (see Mazhar Ali Khan's panorama of 1846, fig. 99) until whitewashed in the late twentieth century.

At the end of the public access stood the Diwan-i Am, entered through its gatehouse, the Naubat Khana (fig. 90), where drums were played to announce the arrival of the emperor into the Red Fort. Although pillared halls were integral to Persian architectural vocabulary, this arrangement followed an architectural vocabulary first seen in Delhi at Chaunsath Khambha, the tomb of Mirza Aziz Kokaltash, the foster brother of Emperor Akbar, standing in the Hazrat Nizamuddin Basti.

The Diwan-i Am was enclosed within an arcaded court, destroyed after the large-scale demolitions in the aftermath of the first war of independence in 1857, but the foundations of which still survive. Also in the twentieth century the fine layer of white lime plaster was scraped off the Diwan-i Am to reveal the more fashionable red sandstone. However, the white shining plaster prepared by mixing and grinding lime mortar with marble dust and egg white for several months was meant to give a 'marble-like' appearance to the red-sandstone building. Mazhar Ali Khan's remarkable painting shows the striking white Diwan-i Am in its courtyard (fig. 99) and the intricate ornamentation on the walls of the octagonal courtyard of the bazaar.

The emperor seated on his throne would have seen visitors assembled as per their rank both within the Diwan-i Am, the floor of which would have been covered with priceless carpets, and spilling into the courtyard up till the arcaded enclosure and shaded from the sun in the summers with a vast awning that covered 3200 square yards. Supported by four silver poles, an audience of almost 10,000 people could be accommodated under this huge velvet awning.

Shahjahan, unlike his father Jahangir who was much influenced by European art, sought to limit architectural decoration to Islamic norms that permitted only geometric patterns or plant forms. Yet, in a departure that has only been explained as a desire to mimic the flying throne of King Solomon, the throne platform or Jarokha at the Diwan-i Am has a background depicting the mythological Orpheus playing music to beasts and several birds adorning the surrounding panels. Noted historian Ebba Koch notes: 'it seems that the technique of inlaying with stones or parchin kari, as the Mughals called it, carried in itself a Solomonic connotation. The animal imagery of the Solomonic throne (the birds and the lions), is projected on the pietre dure wall, where … a Solomonic

Following pages: Fig. 87: THE DIWAN-I KHAS IN THE PALACE IN THE RED FORT, by Ghulam Ali Khan, 1817. Ghulam Ali Khan's view of the Diwan-i Khas breaks free of the conventions of these architectural drawings and is instead a complete picture of the residence of the emperor with the appropriate shamianas and qanats and active participants in the scene. The viewpoint is centred just to the left of the north façade. His handling of the main building is masterly but less so is his inability to control the perspective of the façades of the buildings on the right. This view became a model for later paintings of the Diwan-i Khas.
Watercolour and bodycolour, British Library, London, Add.Or.4694.

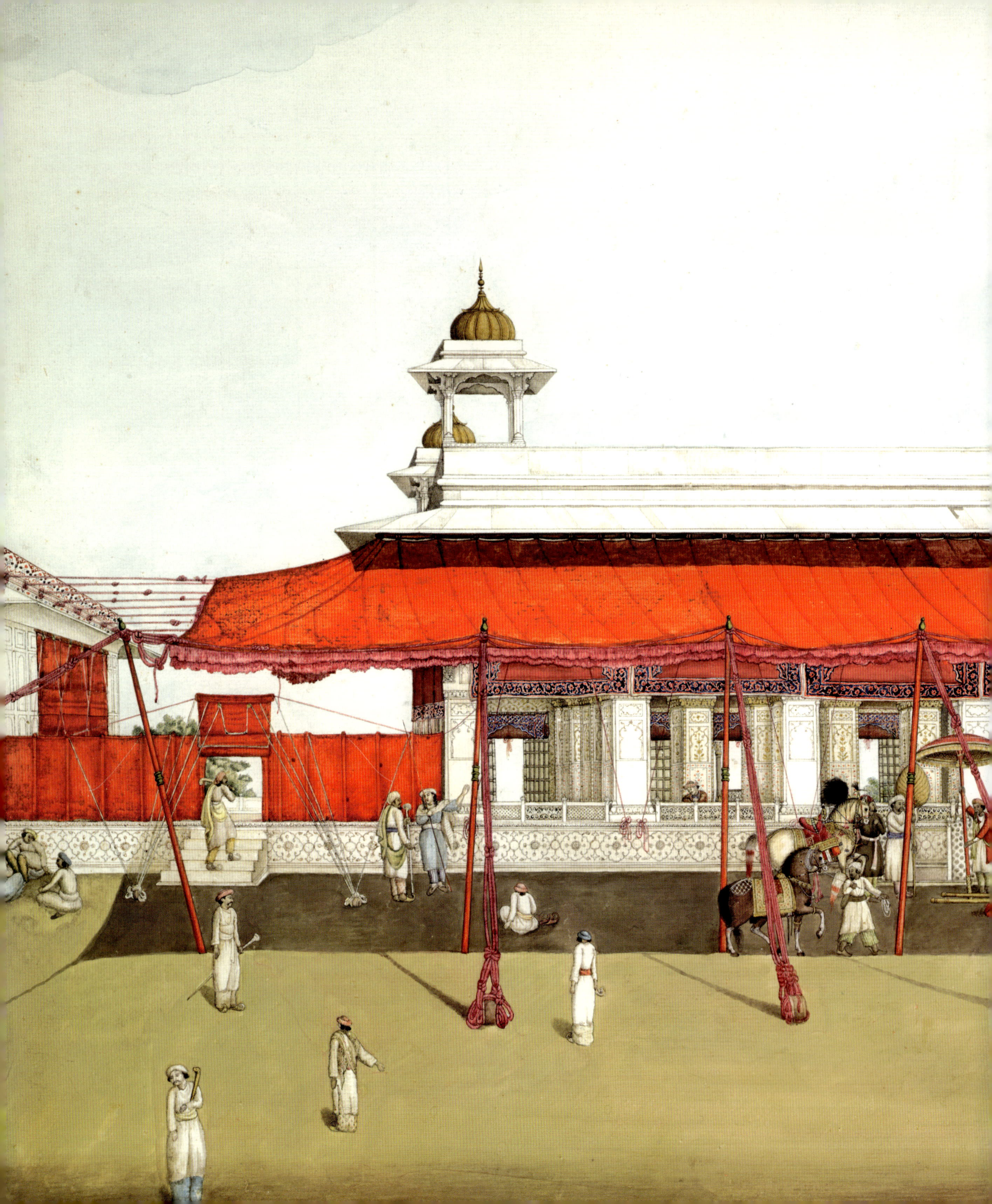

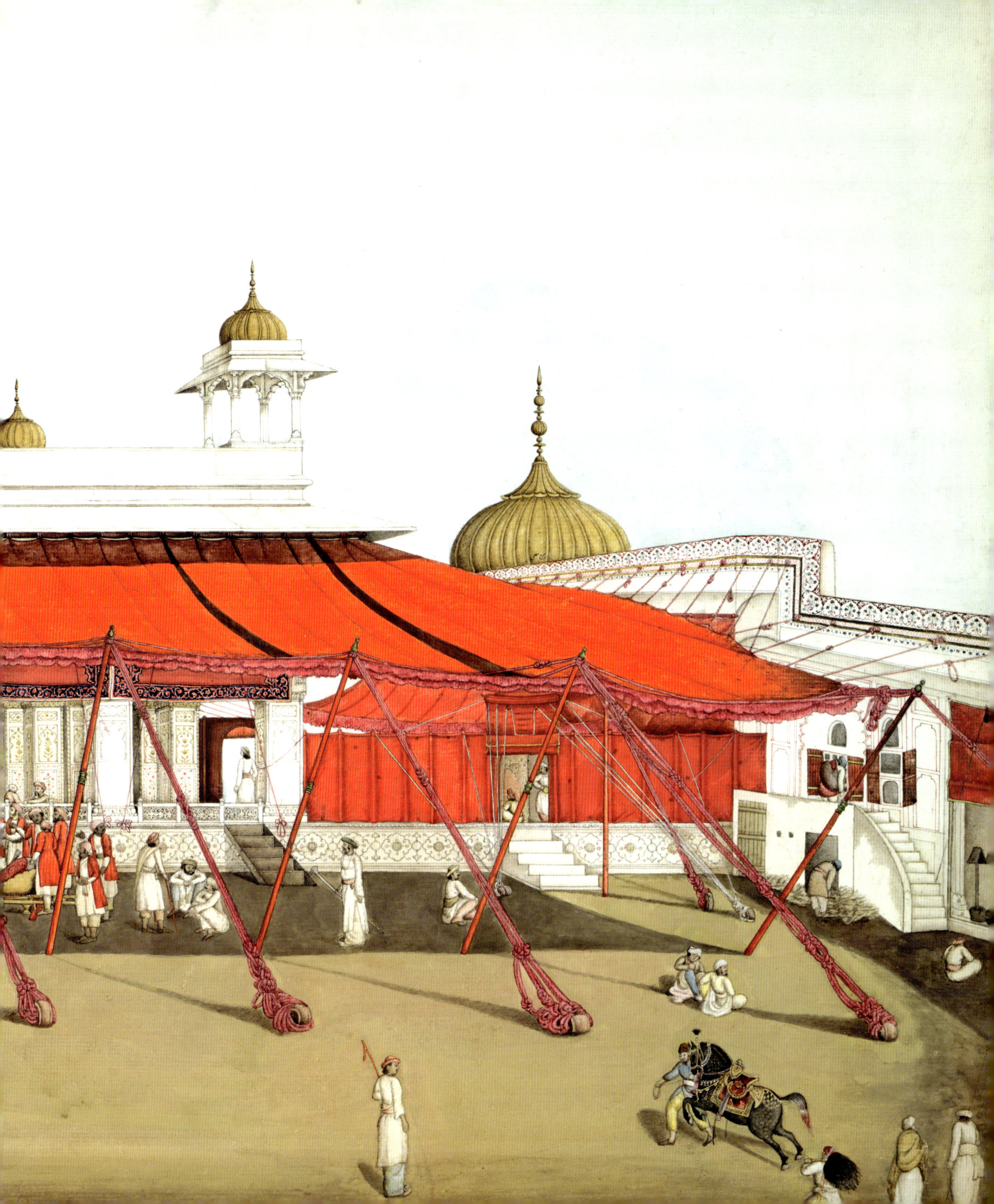

164

Fig. 89: ELEPHANT RIDERS FROM THE DELHI GATE, photography by Joseph Beglar, 1870-80. From the Archaeological Survey of India collection. The sculptures are of the two riders, Jaimal and Patta, heroic Rajput chiefs who defended the fortress of Chittor against Akbar. They were made of red sandstone and had separated from their elephant mounts which once stood outside the Delhi Gate of the Red Fort (see facing page). They are shown displayed at either side of the entrance to an unidentified house. The figures are of the upper half only, with curved bases which would be seated on the backs of the elephants.
British Library, London, Photo 1003/(878).

Facing page: Fig. 88: ELEPHANT FROM DELHI GATE, photograph by Joseph Beglar, 1870-80. From the Archaeological Survey of India collection. This is one of the pair of life-sized black marble elephants which once stood outside the Delhi Gate of the Red Fort. They were once mounted by riders Jaimal and Patta. They originally stood outside the fort at Agra and were brought from there to Delhi by Shahjahan only to be removed by Aurangzeb. They were later reinstated by Lord Curzon, viceroy of India between 1899 and 1905.
British Library, London, Photo 1003/(877).

Fig. 90: THE NAQQAR KHANA AND LAHORE GATE, photograph by Robert and Harriet Tytler, 1858. The view is taken from the roof of the Diwan-i Am looking towards the west side of the great chowk that formerly existed here surrounded by an arcaded cloister. The west side was pierced by two smaller gateways near the corners as marked in fig. 86 and as recorded here as well as by the Naqqar Khana itself. Beyond is the Jilau Khana, the court at the crossroads of the palace.
British Library, London, Photo 53/(17).

throne wall is created within the arched niche' (In 'Shah Jahan and Orpheus: The Pietre Dura Decoration and the Programme of the throne in the Hall of Public Audiences at the Red Fort of Delhi' in *Mughal Art and the Imperial Ideology*, Oxford 2001).

The public east-west axis of the Red Fort was a continuation of Chandni Chowk until Aurangzeb added a barbican and as was famously said, put a 'veil' around the fort. This public axis met the private or royal north-south axis of the fort at the Diwan-i Am.

The Diwan-i Khas or the 'hall of private audience' of the emperor was easily the finest building in the Red Fort. This is where the emperor held his special audiences with his most trusted courtiers and this is where he received his most important guests, sitting on the famed Peacock Throne. Shahjahani ideals of symmetry, beauty, elegance, intimacy were combined to create grandeur. The façade of five cusped arches supported

Fig. 91: INTERIOR OF THE LAHORE GATE, photograph by Robert and Harriet Tytler, 1858. The Lahore Gate had been where resided the commandant of the fort, appointed by the British, and the gateway has been remodelled on this side to provide accommodation for him. The Chatta bazaar extends from the gateway on the left and massed cannon have taken over from the gardens formerly here.
British Library, London, Photo 193/(11).

by square marble piers decorated with inlay of semi-precious jewels led to a gilded ceiling interior.

Adjoining the Diwan-i Khas were the emperor's personal quarters, the Khas Mahal and the harem – covering almost a third of the area of the Red Fort. The Khas Mahal epitomized privacy, while bringing the outdoors into the pavilion with the cooling waters of the Nahr-i Bihisht (fig. 101). The central portion of the pavilion, the Khwabgah, was enclosed by the finest marble lattice screen known in India, badly damaged in recent years, its breathtaking carving is topped with a 'scales of justice' placed on a crescent moon and other heavenly bodies. On the river face, the Khas Mahal's most decorated room was the domed, semi-octagonal tower known as the Mussaman Burj, in the opening of which the emperor gave his daily 'darshan' to crowds gathered on the river's embankment.

Restoration of Sunder Nursery

The vast open space that stood between Humayun's Tomb and his fort – Purana Qila – was locally known as Azim Bagh possibly due to the early Mughal era Serai of Azimganj that stands here. Bound by the river on the east and the Grand Trunk road on the west, this land stood in close proximity to the dargah of Hazrat Nizamuddin Auliya and since it is considered to be auspicious to be buried near a saint's grave a profusion of tomb building happened here, especially during the Akbari era.

In the early twentieth century this area was used to experiment and grow plants for the upcoming British city of New Delhi thus establishing the Sunder Nursery. Since 2007, the Aga Khan Trust for Culture in consultation with the Central Public Works Department and the Archaeological Survey of India is developing a city park which will define the

Fig. 92: SUNDER NURSERY was laid out by Percy-Lancaster to provide for trees in New Delhi. Located in the heart of the national capital, the Aga Khan Trust for Culture is presently landscaping the nursery and undertaking conservation work on the monuments that stand here.
Sketch by Himanish Das, The Aga Khan Trust for Culture

buffer zone of the World Heritage Site. It is aimed to create a major landscaped space of truly urban scale, deriving inspiration from the traditional Indian concept of congruency between nature, garden and utility coupled with environmental conservation. The space will also provide a major new green space for public recreation.

The 70-acre Sunder Nursery is home to nine Mughal period structures and the grand Mughal Azimganj Serai abutting it on the north, all of which are undergoing careful conservation work with master craftsmen. Similarly the three early Mughal tombs standing in the adjoining 17 acre Batashewala Complex are being conserved using traditional building crafts, tools, and techniques by master craftsmen. As part of the project, the planned micro-habitat zone/arboretum will simulate a microcosm of Delhi's fast disappearing biodiversity, including *kohi* (hill), *khadar* (riverine), *bangar* (alluvial) and *dabar* (marshy) zones.

On completion, the three project zones of Humayun's Tomb, Nizamuddin Basti will be interconnected by nature trails and heritage walks.

Fig. 93: The Mughal-era Grand Trunk road passed through present-day Sunder Nursery; the proposed landscape plan now aims to create an ecological heritage zone of truly urban scale, deriving inspiration from the traditional Indian concept of congruency between nature, garden, and utility coupled with environmental conservation.
The Aga Khan Trust for Culture

Though today standing exposed to one another, historically, the luxurious pavilions of the Diwan-i Khas, the hammans, Khas Mahal, Rang Mahal, Mumtaz Mahal (fig. 20) were all enclosed with their courtyards and their own gardens allowing no simultaneous visual linkage despite the Nahr-i Bihisht flowing down the centre of them all.

Rang Mahal, known after its painted wall surface was the principal building of the harem. As with the Diwan-i Khas, the façade had five great cusped arches with the Nahr-i Bihisht pouring out into the gardens from the wider central arch while the niches were lit by candles glowing behind the sparkling water. The *tehkhanas* below were kept ventilated with air passing through marble screens. In the centre of the building was the most magnificent lotus shaped marble pool with deep borders which would have held pietra dura floral inlay, with coloured water from gurgling fountains flowing into it.

On the north of the Diwan-i Khas was the hammam, favoured by the Mughal emperors to escape the 'dust and heat' of Hindustan. With rooms for hot and cold baths and special rooms for the royal children, the hammam had three main apartments. Marble, inlaid with semi precious stones in floral patterns, was the favoured material for the flooring, reservoirs, vapour slabs, and the walls.

Though the entire palace-fort was of a garden layout, of the principal formal gardens – Hayat Bakhsh and Mahtab Bagh (fig. 26) – only half of the Hayat Bakhsh now survives. Over the rest were erected the barracks of the British forces in the nineteenth century. The gardens had large tanks and made extensive use of water brought in using an ingenious system of irrigation and circulation. The complex geometry of the gardens exploited the direction of movement which was coupled with possibilities of extended views over the river to generate a feeling of spaciousness, with the building pavilions protected by awnings, stone lattice screens, arcades, and elaborate plinths.

Hazrat Amir Khusrau, the celebrated early fourteenth-century poet, had written of the area in Delhi where lived the revered Sufi saint, Hazrat Nizamuddin Auliya, 'if on earth there be paradise/ O it is here, it is here, it is here' – a verse that Shahjahan had inscribed on the Diwan-i Khas of his palace-fort. Though the principal buildings survive, their setting was destroyed by British forces in 1857. The present form of the fort is therefore very different from its original conception.

JAMA MASJID

In Shahjahanabad were built a considerable number of mosques leading to historians referring to Shahjahan's period as the 'golden age of mosque construction'. Mosques played a pivotal role in urban life at Shahjahanabad and religious endowments ensured a mosque in every street, bazaar, and square.

Besides the imperial congregational mosque of Jama Masjid, there were neighbourhood mosques attached to the major havelis and the mosques built with royal patronage such as Masjid Fatehpuri (fig. 85), Masjid Akbarabadi (fig. 94), Masjid Sirhindi, Masjid Aurangabadi, Zinat al-Masajid (fig. 18), and the Sunhari Masjid, amongst others.

Essentially, a mosque is aligned with the cardinal axis in a manner that allows the faithful to face the holy shrine of the Prophet in Mecca and two main styles can be discerned. The first has with a large prayer hall with a *pishtaq* (large arched opening) surmounted by either three or five domes and mostly with attached minarets. The second type comprising neighbourhood mosques or those for private royal use were based on the additive grid system of vaulted bays, with a prominent central bay.

Shahjahan's Jama Masjid, construction of which commenced in AD 1650 after consulting astrologers, remains India's largest and most well-known mosque. Built on a rocky outcrop, the red sandstone plinth is over 10 metres higher than the surrounding ground and is reached by a flight of steep sandstone steps from the north (figs 17, 81), south, and east. The courtyard of the mosque today accommodates over 25,000 worshippers and is enclosed by an open arcade.

The main structure of the mosque, the prayer hall on the western side, stands on another slightly raised platform and is surmounted by three bulbous domes covered with white and black marble stripes (figs 19, 35). The eastern façade of the prayer-hall has two towering minarets topped with Mughal-style canopies, as seen at Humayun's Tomb, while four smaller minarets are attached to the rear, western façade.

As with the Jama Masjid outside the Red Fort Agra, commissioned by Shahjahan's daughter Jahanara, the main prayer hall is two bay deep at the Jama Masjid in Delhi, thereby significantly enhancing the depth and in turn grandeur of the lofty central archway. The five arched openings on the façade on either side of the central opening carry inscriptions glorifying the emperor and eulogizing the architecture of the mosque with quotes such as: '*The* shamsa (sunburst on the central archway) of the central portico is more brilliant than the shining lamps of heaven and the kalasha (finial on the domes) bestows a glow of radiance upon the celestial lamps of paradise.' The five arched openings on each side of the main façade in turn lead to three arched openings leading into the three chambers of the second bay of the prayer hall, the central one of which is roofed by a dome.

The Jama Masjid towers over the urban and religious landscape of Shahjahanabad and it is believed that its plinth is higher than the ramparts of the Red Fort.

HAVELIS

Just as the Indian royalty were expected to build 'palaces' in the British city of New Delhi, in Shahjahanabad, where the emperor led the way, the nobility – who were allotted lands when the city walls were being built – was bound to follow. Though the British architects laid down strict guidelines and architectural controls, in Shajahanabad, the Red Fort was the inspiration for the architectural spirit for the rest of the city.

Fig. 94: THE AKBARABADI MASJID, Mirza Shah Rukh Beg, 1847. This is a woodcut print from Syed Ahmed Khan's *Asar al-Sanadid* and the only representation before its destruction in 1858 of the Akbarabadi Masjid which stood on the west side of Sadatallah Chowk at the beginning of the Faiz Bazaar. It was one of the large mosques erected in Shahjahanabad in 1650 by a queen of Shahjahan, in this case the Akbarabadi Begum. It follows the pattern of the Jama Masjid on a smaller scale but with seven bays instead of eleven. It had been severely damaged in some of the assaults on Delhi in the previous century and has lost its gateway and enclosing wall as well as half of its northern minaret. To the right is the Sonehri Masjid or Golden Mosque of Nawab Javed Khan (fig. 16).
Woodcut print, 20 x 32 cm. British Library, London, 14109.c.1.

Fig. 95: THE SHAH BURJ IN THE RED FORT AND INLAID WORK IN THE FLOOR, studio of Mazhar Ali Khan, c. 1840. From Metcalfe's Delhi Book.
The Shah Burj stands at the northern end of the palace range in the Red Fort and from its Bengali-roofed pavilion ran the Nahr-i Bihisht, fed by a branch of Ali Mardan Khan's canal, linking the pavilions along the terrace. The cupola was destroyed in 1857 and never replaced. The beautiful decorative panel below is the basin of a fountain that stood within the Shah Burj.
Watercolour, folio size 25.8 x 19 cm. British Library, London, Add.Or.5475, f.42.

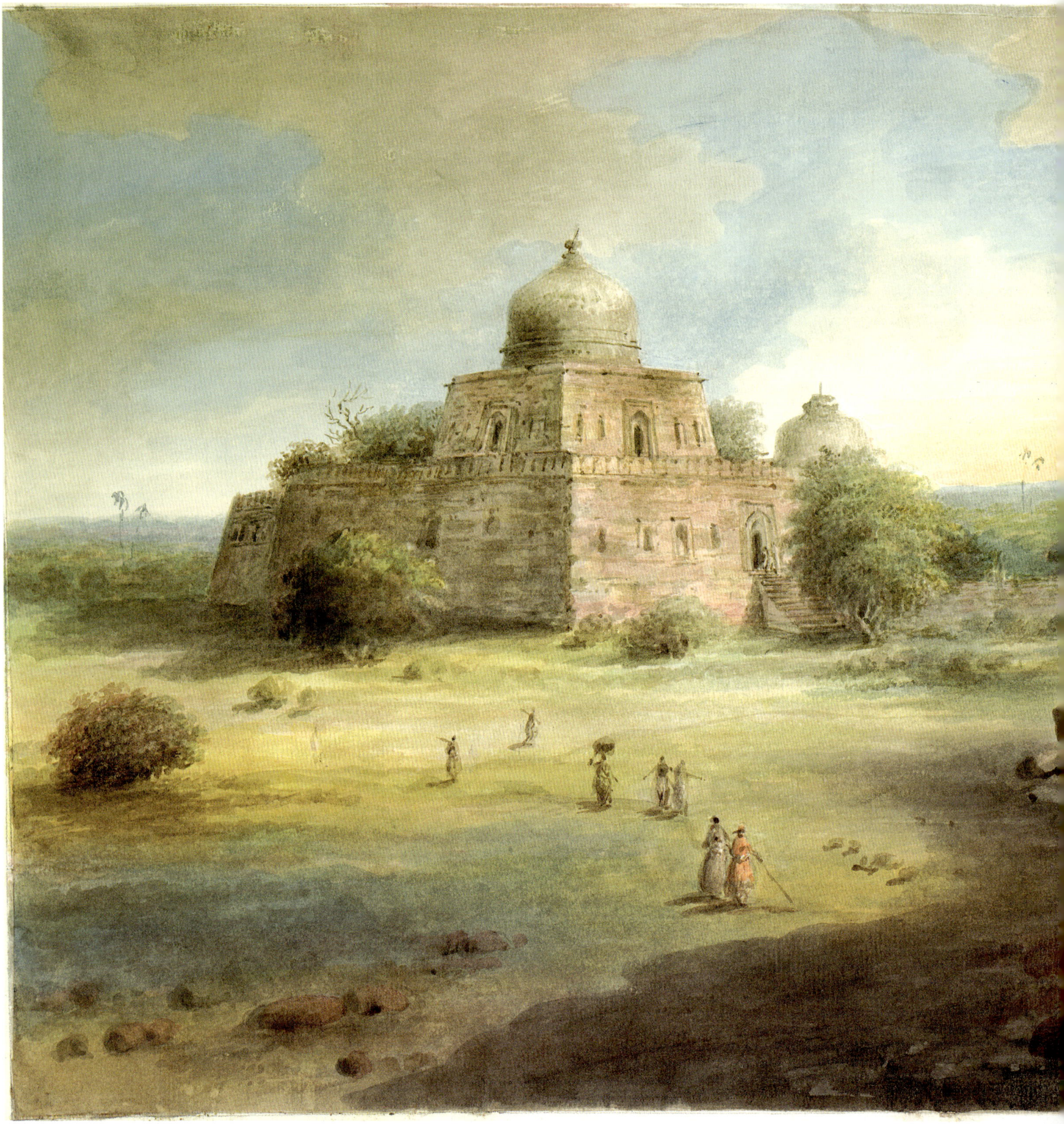

Fig. 96: GHIYASUDDIN TUGHLUQ'S TOMB AND THE WALLS OF TUGHLUQABAD, by Sita Ram, 1815. From the albums of drawings done by Sita Ram for Lord Hastings 1814-15. The citadel and city of Tughluqabad was built by Ghiyas al-Din Tughluq (1320-1325), east of the Qutb Minar. The fortress stands on a high outcrop of rock with rubble-built walls, surviving intact all along the seven kilometre perimeter, with a reservoir on the south. Beside his citadel and linked to it by a causeway is his tomb built in an equally military style, the domed structure with battered walls standing in its own little citadel originally within a reservoir.
Watercolour, 29.6 x 50.5 cm. British Library, London, Add.Or.4834.

Fig. 97: JAMA MASJID VIEW FROM EAST, photograph by Robert and Harriet Tytler, 1858. The view is looking west along the Khas Bazaar with the buildings in the course of demolition.
British Library, London, Photo 53/(21).

Shahjahanabad was divided into homogeneous *mohallas* or wards that were gated communities and thus could be effectively secured. Following the transition from public to private in the Red Fort, the gate of each *mohalla* marked the entry into a semi-private space from the public streets. The principal haveli in each *mohalla* could have several courtyards leading from the public *baithak* or sitting rooms on the street side, to the first courtyard where the public functions were held and eventually the most private zenana court. The public court were usually styled on the Diwan-i Am with cusped arches and fluted columns and the side chambers had mezzanine floors where women, sitting behind elaborate stone lattice screens could observe meetings or a nautch.

As with the Red Fort the exterior walls of the havelis were mostly bare except for the ornate gateways, giving little clue of the splendour that lay behind those imposing walls.

Fig. 98: JAMA MASJID FROM THE NORTH-EAST, photograph by John Murray, 1858. The view is taken over the buildings in the Kucha Bulaqi Begum before their demolition.
British Library, London, Photo 52/(23).

Each haveli stood amidst a dependent neighbourhood, where the nobleman's retinue lived and carried out business. As with structures in the Red Fort, havelis continuously extended themselves with additional linked courtyards surrounded by rooms.

Each of the courtyards was well lit but the harsh rays of the sun did not penetrate the verandahs. Instead, the breeze was captured and passed through the haveli ensuring comfort for all rooms especially the *tehkhanas* or the basement chambers (fig. 36) – integral to the residential quarters to where the family could retreat during the long summer days. Room heights within the haveli varied to allow the much used terraces at several levels and thus ensuring a greater degree of privacy, further enhanced by terrace pavilions.

A luxurious hammam or bath was attached to most havelis. As with the Red Fort, these were mostly built of marble and their shallow pools were fed with water drawn from wells – of which 678 were counted in 1847.

THE BRITISH AT SHAHJAHANABAD

Shahjahanabad and the Red Fort functioned as planned for almost 200 years despite the power of the Mughal Empire declining significantly in the eighteenth century. This in turn led to a decrease in trade and population bringing building activity almost to a complete halt.

From 1803 onwards the British Resident occupied the northern portion of the city where, in 1826 the St. James Church was built amidst other important buildings (figs 102, 103).

The basic features of Shahjahan's city would have remained intact into the twentieth century had the British not unleashed widespread destruction following the first war of independence that commenced with the crowning of the last Mughal emperor as king of India at the Diwan-i Khas.

Almost 80 per cent of the Red Fort was levelled to the ground. Not only were buildings lost but the original context and sequence of movement disfigured. Similarly, large parts of the urban fabric surrounding the Jama Masjid, including the Akbarabadi mosque of the Shahjahani era, were demolished. The fort and the city which had been functionally, spatially, and visually integrated, had all these connections severed.

Soon after, Jahanara Begum's gardens, north of the Chandni Chowk, were taken over to lay railway tracks and build the railway station earlier planned to be outside the walled city or even east of the river. The railway destroyed a large part of the city and cut through the Salimgarh citadel and parts of the Red Fort, further changing the immediate surroundings of the fort.

The demolition of the Red Fort buildings in the aftermath of 1857 was also coupled with looting of what remained after the repeated raids of the eighteenth century. The famed inlaid panels of the Diwan-i Am were removed and taken to England. They were, however, brought back in 1902 at the insistence of Lord Curzon who also brought in Italian craftsmen to restore them to the Diwan-i Am.

CONSERVATION NEEDS OF THE TWENTY-FIRST CENTURY

It is a reflection on the times we live in or India's attitude towards her glorious past when Shahjahan's great city is today officially designated a 'slum'. This despite the fact that much of the historic fabric remains and that there are still families inhabiting the havelis who can trace their descent from nobles who were allotted the land by Shahjahan.

In the last three decades portions of the city have become wholesale markets due to the proximity of the two major railway stations and the poor implementation of building regulations and no control on prohibited activities such as storage of hazardous chemicals. This has led to a gradual migration of residents from organic Shahjahanabad to the planned neighbourhoods of post-independence era.

Time and again one hears of the desire to restore the past glory of Chandni Chowk but what is required in the urban context is not concern with 'past glory' but concern with what we have made out of our inheritance. Streets that would have once stood unrivalled in the world for the quality of life they provided are today chaotic and inaccessible.

Isolated conservation efforts have had no impact or even failed since these are seen as elitist, when we in India should be more concerned with improving the quality of life through conservation effort than preserving authenticity. To make conservation efforts meaningful to the residents of Shahjahanabad, expeditious action is required in areas such as generating public awareness, pilot conservation projects, urban renewal schemes, traffic management, infrastructure improvements, environmental development, and waste management around key heritage locations and with the participation of the resident community.

Street improvements, safer pedestrian access to important sites needs to be coupled with significant incentives for owners of heritage properties for preservation, upkeep and reuse where required. Simultaneously, existing laws and building regulations need to be implemented with consistency.

More than 150 years since the Red Fort was savagely mutilated and 65 years since Independence it continues to present a poor reflection of what it once was. If nothing else poor conservation attempts such as the attempted restoration of the northern end of the Nahr-i Bihisht in 2003-4 have only further disfigured the historic character. This despite the palace-fort being designated a UNESCO World Heritage site in 2007.

A comprehensive plan to restore not only the buildings but also their attached gardens and enclosures needs to be taken in hand now that the Indian Army has vacated large portions of the fort it had continued to occupy till the twenty-first century. Demolition of a few British-era barracks can lead to the restoration of the Hayat Bakhsh and the Mahtab baghs. The significant green space liberated from parking lots and transit camps on the east and west of the Red Fort needs to be planted in a more balanced manner allowing Mughal-style orchards to exist with open green space used for festive occasions.

Though Shahjahani grandeur might no longer be possible, dignity should be easily achieved and with it pride both for the inhabitants and visitors from worldwide.

Fig. 99: PANORAMA OF DELHI FROM THE LAHORE GATE OF THE RED FORT, by Mazhar Ali Khan, dated 25th November 1846. For the complete publication of this unique document, see JP Losty, *Delhi 360°*, Roli Books, Delhi, 2011.
Watercolour and bodycolour, 66 x 490 cm. British Library, London, Add.Or.4126.

Tirpolea Bagh Hiat Bux | Jumma Mote Musjid | Durwazah Jalee | Chyattah Durwazah Lahori Mirzah Meerza Babar | Mosahnumun Burj | Durwazah Nakarkhanah Deewan Am | Chok Deewan Am | Mukan Meerza Wulee Ahd | Baghchah Peah-i-Durwazah | Musjidi Futah Poore | Chok Nakar Khanah | Harwailee Munwail | Makamat Meerza Sultan Bahadur Tirpolea | Duya Mukul Meera Shah Rookh | Makamat Biayh | Asud Burj Bazee noorahin | Fozel i Killah | Kutorah Mirzah Nadir Mhamur New Muhla | Durwazah New Muhla Musjid i Bernad | Musjid Nokcha

Tirpolea bar | Musjid | Makamat Chota Dareebu | Bazentur kee Dookan eebee Dareebar ker | Koocha Boola Ker Begum | Saruk je Killachay to bare e Durwazah tuk bay | Musjidi Fatah Poore | Harwailee Munwail | Deo Kanain Chandnee Chouk | Musjid | Saruk i Neezumbood | Koothee Begum Sumroo | Saruk | Koothee Nawb Khan Allekhan | Koothee Hindoroo | Dursah | Tauwalah Bank Dehlee Bank | Musjid zer Killah 5th November Church yonee Girjagh

Fig. 100: DIWAN-I KHAS WITH CRYSTAL THRONE PACKED FOR TRANSPORT, photograph by Charles Moravia, 1858. The photograph comes from the album of Edward Campbell, who was ADC to the Governor General Lord Canning and was also Prize Officer after the siege of Delhi. The crystal throne was placed in the centre of the river façade of the Diwan-i Khas. It no doubt replaced the Peacock Throne after it had been carted off to Persia by Nadir Shah in 1739. Earlier descriptions, including William Francklin's and Thomas Twining's, both of whom saw it 1794, suggest that it was covered with cushions with a canopy above supported by silver pillars, as in fig. 71. Emily Clive Bayley records seeing the block of crystal 1848-50 'on the top of which luxurious cushions of cloth of gold used to be spread for the King to sit on' (Kaye 1980, pp. 205-06).
Private collection, London.

Facing page: Fig. 101: SCALES OF JUSTICE SCREEN, photograph by Joseph Beglar, 1870-80. From the Archaeological Survey of India collection. This beautiful jali is in the Tasbih Khana facing the south side of the Diwan-i Khas and is placed over the Nahr-i Bihisht which runs underneath it. The upper semi-circular panel depicts a crescent moon, stars and the scales of justice, the latter used as a regal emblem. The lower section is carved in an intricate floral and lattice work design. Here seated on an improvised throne in front of the screen Bahadur Shah was declared emperor in 1837.
British Library, London, Photo 1003/(876)

183

Fig. 102: THE INTERIOR OF ST JAMES'S CHURCH, by a Delhi artist, perhaps Mazhar Ali Khan, 1836-40. The octagonal drum of the dome is supported by the massive arches within the church also supporting a smaller inner dome while the outer walls also form an octagon with doors at the angles between the arms of the cross. This is a spectacularly difficult view for an Indian artist untrained in western perspective. Perhaps only Mazhar Ali Khan himself could have pulled this off in view of his other difficult perspective views (figs 35 and 99). The view is towards the chancel through the central arches where obviously the congregation mostly sat since this is where the punkahs are and past the twin pulpits.
Watercolour, National Army Museum, London, 1956-02-27-4.

Fig. 103: ST JAMES'S CHURCH, by a Delhi artist, 1836-40. St James's Church was commissioned by Colonel James Skinner (1778-1841), famous for the cavalry regiment Skinner's Horse. While lying wounded on the field of battle he made a vow that if he survived he would build a church in thanks for his life being saved. The church was eventually started in 1826 and completed ten years later. It is in the form of a Greek cross surmounted by a dome with porticos closing off three of the arms of the cross and the chancel forming the fourth. The drawing is normally attributed to Ghulam Ali Khan, who had worked for Skinner in the 1820s, but it cannot be said that it really resembles his earlier work.
Watercolour, National Army Museum, London, 1956-02-27-5.

Fig. 104: PALACE OF RAJA BAHADUR OUTSIDE DELHI, by a Faizabad draughtsman, 1774. Inscribed above: *Maison du raja Bahadour hors Delhi et bords du Gemma*.
This is one of the group of fourteen drawings of palaces and other buildings in Delhi done for Col. Gentil in 1774. Most of the drawings are simple elevations without any perspective, but in this one, the Faizabad artist manages to suggest a courtyard behind his completely symmetrical facade.
Pen-and-ink and watercolour, 48 x 179 cm. Bibliothèque Nationale de France, Paris, Éstampes Od 63/5

hors Dely et bords du Gemna.

Fig. 105: THE MAGAZINE AND CHRISTIAN CEMETERY AT DELHI, photograph by Robert and Harriet Tytler, 1858. The magazine for munitions occupied the southern part of the former mansion of Dara Shikoh on the river north of the Red Fort. The magazine itself was blown up by its defenders in 1857 but the walls survived to be photographed. They have been fortified in an extraordinarily mediaeval European way reminiscent of an Italian fortress. At the south end is an old Christian cemetery.
British Library, London, Photo 193/(3).

Fig. 106: LUDLOW CASTLE, photograph by Robert and Harriet Tytler, 1858. Ludlow Castle served as the Residency for Thomas Metcalfe and his successor until 1857. The building seems to have escaped serious damage in 1857.
British Library, London, Photo 193/(7).

Making of New Delhi

Malvika Singh

The walled city of Delhi, built by Shahjahan, was a jewel in the Mughal crown. Fashioned with much love and care, the fine workmanship reflects the aesthetic sensibilities of that age as well as the well-honed 'eye' of extraordinary patronage. From the deft carving of stone, to delicate embellishments in pietra dura on the inner walls of the Diwan-i Khas and the Diwan-i Am as well as on other splendid baradaris, to the canals and waterways that kept the cool, lined by paved paths shaded by well entrenched, lush and rooted trees. This private realm of the Emperor of Hindustan was opulent and spectacular. A 'pearl' of a mosque and the living quarters of the extended royal family was the core of this magic space. The Red Fort, pinnacle of power, stood segregated from the city that grew around it. The majestic and unmatched Jama Masjid, at the edge of Chandni Chowk, beckoned the faithful to prayer. Grand and less-grand havelis, leading off Chandni Chowk, housed the Dilliwallahs, the diwans, the poets, the business people, the artisans who worked in silver and gold, brass and copper, the artists who were the visual chroniclers of their time. This city was the 'atelier' of its period, integrating all the ingredients that made Dilli so special.

In 1857, a page of history was turned.

Shahjahanabad was devastated and severely injured by marauding British troops that trampled upon a vibrant culture and a political dispensation, albeit a declining one. Having rampaged a great city of north India, a repository of a living culture, the 'invaders' positioned their first 'British outpost' on the outskirts of that 'old' city, profoundly insecure and disturbed because of the deep anger the people felt towards them following the assault on their capital. There was an encompassing pall of anger that hung over this capital of the Mughal Empire. The 'British' part of town remained static and sterile, waiting patiently for some glimmer of a change in attitude, hoping for a move towards a rejuvenation of spirit and a reinvention of supremacy.

In circa 1900, Calcutta was the seat of colonial power and Lord Curzon was well entrenched there, with no intention to move. He was a man of strong views, beliefs, and firm, unwavering conviction. He played his role with pride and determined force. He studied India, her cultural patterns, her layered realities and her diverse people. He may have even envied the splendid pomp and show, the riches and supreme power of her pantheon of rulers, nearly as many as her gods. It was possibly this understanding of India that compelled Lord Curzon to create and detail the blueprint for the spectacular Durbar of 1903 (figs 107, 108) without recognizing that the successful, talked about event, could have been the precursor to the idea of shifting the imperial capital from Calcutta to Delhi.

The Delhi Durbar was conceived by Lord Curzon to proclaim and honour the coronation of King Edward VII and Queen Alexandra, Emperor and Empress of India. He had sincerely hoped the emperor and his consort would attend the grand event on 1 January 1903 but that was not to be. Instead, the Duke and Duchess of Connaught, younger brother of the king, represented the Crown. The open plains on the outskirts of Delhi housed the elaborate campsite that was planned with meticulous precision to ensure efficient service and much comfort. From incorporating an elaborate drainage system to handle the extensive tented accommodation, to specially designed police uniforms, a special postage stamp and medals to commemorate the occasion, a map of the 'site' and guidebooks for all the guests, and Brooke Bond Tea, the official beverage, Lord Curzon was determined to make this event incomparable.

Parallel to the official procession that Lord Curzon (fig. 109) led along with the Duke and Duchess of Connaught, he had crafted one that represented 'India' and the Indian people, accompanied by musicians, performers and acrobats, and all the other magical paraphernalia that make this civilization so unique and like no other. He set up a historic, comprehensive exhibit at Qudsiya Gardens that showcased the best of India's arts and crafts tradition and published a catalogue of the artifacts in the many galleries.

Following pages: Fig. 107: DELHI DURBAR, by a Delhi artist, 1877. This was the first of the British imperial durbars held at Delhi, in an amphitheatre north of Shahjahanabad subsequently called Coronation Park. The Viceroy Lord Lytton proclaimed Queen Victoria Empress of India in front of a large number of the Indian princes, who were photographed for the occasion. The durbar was organized by J. Talboys Wheeler, who subsequently published his *The History of the Imperial Assemblage at Delhi* (London, 1877). *Watercolour, Red Fort Museum, Delhi.*

Pages 194-195: Fig. 108: DELHI DURBAR OF 1903, an oil painting by Roderick Mackenzie. The painting commemorates the coronation of King Edward VII, which was celebrated with a procession led by the Viceroy Lord Curzon and his wife, then followed by the Duke of Connaught and his wife, and then the Maharajas. *Corbis: IX003119*

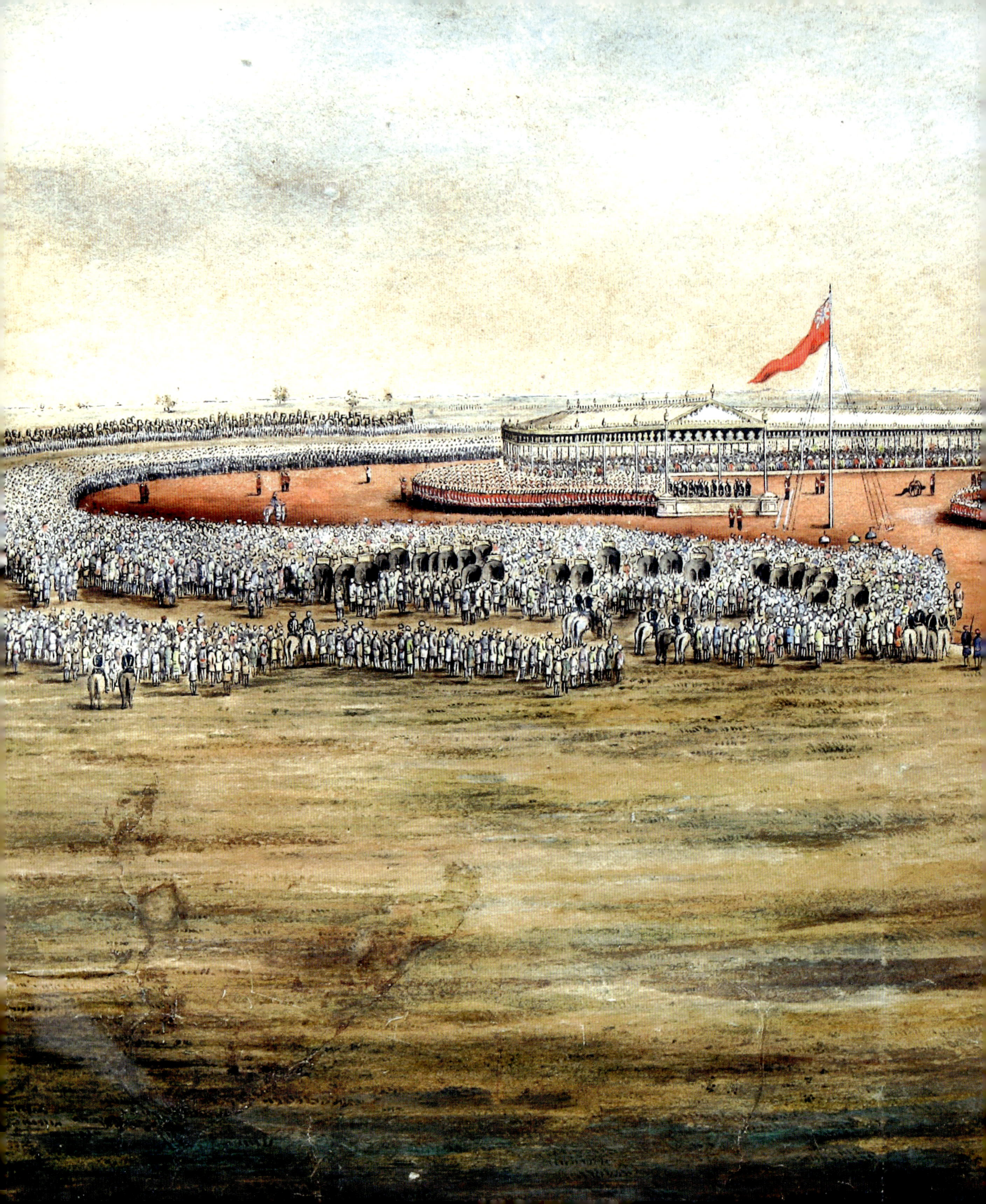

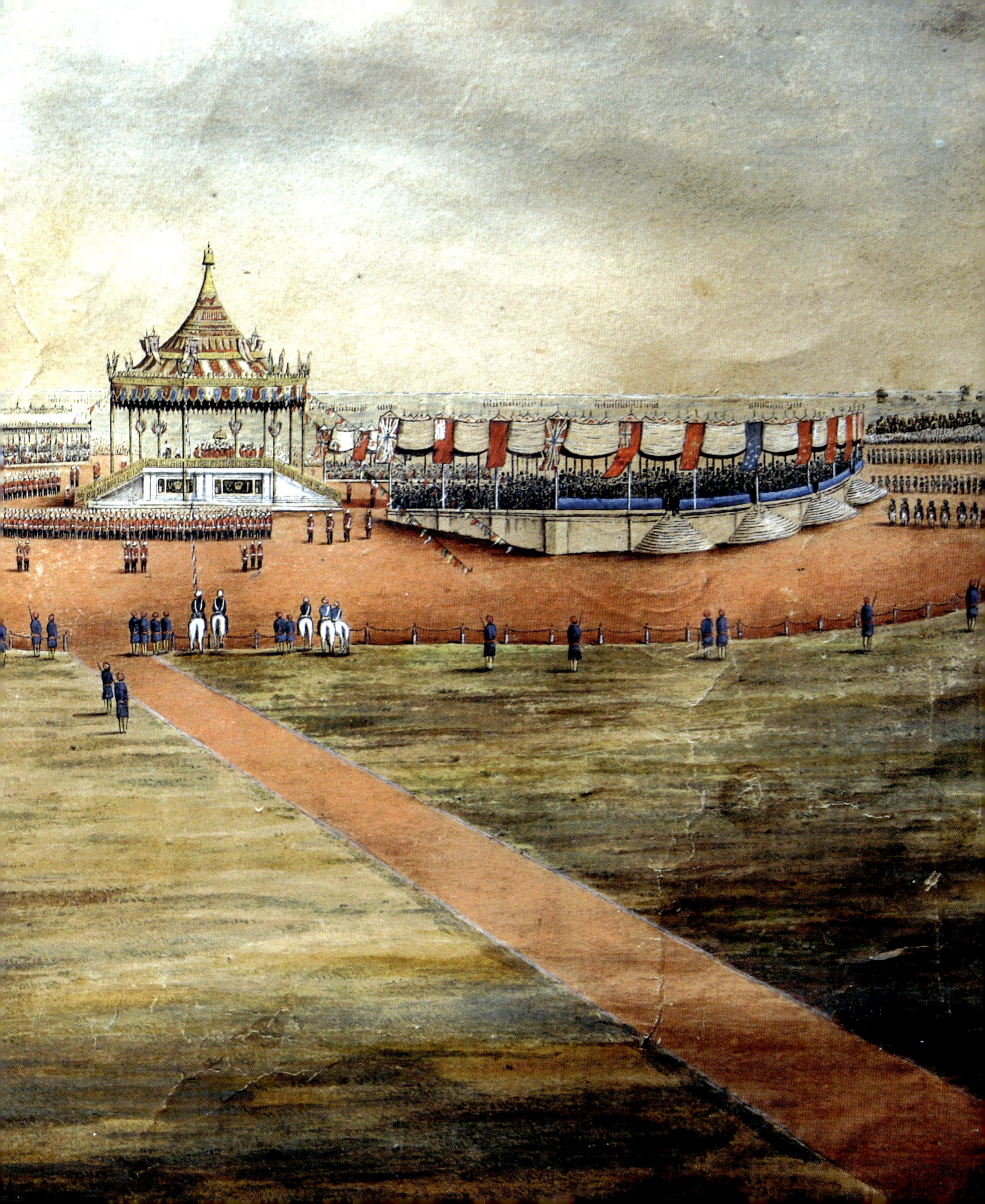

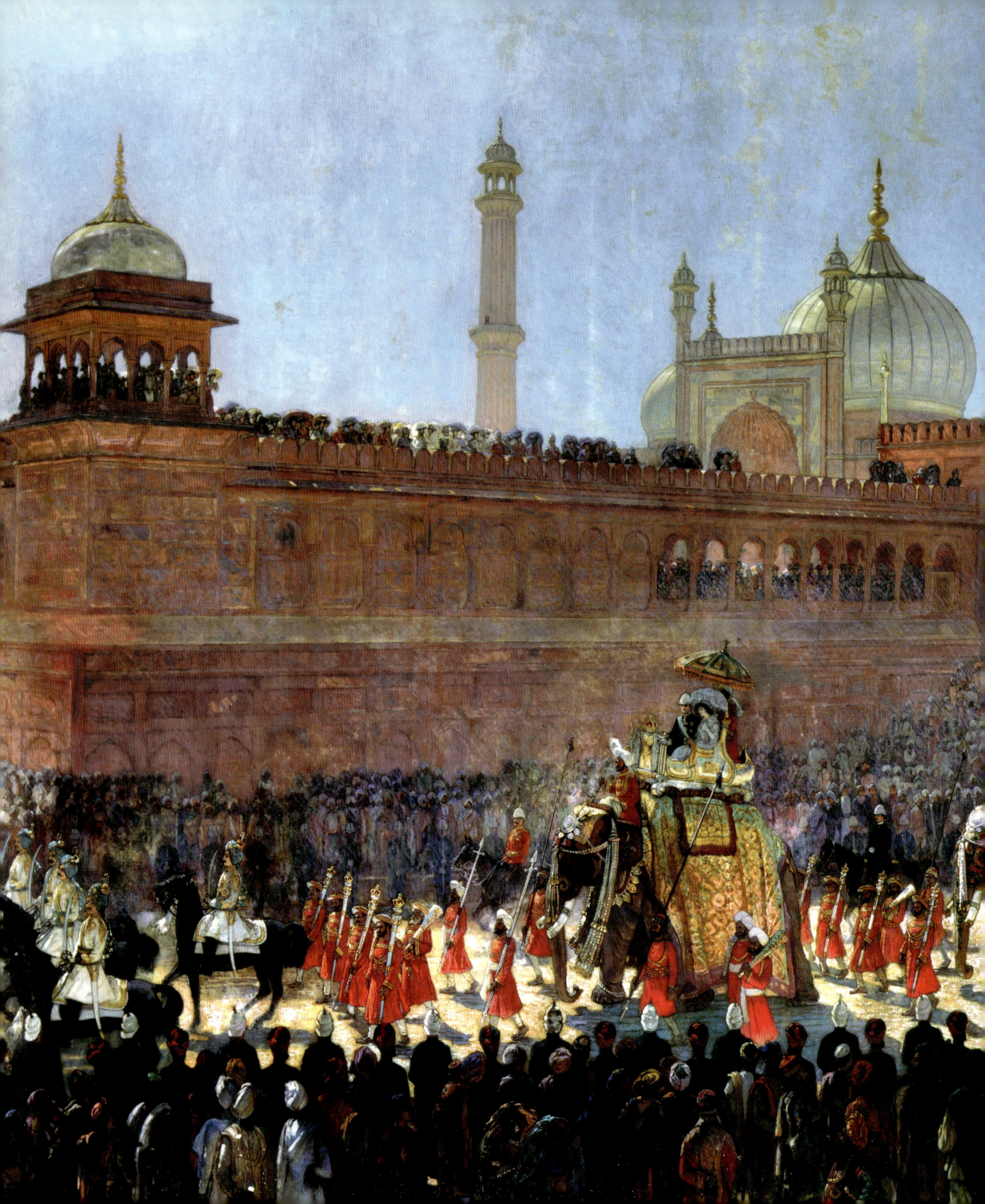

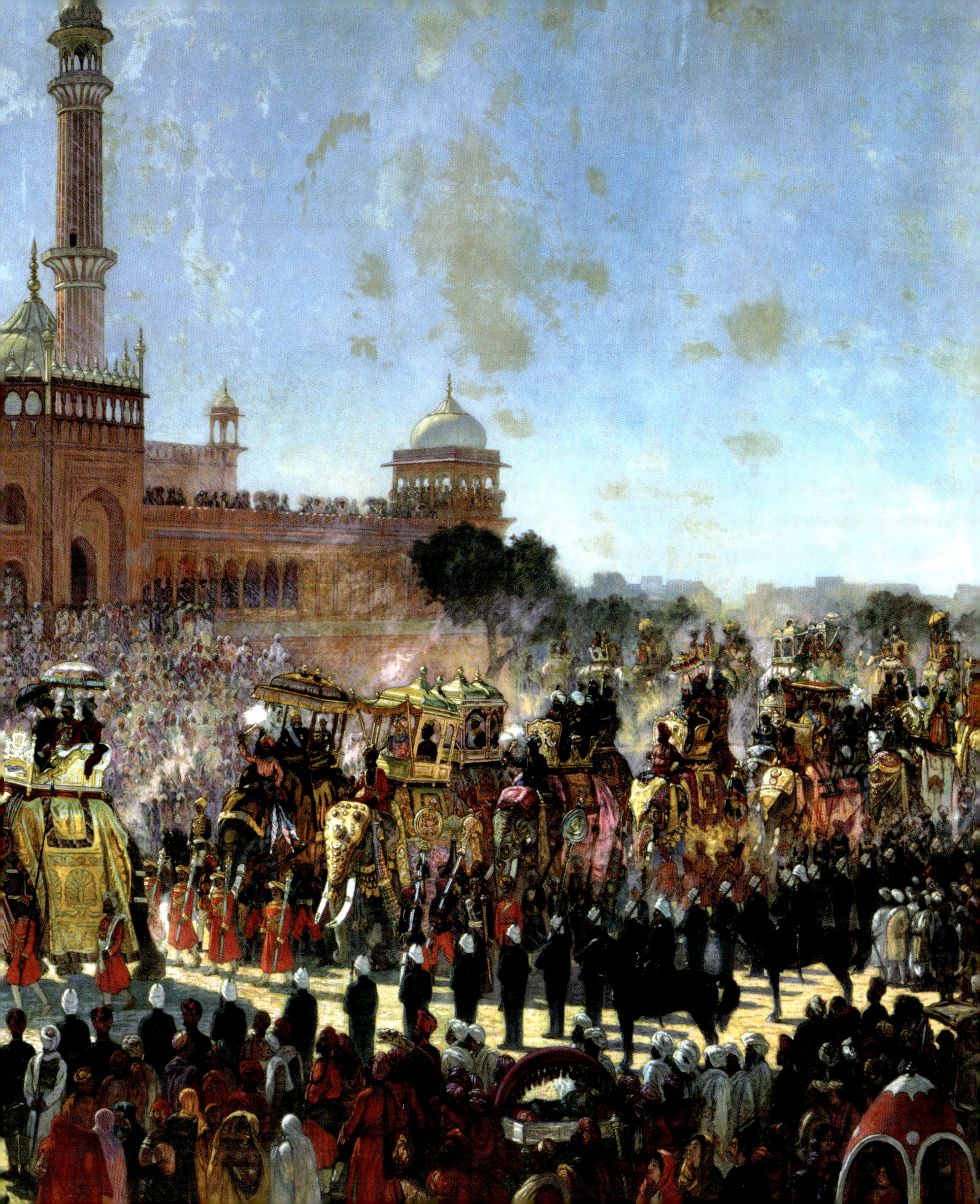

He attempted, in his very personalized style, to synthesize the strengths of both Britain and India in the larger display of both traditions and cultures.

Invitations had gone out to friends and family luring them into visiting the jewel in the crown for the grand durbar of 1903 in Delhi, away from the seat of Imperial power that was Calcutta. Curzon had felt that the location for the Durbar needed to be set in the spectacular capital of the Mughals, Shahjahanabad the city that housed the Red Fort and the Jama Masjid. Dilli was being readied for an extravaganza that would remain unmatched in historic pomp and spectacle. A vast stretch of land was levelled for pitching a tented city with all the facilities that would make the experience memorable and one of a kind. The entire 'pantheon' of Indian rulers, extraordinary and stately, was preparing to arrive at this venue, in all their refined attire with spectacular accoutrements, to partake in the celebrations that were planned to mark the coronation. Painters, photographers, and writers converged on Delhi, some of them having spent time travelling through exotic parts of the country months ahead of 1 January 1903.

Mortimer Menpes was one distinguished artist who visited India to paint the Durbar of 1903. His first impression of the city was this: 'Delhi is not a red city brilliant and full of colour. It is a gray city. The sky though blue, was a sad blue. The streets, the buildings, the earth, the dust, all were gray. What setting could be more exquisite for the jewels before me, what background more perfect for the pictures to come, the gorgeous pageantry that was to sweep over this colourless canvas?' He put together a wonderful set of personal impressions through a series of paintings, and water-colours, with an accompanying text. His descriptions were varied, ranging from vivid accounts of sumptuous, luxurious royal India, of imperial pageantry, to the ordinary, but hugely unusual, realism of a magical country (from *The Durbar* by Mortimer Menpes and Dorothy Menpes).

The written word, paintings and photographs captured the special moment. I have liberally quoted from Mortimer Menpes and Ruby Madden, an Australian guest at the Durbar, two individuals from far ends of the globe, to present a true, albeit personalized account of the grand and opulent event. All the guests stayed in large, well-appointed tents that had attached sitting rooms and bathrooms. There were dining tents, and an entire Press section that was the hub for not merely sharing news but also as a place where the drinks carried on late into the night, where there was a constant feeling of action in a café environment. It was an extraordinary congregation that reached out to envelop the best of India!

To begin at the beginning – Menpes describes the viceroy's procession as it entered Delhi, marking the inauguration of the 1903 Durbar – 'One felt a thrill of patriotism as a magnificent elephant towering high above the rest came into view, the handsomest and finest of all, at sight of which thousands of voices as though from one throat murmured, "The Viceroy"! Every hat was raised, every turbaned head bent low, before that youthful, joyous figure under the glittering golden umbrella (fig. 109).'

And there was more – 'Every now and then an elephant would rise clear and tangible from this Arabian nights, and one would catch for a moment a glimpse of some historic potentate, only to be lost the next moment as he passed into the throng of his fellows. For hours that seemed unending the great procession dragged its glittering pageantry along. The different races gathered together from the length and breadth of India were singularly impressive. Fierce white-robed Pathan and Baluch chiefs who had never even seen one another before, riding side by side with European officers what a contrast!'

Menpes was staggered by the visual impact of the great Jama Masjid – 'I shall never forget my first sight of the Jumma Masjid. It was worth coming to the ends of the earth to see. What was it like? What can I compare it to? Anything that we in England have ever seen? I think not. Perhaps a garden is nearest to it, not a surrey garden planted with stocks and mignonette, but an ideal garden such as we have all dreamed of, with banks studded with gorgeous flaming tropical flowers. No: that will not do: it must be a garden of jewels, a garden set with jewels, with pearls, sapphires, rubies and diamonds. How impossible is this scene to paint, impossible to imagine, impossible to describe! The streets, the houses, the roofs, the steps, and the benches massed about the Jumma Masjid teemed and vibrated with colour; the flowerbeds stretched as far as the eye could see; it was a garden for a fairy princess. Poor painters, poor palettes! How futile your efforts must be!'

The other guest at the Durbar of 1903 was Ruby Madden, daughter of Sir John Madden, Chief Justice and Lieutenant Governor of Victoria, who sailed to Bombay all the way from Australia to attend what was going to be the most magnificent gathering ever held. She stayed for ten months and her letters home told an extraordinary story of fearless travel to unknown and mysterious shores at a young and impressionable age, laced with unusual perceptions of India, jewel in the British Crown, padded with marvellous descriptions of life at the Curzon Camp! (from *A Season in India: Letters of Ruby Madden, Experiences of an Australian Girl at the Great Coronation Durbar*, 1903)

'Sunday we went to service again at the Viceroy's tent and had a divine service with oh such lovely hymns on a string band they sound beautiful … Mortimer was waiting to show us around the Duchess's and guests' tents. Claude and I were personally conducted by him through the Connaughts' home, just like a lovely house, furnished beautifully … they have lovely big sitting rooms and a huge dining hall where they all dine together. The Viceroy has his own house built especially for this ten days and costing at least 10,000 pounds. I never knew anybody quite so unpopular as he is. He is loathed by everybody, soldier and civilian alike, and they say this show was merely got up for his glorification … the kitchens are wonderfully arranged with 150 cooks and big cases heated with charcoal, slung on poles in which to carry breakfast to anyone who does not want to get up for that meal … Claude drove me out to hear massed bands at the Polo ground in the afternoon. It was simply glorious, 2000 performers playing the Lost Chord.

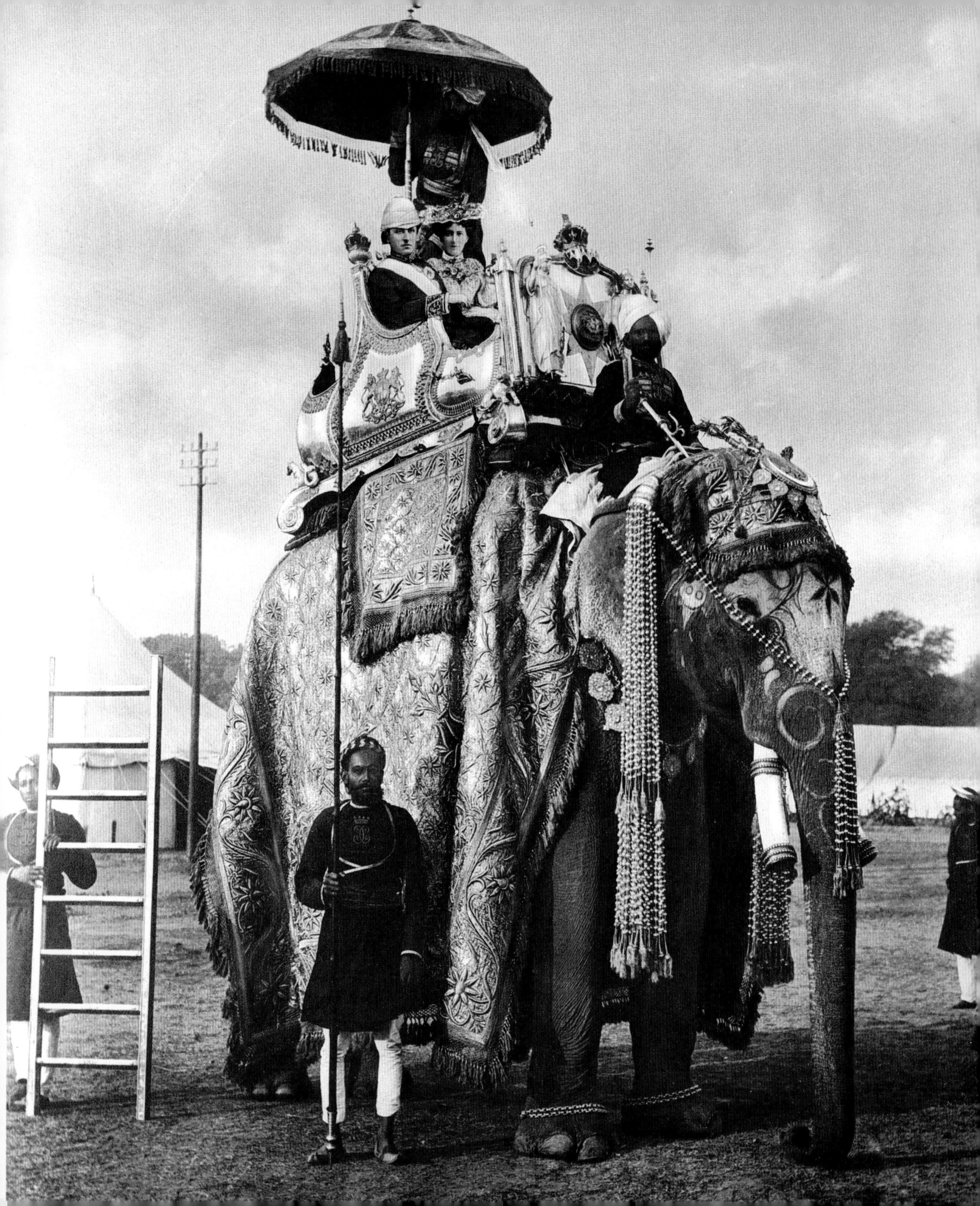

'Monday was the great procession day. We had seats in the Jumma Musjed, the Mohammedan temple, which was the swagger place to go and is the most lovely building itself ... the streets were a lovely sight to see with the crowds dressed in their different colors ... the procession was a wonderful sight ... the native never cheers so they went along in solemn silence and made it so depressing. Ld. Curzon is just like a groom but Lady C looked lovely seated beside him on the elephant with a huge gold umbrella held over her head and dressed in mauve with a hat made entirely of mauve orchids ... the Rajahs looked lovely, a mass of jewels, and seated on their gold and silver howdahs ... .'

Her description of the line of royals at the investiture ceremony deserves to be quoted here to present a delightful flavour of the event. 'Then the Viceroy made a long speech which was excellent but dull ... Then all the Rajas were presented in order of precedence which took some time but was highly interesting as their different costumes were so wonderful. Bikanir looked very well. He is tall and good looking and has been educated at home and likes to be as English as possible. He was dressed in pink satin embroidered in gold with pale green gauze turban, one mass of diamonds. Some of them looked so weird and awful. One was in a white muslin ballet shirt with orange jacket and tight orange pantaloons, ending up with elastic side boots. The Begum of Bhopal insisted on appearing too, dressed in gold with a blue lace veil like a lampshade over her face and a gold crown on her head. She was escorted by 2 huge men in black and gold. It was a great honour her coming and she laid a gold casket at the Viceroy's feet ... the show ended ... it certainly was a marvelous sight and one to be remembered for ever ....

'Went to watch polo early as there were two good matches between the 15th Hussars and the 4th Dragoon Guards and between Alwar and the I.C.C. ... I simple loved the game altho' the Cadet Corps got beaten. Alwar was hopelessly strong. The Raja plays himself and is a marvellous hitter ... I think the 15th won their game but had six falls which rather upset them ... In the evening we went to the fireworks and saw it from the Jumma Masjid ... We got excellent seats on the highest point and enjoyed the wonderful sight ... some of the rockets were too beautiful .... We got home about 1.30, the traffic is always the difficulty, the police are worse than useless, and the native driver is hopeless and the crowds are far worse than the Jubilee in London ... At the Investiture everybody wore all the jewels they possessed and the Rajahs literally made you blink when you looked at them ... The evening was the State Ball ... we got there without the slightest difficulty thro' the Lahore Gate (Red Fort) ... I was wildly excited for it looked such a gorgeous scene as we drove up to the steps ... the dressing was magnificent ... the men

Facing page, Fig. 109: LORD AND LADY CURZON, Luchman Prasad had the honour of carrying the Viceroy and Lady Curzon to the Durbar arena. Over his back was mounted a howdah of burnished silver as an umbrella of silk and gold hung over the crimson, velvet seats. A scarlet velvet housing (jhul), heavy and stiff with gold embroidery, swept to the ground. Lord Curzon, ever aware of the role he had in life, had chosen to ride an elephant to emphasize that the pomp of the Mughals was now the preserve of India's British rulers.
Private Collection

divine in their uniforms ... the Rajahs surpassed themselves in jewels and looked like moving jewellers shops ... The most wonderful sight was the Dewan-i-Cas where supper was served in the most sumptuous style, it adjoins the Dewan-i-Am where we danced by long passages which were lined by 5th Dragoon Guards in their tin helmets and plumes and full uniform. It was originally used as the zenana and is entirely of white marble inlaid with precious stones, the same as the Peacock Throne.'

The British serving officers lived on Civil Lines in those days, in colonial bungalows, segregated from the Dilliwallahs, living with their extended families in rambling havelis in Shahjahanabad, and some who worked for the new masters, in copy-cat 'modern colonial' structures on the outskirts of the walled city. The Maidens Hotel (fig. 125) was the first of its kind and was situated near the Secretariat offices. Exchange Stores supplied the household needs of these families and life was simple and comfortable! When the scorching summer descended on the plains of Delhi, the British moved 'house' to the hills beyond, to Simla, Mussourie, Nainital, Kasauli, and suchlike.

Dilliwallahs, in contrast, just changed the rhythm of their daily life. They woke up with the first ray of light, did their domestic chores in the cool of the morning, stayed indoors from midday on till the sun began its retreat into dusk, defeating the harsh, dry and impossibly hot hours of the day. Evenings brought the city back to life. The streets and bazaars bristled with heightened activity. Families visited one another; trade was brisk, socializing at its height. Sleeping under a canopy of stars was normal. If it was really very hot, the floor of the flat roofs was drenched in water, the sheets too, and sleep came easier in a moist wrap. By the early hours of the morning the cool would briefly envelop the city, enter the courtyards and rooms to be captured for as long as it deign stay. Vetiver blinds, constantly watered, conditioned and cooled the hot air as it drifted into the house through the slats of these special *khas ki taatis*.

The British created a 'civil lines' in all the towns they went to in India. They put in the infrastructure of amenities they required, down to the club with its tennis courts and swimming pool. They adopted all the 'Indian' devices to keep their homes cool in the summer, slept under the stars, fell asleep to the music of jackals and koels calling, awoke at sunrise, slept through the very warm and still afternoons with the punkhawallah fanning them, went clubbing in the evening and usually came home to a three-course dinner prepared by the Mug cook from Bengal and his helper. They absorbed India and survived India.

Since Calcutta was the capital, British Delhi did not grow into a large city within a city. It had an adequate infrastructure and a clearly defined comfort zone. Lord Curzon who 'ruled' from Calcutta, had a profound attachment to that city but was awed by Delhi and its layered, tumultuous history which is why he had chosen it as the venue for the great Durbar of 1903 which was an extravagant success, encompassing the best of Britain and India.

The Durbar of 1911 (fig. 110) was nothing like the earlier durbars of 1877 or 1903! The motor-car had replaced the elephant and time had moved on. It had been said of the learned well from his friend, teacher and guide, Gertrude Jekyll, an influential British garden designer who worked very closely with the arts and crafts movement.

Edwin Lutyens wrote regularly to his wife describing the progress of the imperial capital as it rose out of the dry landscape. Anecdotes of his fleeting experiences with the bizarre, the funny, and the aggravating incidents that happened around him, were an intrinsic part of his missives to her where he voiced his feelings openly and without any hesitation or the otherwise mandatory 'correctness'.

In January 1929 he wrote to her: 'Baker has collared the emblems of the colonies for his babu court instead of my Great Place, where they ought to be and H.E. agrees with me. But again I am too late as Baker has been to all the Governors etc. for their consent. I suppose if I did no work and only wire pulled I could do the same … Mustoe has done extraordinarily good for the gardens. Last winter they were a desert and a debris one at that. Now full of roses and beautiful roses. The tanks run and reflect and ripple and my rainbow in the deep fountain has come off – a vivid rainbow and children can find its start …-

'It is very tiring going over the buildings … they are very careless and the Indians are for ever damaging things and the messes they make! 'orrible! Parker, the sanitary engineer, an Englishman, said this morning: it looks, referring to Government House, "very different from what I expected". I said, "what did you expect?" He answered, "I don't know". This after seventeen years working on the plans!… the Irwins seem very happy and long to get into it.'

On Christmas Day 1929 Lutyens was giving final touches to the residence of the viceroy of India, Lord Irwin. He writes: 'the most tiring week I ever had – arranging furniture, seeing to things and driving men, hanging pictures. But Monday the 23rd came. The viceroy arrived at 8 a.m.. We had to get up at 7 in tailcoats. It was raining which stopped in time but a thick white fog enveloped everything. At about 8 a very white sun peered through and made the world a ghost. We heard the booming of guns – some heard the bomb and it was not until after H.E.'s arrival that we heard his train had been bombed. The bodyguard did soldier-like things, bugles blew and out of the fog H.E.'s car emerged. The guard was inspected. He then came up the great portico where I was presented to him and others on the work … and they, Lady Irwin and H.E. went into the house and we left them alone and for the first time in 17 years the house closed on me.'

There were many unusual, amusing incidents that brought a sense of surprise and wonder for the Dilliwallahs during those years leading up to the completion of the

Facing page, Fig. 110: KING GEORGE V AND QUEEN MARY ON THE DAIS DURING THE DELHI DURBAR OF 1911, photograph by Vernon & Co., 1911.
King George V and Queen Mary were the only reigning monarchs to visit their Indian empire. The King is wearing the Imperial Crown of India, made especially for the occasion and the only time it has ever been worn. This durbar was the most lavish of all the imperial assemblages and its crowning stroke was the announcement by the King of the transfer of the capital from Calcutta to Delhi.
British Library, London, Photo 1/14 (22)

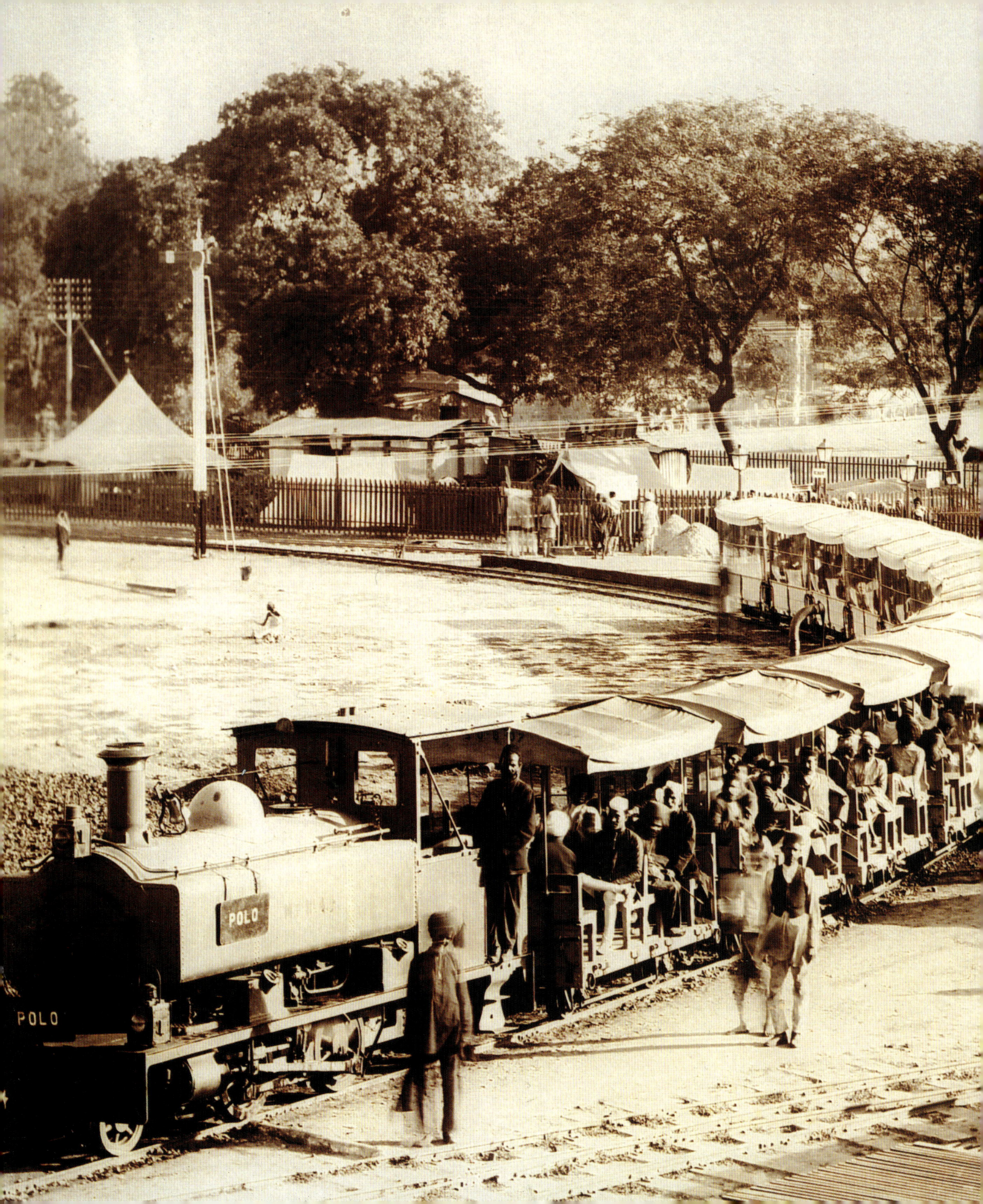
POLO
POLO

Fig. 111: THE TIS HAZARI RAILWAY STATION, 1911, anticipated the Metro, being one of several small stations built to link the venue of the 1911-1912 Coronation Durbar, extending from Kashmiri Gate to Azadpur.
Bates and Hindmarch, Private Collection.

Fig. 112: GOVERNMENT HOUSE FLANKED BY SECRETARIAT BLOCKS:
Impression of the forecourt. Notice the in-scale elephants in the secretariat building that fused arcadia with modernity in the imperial imagination.
Private Collection

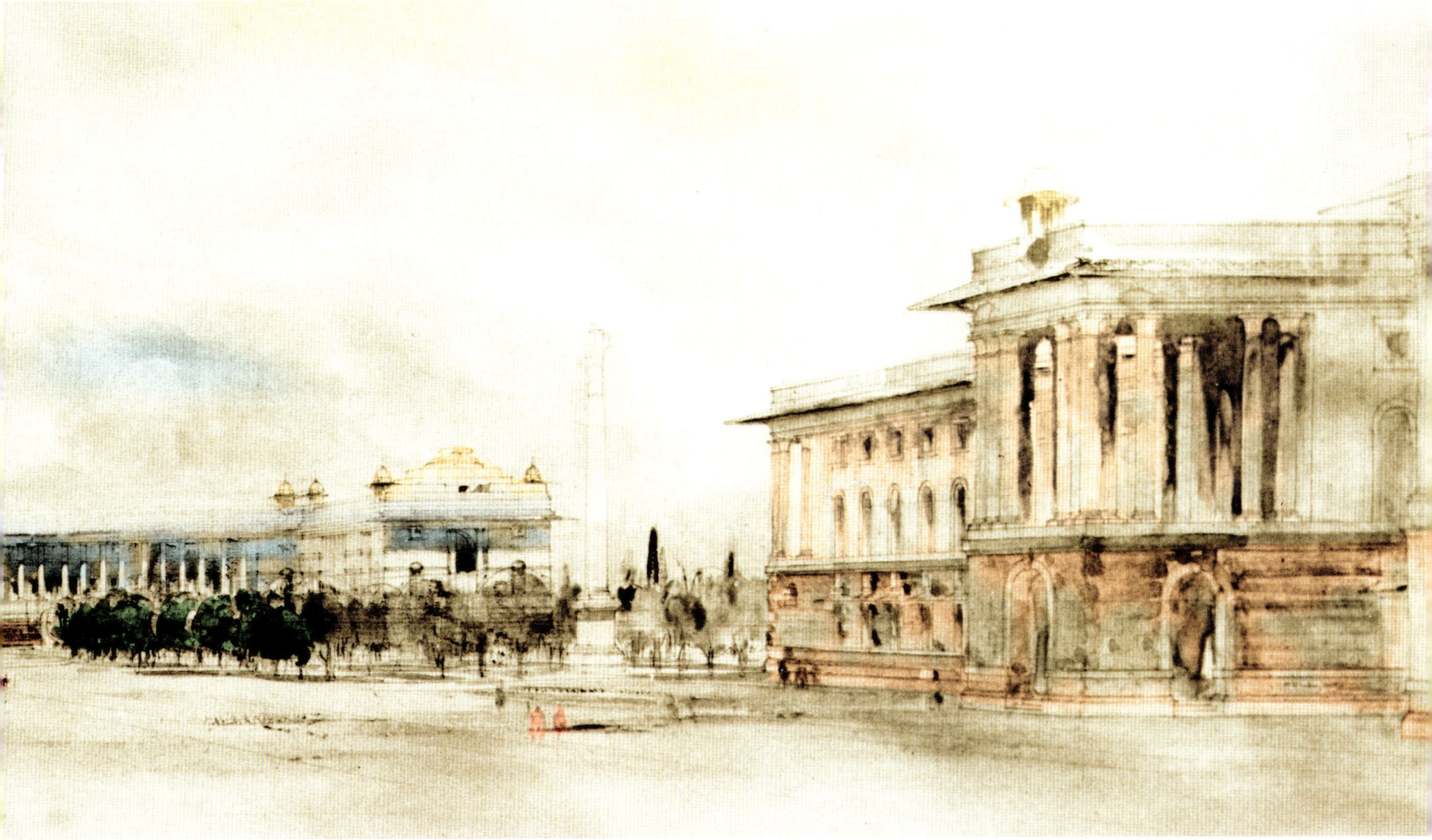

Fig. 113: GOVERNMENT HOUSE: Baker and Lutyens drew elaborate and highly detailed charcoals and watercolours, respectively, which visualized the architects' impressions of the new city.
Private collection

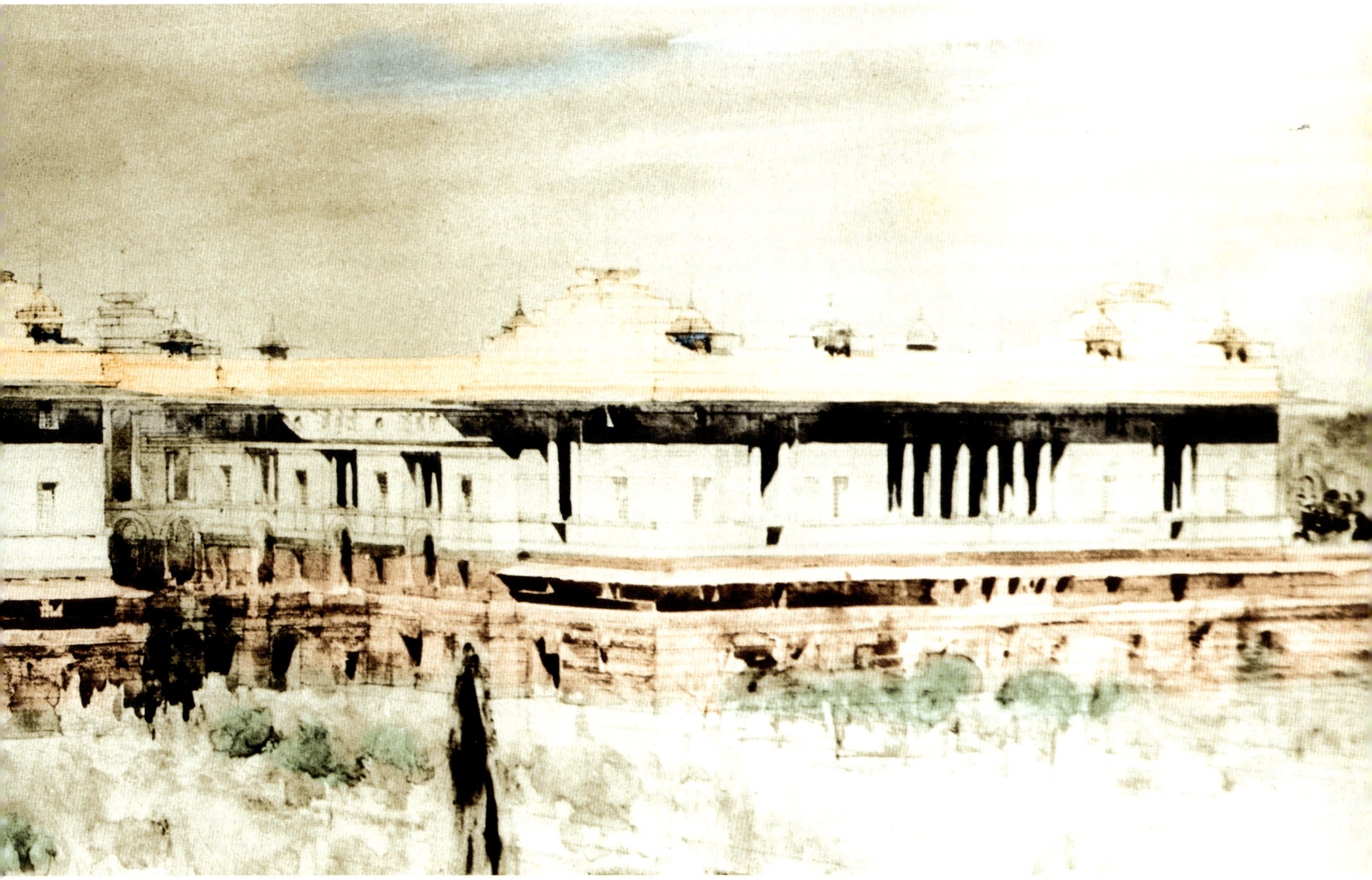

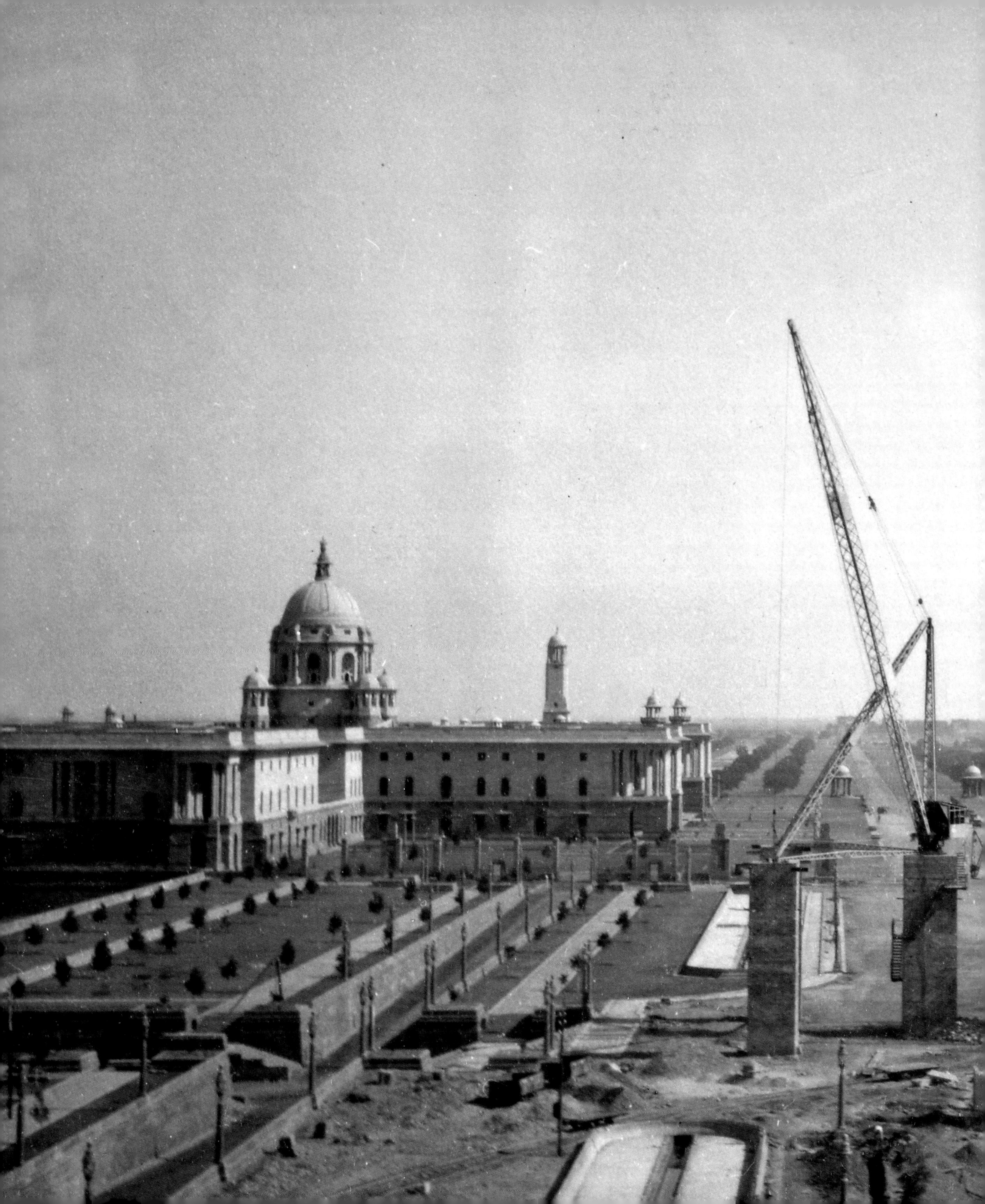

Fig. 114: NORTH AND SOUTH BLOCK: A view of the North and South Block buildings taken from the Government House. The base of the Jaipur Column in the forecourt is wrapped in scaffolding. Despite the apparent mess, the vista along Kingsway (now Rajpath) is clearly visible.
British Library

imperial capital! On 10 January 1927, Sir Samuel Hoare flew into India and landed at the Delhi aerodrome. Upon landing, and in his short speech, he spoke of the intention of the Imperial Airways Company to name the aeroplanes that will fly from London to India after the cities en route. The many awaiting his arrival at the airport including the viceroy and the vicereine, applauded the idea. Lord Irwin then requested his wife to pull a cord from under the aircraft and reveal, on a banner that floated forth, the name of this aircraft as the first of many christenings – 'City of Delhi'. All those assembled that day were taken on 'short joy rides', says the *Times of London*!

On 10 February 1931, 'New Delhi', was inaugurated by the viceroy, Lord Irwin, and Lady Irwin. The occasion was celebrated with much pomp and ceremony, heralding a new beginning in this ancient capital that had seen many avatars. A quote from the *Times* London describes the event: 'thirty-one guns thundered out a salute from the Ridge when Lord Irwin left the Viceroy's House this morning at 11 to perform what was virtually the inauguration ceremony of the Imperial Capital of New Delhi. The cold weather sunlight shone down on a brilliant spectacle staged between the north and south blocks of the twin secretariats …'. New Delhi unfolded into a young, contained city, seat of government, with all the ingredients, hotels, clubs, recreation centres, sports grounds, shopping arcades, residences and parks, hospitals and religious places, that come together in the design and creation of a comfortable 'settlement' with all conceivable amenities.

The Indian professional contractors, who built New Delhi with Edwin Lutyens and Herbert Baker, had come from Sindh, Sargodha and beyond. They saw the prospect of large contracts that would be awarded for engineering, for the supply of stone and bricks, for the construction of the buildings, homes and offices of the imperial government, for the crafting of the embellishments both external decorative symbols as well as the carpets and furniture, lamps, and mobiles, which would further their already established, prosperous businesses back home. They worked with commitment and a missionary zeal, adding value to this mammoth project.

Most of them who came to Delhi, did not return to the lands of their birth and put down fresh roots in this new city, a city of opportunity and the future. It turned out to be a wise decision because with the partitioning of our subcontinent, those who had homes across what is now the border of a sadly divided land, lost everything they owned, everything they had nurtured and built with care. The Indian builders in the Lutyens-Baker team became the First Families of New Delhi! They bought land and built their first homes next to each other on what is today Jantar Mantar road, embraced the new city they were building and worked relentlessly at identifying with it to start life anew.

Plots of land were their jewels, that later became family heirlooms. There are some delightful orally-handed-down accounts of how Sir Sobha Singh took every offer the British made to him and turned it into a fruitful opportunity and investment. When he was asked to build Sujan Singh Park, a complex of residential flats built around two garden quadrangles, at his own cost, because it was urgently required to house British army officers for as long as needed through the War years, he, without hesitation, accepted the offer. It is believed his wife was up in arms saying that he never bothered to buy her a piece of jewellery but always found the money to buy land and build, and this time, not even for himself. A wise and practical man, he assured her that wars do not go on forever and that it would soon be over, and the eighty-four flats, with quarters for the staff of those living there as well as many open, green spaces, would revert to him! It did, and it is in this complex that his children, grandchildren, great-grandchildren and great, great-grandchildren continue to live as a large, rambling, 'undivided' family, but individual, independent apartments!

The major luxury hotel that sat on Queensway, now Janpath, the Imperial (fig. 126), was designed by one of Edwin Lutyens team, D.J. Bromfield, for the builder – SBS Ranjit Singh. As you entered the imposing gates then as now, a line of palm trees led you to the porch and into a rather sumptuous space organized carefully with long, formal corridors, atriums, spacious rooms, verandas, and gardens. The most famous restaurant, the Tavern, has found a place in the list of Delhi's legendary landmarks. A live band played in an ambience of soft lights, elegant décor, with great food and drink. It was here that young and old couples held hands, which was daring in those days, romanced and then danced into the early hours of the morning!

Further down the road, Scindia House stood at the edge of Janpath and the outer circle of Connaught Place that was an imposing, rather grand, circular pillared shopping arcade with residential flats on the first floor. It remains an iconic landmark of the city. 'Cooke and Kelvey' was a shop renowned for its quality silverware, founded by Robert Thomas Cooke and Charles Kelvey in Calcutta post 1857. They opened their showroom and shop in Scindia House, and continues to be the most favoured and trusted for quality silver. From silver tea service, trays, fine cutlery to picture frames and key chains, it retains the style and mood of an age gone by. Girdhari Lal jewellers and Kanji Mal were traditional 'family jewellers', trusted and renowned. Glamour had the finest selection of saris and textiles, a 'must-visit' destination for a bride-to-be. Harnarain Gopinath had the best pickles and preserves in town that titillated the taste buds much like a grandmother's secret recipe. Oriental Fruit Mart was where you went for exotic fruits and vegetables like avacados and asparagus, bull's eye sweets, cans of sardines and kippers, and more. Vaish Brothers in Regal Building and Lokenath were the equivalent of Delhi's 'Saville Row'-type tailors; Snowhite were the drycleaners; Pandit Brothers, owned and run by a prominent family from Kashmir, had the best bedsheets and towels! Godin and Company, the musical instruments shop; Kinsey Brothers, the studio photographers; MR Stores, the hardware merchants; Empire Stores that sold all household provisions; Chinese Art Palace where you could rummage about a pick up an authentic ginger jar and blue and white garden stools; and many more, set up shop in Connaught place (figs 129, 130) It was the new commercial hub and the core of the new city of Delhi.

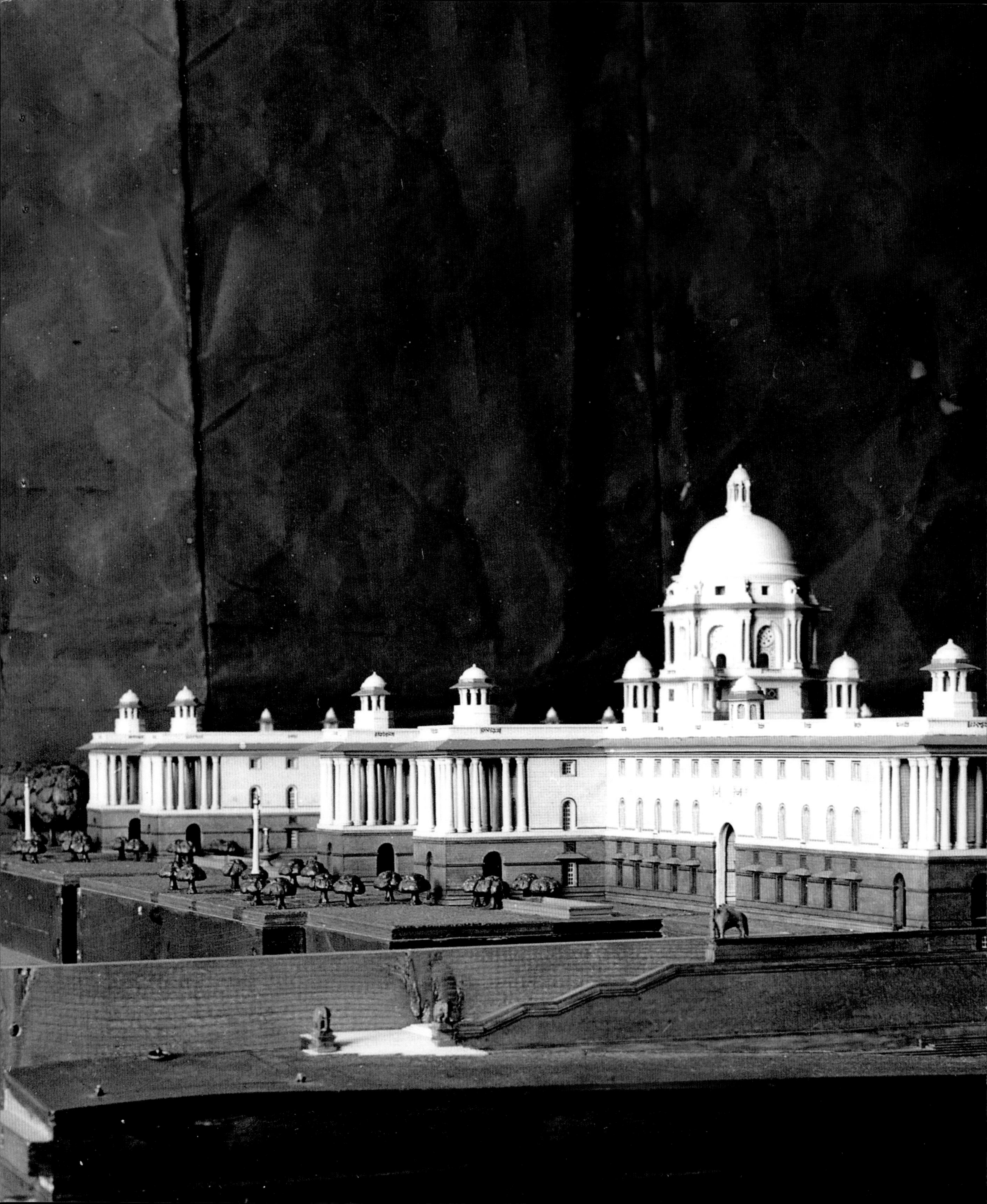

Fig. 115: VICEROY HOUSE, model of the proposed secretariat blocks of the Viceroy's House, New Delhi, by Sir Herbert Baker. This image comes from an album of photographs of the model of the Government House.
RIBA36022

218

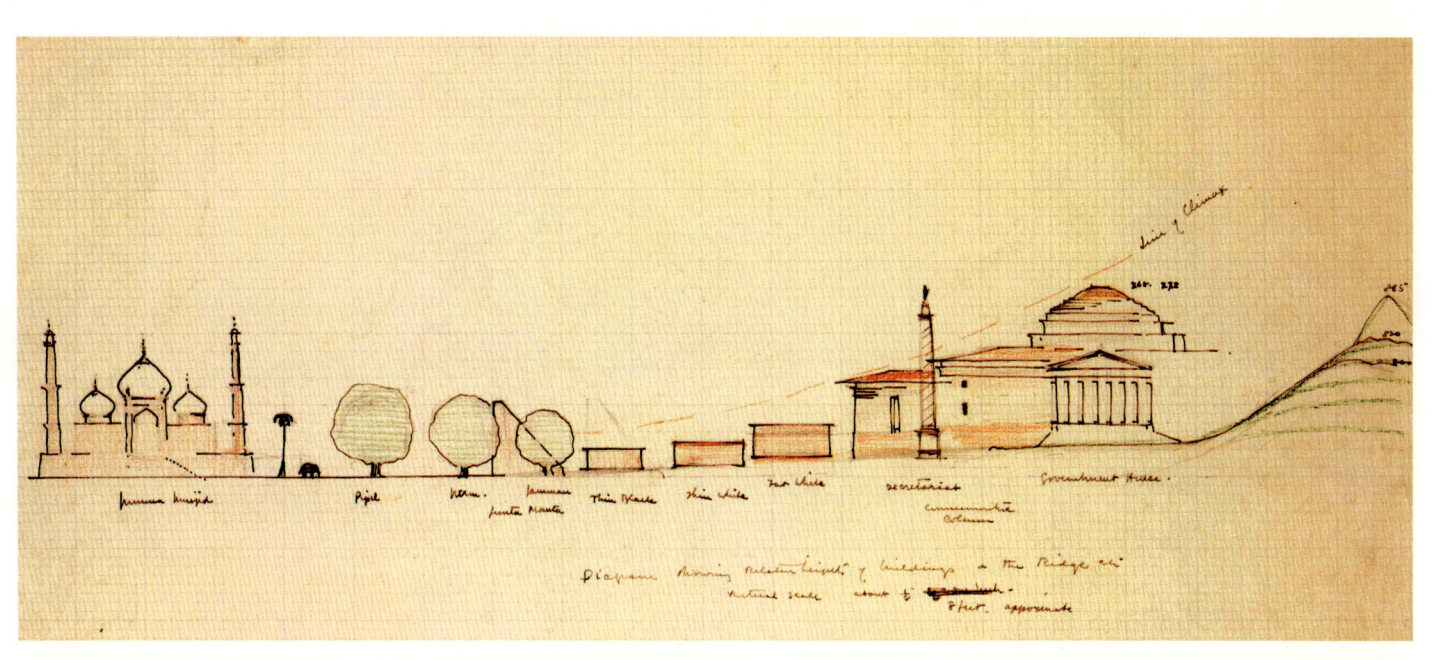

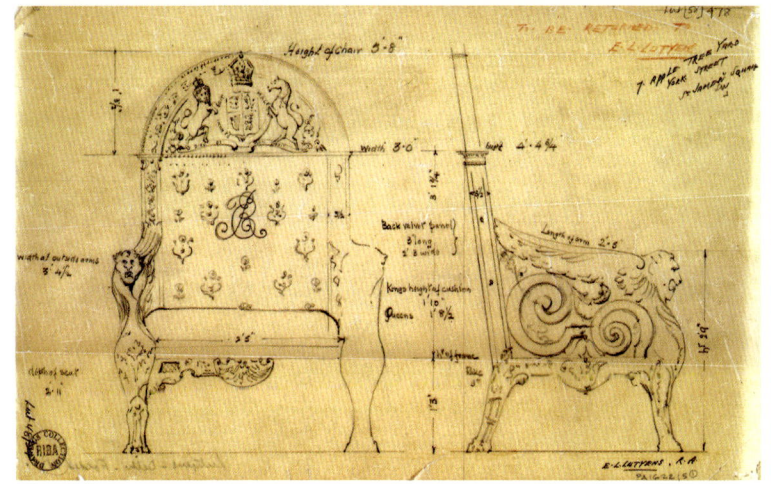

Fig. 120 (above): THE RASHTRAPATI BHAVAN (Presidential House/Palace) or The Official Residence of the Head of the State is the official residence of the President of India, located at Raisina Hill in New Delhi. Until 1950, it was known as 'Viceroy's House' and served as the residence of the Viceroy and Governor General of India. It is amidst an area known as Lutyens' Delhi.
Pavan Varma

Fig. 121 (below): A CARICATURE DEPICTING A CONFRONTATION BETWEEN SIR EDWIN LUTYENS AND SIR HERBERT BAKER. Both men are shown brandishing drawing instruments and have drawing boards strapped to their bodies.
RIBA21576

Facing page: Figs 116, 117, 118 & 119 (clockwise from above): VICEROY'S HOUSE, NEW DELHI. Preliminary study showing relative heights of buildings and the Ridge. Designed by Sir Edwin Landsdeer Lutyens. *RIBA13031*; DESIGN FOR THE ROMAN CATHOLIC CATHEDRAL CHURCH OF THE SACRED HEART. NEW DELHI. South elevation with plan of the south end. Designer: Sir Henry Alexander Nesbitt Medd. *RIBA31017*; VICEROY'S HOUSE, NEW DELHI. Preliminary elevation. Designer: Sir Edwin Landsdeer Lutyens. *RIBA53343*; and DESIGN FOR A CHAIR BEARING THE ROYAL COAT OF ARMS AND THE LETTERS 'E' AND 'R'. Front and side elevations. Designer: Sir Edward Landsdeer Lutyens. *RIBA29823*.

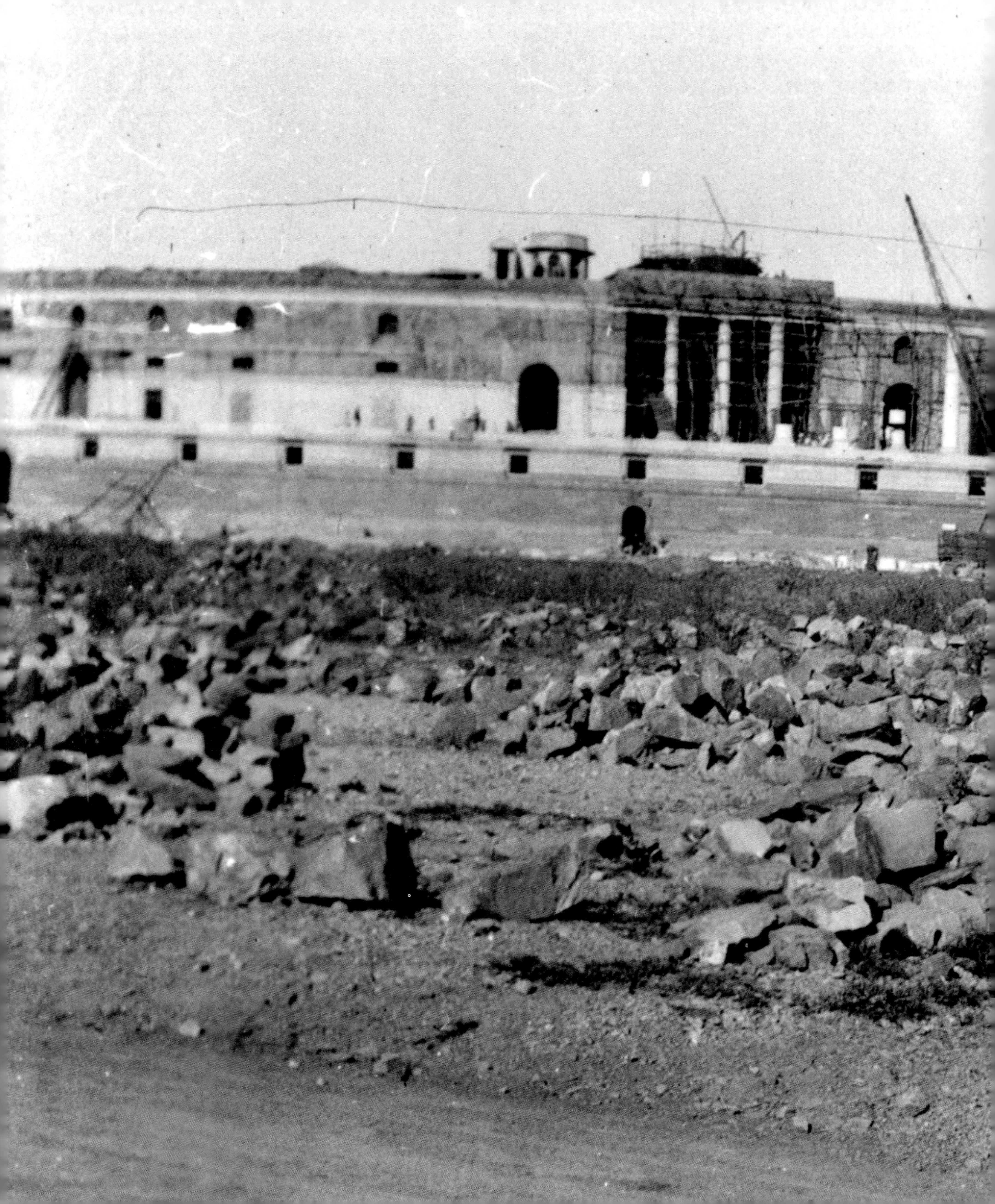

Fig. 122: COUNCIL HOUSE, New Delhi, under construction. Designer: Sir Herbert Baker (1862-1946.
RIBA34039

Fig. 123: COUNCIL HOUSE, NEW DELHI: The central hall. Designer: Sir Herbert Baker.
RIBA34036

Facing page, Fig. 124: COUNCIL HOUSE, NEW DELHI: the Princes' Chamber designed by Sir Herbert Baker.
RIBA28659

Recreation merged with retail therapy. Cinema Houses dotted the grand complex. Regal, with its elaborate walls with stucco work and private boxes for the local gentry; Rivoli, Plaza, and the Odeon played Hollywood and Bollywood films. Matinees were popular, either preceded by brunch or followed by high tea at delightful restaurants like Mikado, Gaylord, Nirula, and Volga. Gradually new entrants ventured into the business of food and leisure. La Boheme, Laguna, and Alps were like the lounge bars of today sans the alcohol. It was where the young met, in a romantic, dimly-lit space, usually surreptitiously, after college en route home. There were also the no-nonsense

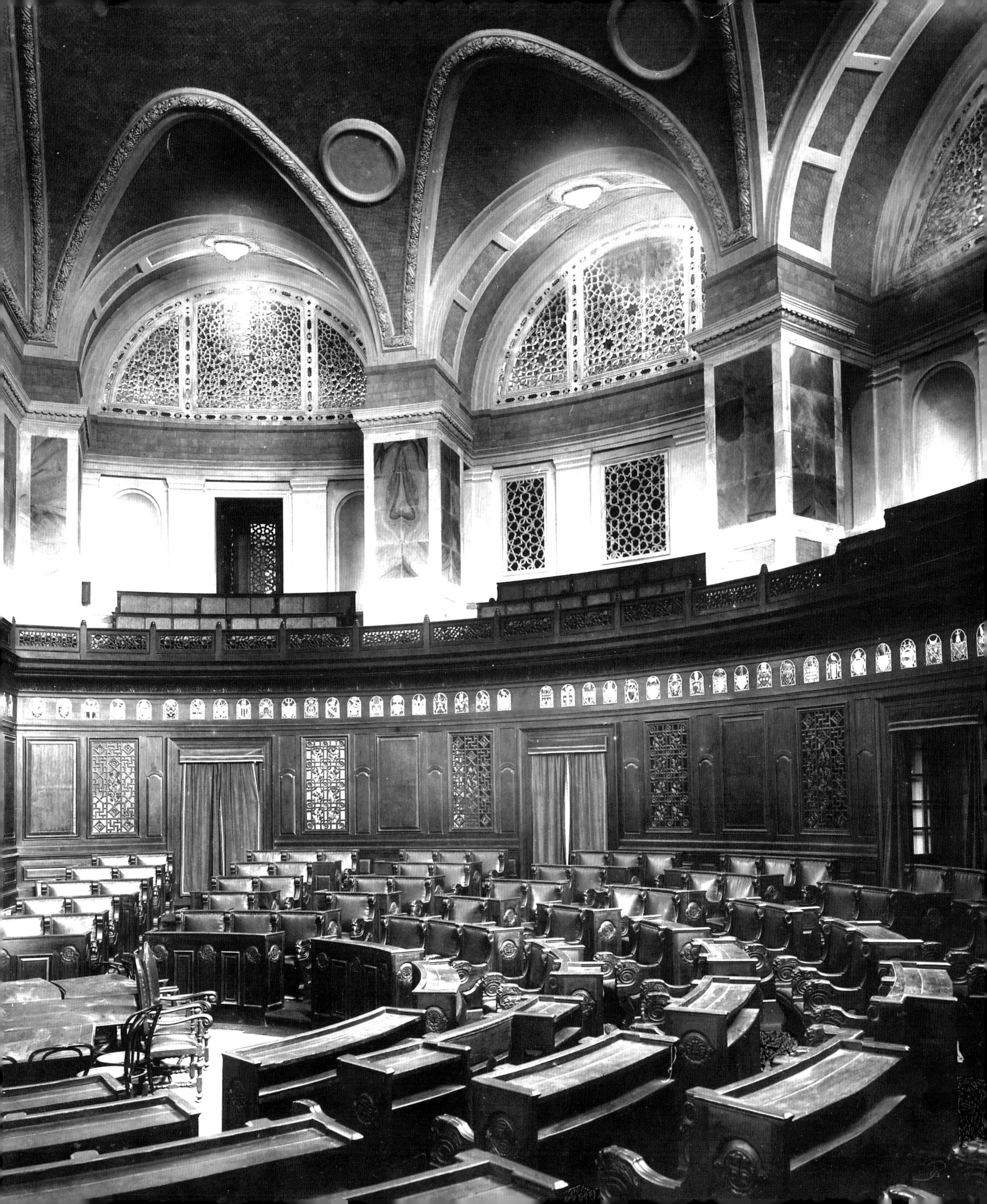

Fig. 125: MAIDENS HOTEL is one of Delhi's oldest hotels built in the early 1900s. It is the close vicinity of the most magnificent Mughal monuments of Delhi, and the famous shopping centre, Chandni Chowk, with its quaint bazaars and meandering lanes. Situated amidst the 'Turn of the Century' bungalows of north Delhi against the river Yamuna on the east; late 19th century architectural elegance is reflected in its architecture and decor.
Oberoi Group

eating places like Standard, United Coffee House, Madras Hotel and others that attracted the working professional for a quick snack or lunch.

Irwin Road, one of the radial roads that led to Gole Market and further to Willingdon Crescent that ran between the Ridge and the Viceroy's Palace, was where the flower, vegetable and fruit vendors displayed their fresh and organic wares for sale, each day of the week. Another, Panchkuin Road, housed the best and famed kulfi shop, Anarkali. Yet another led to Minto Bridge and onto the old city of Shahjahanabad to Jama Masjid and Chandni Chowk, the hub and soul of a proud, culturally confident 'old' Delhi that was watching the 'new' avatar go through its natural growth pangs.

As people settled into their bungalows, social life became more active, clubs became the watering holes for New Delhiites. The Gymkhana Club for the rulers and the Chelmsford club for the ruled! Imitating the days of the Raj, these clubs had card rooms where upper crust housewives would play rummy and bridge, nibbling at cheese straws and cucumber sandwiches, sipping chilled nimbu paani in the summer and hot coffee in the winter. Pre-Independence, New Delhi emptied out during the long hot summer when the government shifted to the salubrious climes of Simla to stay away from the fierce

Fig. 126: IMPERIAL HOTEL opened in 1931 in the newly built capital of the British Raj, the Imperial was the city's first luxury hotel, located on Queen's Way, today's Janpath. The hotel building, designed by the architect D. Bromfield, follows Art Déco lines on the outside, while maintaining a balanced blend of colonial and Victorian styles in its interior. Long corridors and rooms with high ceilings are complemented with an impressive collection of Victorian furniture and 19th-century sketches of Indian monuments.
Imperial Hotel

hot winds, the loo, that swept through the region and ate into everything. Occasional rains would settle the dust, only momentarily and soon the heat would rise again and overwhelm the city. The laburnum, gulmohur and jacaranda trees, bursting into bloom at 45 degrees centigrade and more, gave this dusty city its vibrant colour. The saving grace through the hot and trying season was the cool of the evening that would ignite the fragrance of the jasmine and the raat ki rani. The heady fragrances would break through and infiltrate the oppressive atmosphere and bring joy. Those who stayed on in Delhi through the months of May and June, would sleep under the stars on their flat

Inauguration of New Delhi

It was a true 'irony of history'. Here was a capital city, conceived of and meticulously built by the British with much care taken to ensure fine detailing, completed after eighteen years of building and construction activity, at that very moment in history when the empire had begun beating retreat. Through the 1920s and 30s, the 'revolutionary' call for freedom from British Raj had become vociferous and real. There would be no looking back. Despite the political reality, stiff upper lip, Lord Irwin did not falter in either neglecting the last minute touches that were given to the 'project', or in saluting, with pomp and ceremony, the dedication of New Delhi to India.

The first few days of the second week of February 1931 had been overcast and wet. It was the eve of the Inauguration of 'New Delhi', spread over four days starting on the 10th of the month. Dawn broke that morning and the sun rose high into a clear sky. The four columns, representing the British Dominions, placed along the incline leading down Raisina Hill from the Forecourt of the Viceroy of India's new palace were unveiled. A thirty-one Gun Salute at 11 in the morning heralded the arrival of Lord Irwin in a horse carriage. Lord Hardinge returned to India for this occasion. Commander-in-chief, General Chetwode,

General Currie representing Canada, representatives of the other three dominions, and the ruling Indian princes, were among the guests. It was the first among the formal, celebratory events to mark the moment. On the 11th of February there was a lively and animated fete along the walls of the imposing Red Fort in Shahjahanabad that brought together the diverse and magical soul of India. On the 12th, India Gate, the war memorial arch built by Sir Sobha Singh, was inaugurated with full military honours and ended with the sounding of the Last Post. On the 13th of February 1931, Lord Irwin dedicated the youngest of the many layered cities of Dilli, 'New Delhi', to India and her people in the exalted presence of 5000 specially invited guests. Bands played in the lawns that flanked North and South block, garden parties, lunches, high tea and banquets and polo, interspersed the public ceremonies.

Fig. 127: THE UNVEILING OF THE FOUR DOMINION COLUMNS ON THE GOVERNMENT COURTS marked the inauguration of the secretariat on 10 February 1931. The red sandstone columns, topped by a ship-model, are still draped, as the viceroy arrives to begin the ceremony. This and successive events in New Delhi were covered extensively in the *Illustrated London News* on 7 March 1931.
Mary Evans Picture Library, London

Fig. 128: Following pages: AN AERIAL VIEW OF THE COMPLETED CITY WITH THE WAR MEMORIAL AT THE END OF KINGSWAY. Ironically, this imperial avenue has become the site for one of India's biggest national functions. The 'king's way', or Rajpath, is now used for the Republic Day Parade and other important processions.
Centre for South Asian Studies, University of Cambridge

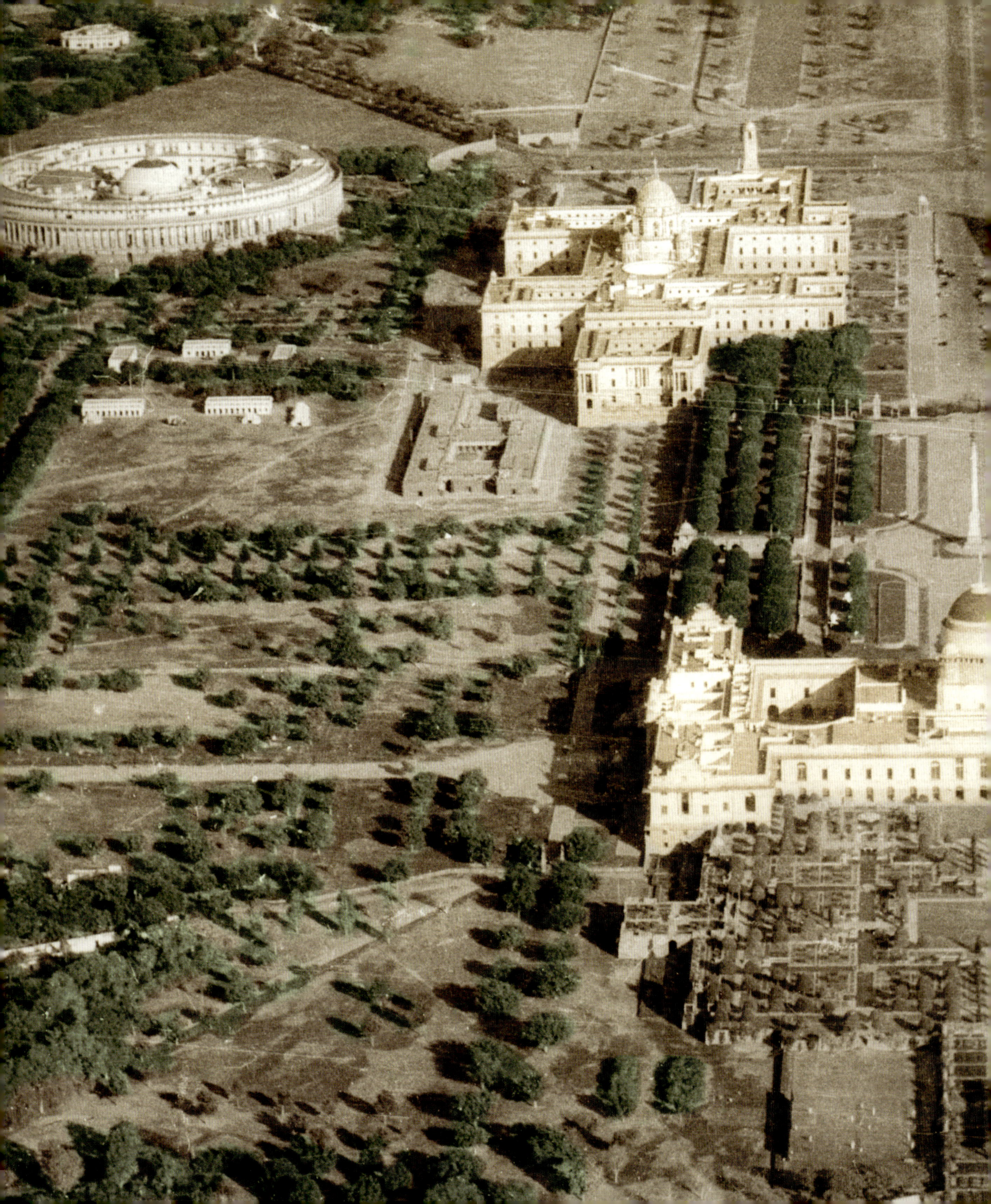

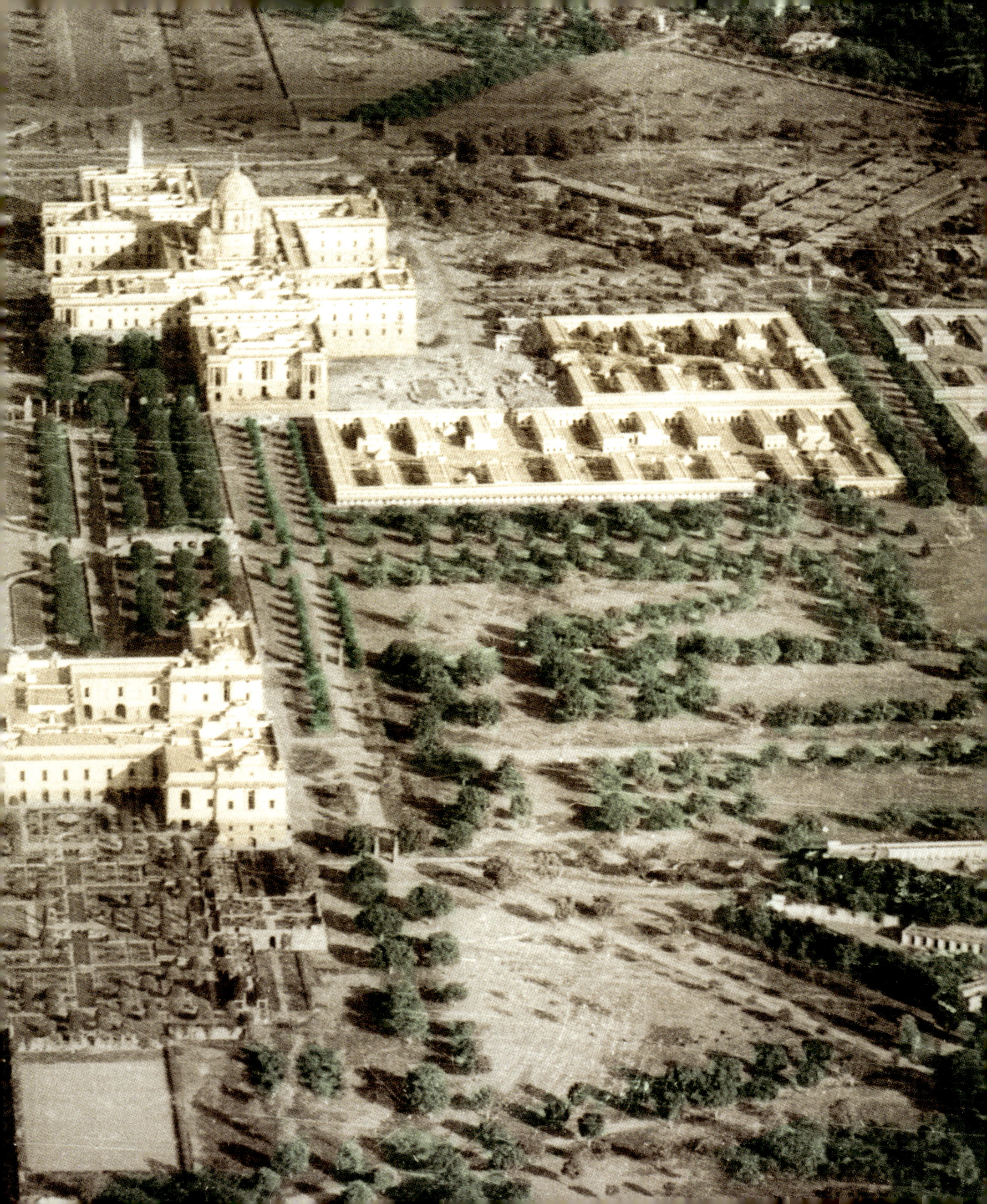

Fig. 129: CONNAUGHT PLACE, The British constructed Central New Delhi with its well-planned layout, just prior to the onset of World War I. Connaught Place, once the commercial heart of the British Raj, is today a busy tourist area that bears little resemblance to the thatched-roof colonial district it used to be; home to a wide variety of international shops and restaurants, attracting the town's Western visitors.
Hindustan Times Archives

roofs or under mosquito nets in their lawns having dampened their sheets to keep the cool till they fell into deep slumber to be woken in the early hours of the morning by birdsong and the gentle rays of a fast hotting up sun.

With the arrival of autumn the sahibs and their memsahibs would return to savour the oncoming winter, with crisp sunny days leading on to a flower infested spring. All the rotaries that linked Delhi roads would be aflame with a myriad colours and gentle scents. This was a time for visits from overseas, official, military and private. Sporting events such as polo and cricket were weekend happenings, followed by high tea and rollicking dance parties. It was the season to go off on picnics to explore the remains of other erstwhile empires that lay scattered around making the extended area of Delhi very special.

This routine of disappearing from Delhi in May and June continued for the privileged and well heeled. Kashmir became the summer haven and families would rent huts in Gulmarg for the season and move there, lock, stock and barrel, with cooks and bearers,

Fig. 130: PLAZA CINEMA, most of the cinema halls of British New Delhi had European names. The great days of Plaza, Regal, and Rivoli, as of Connaught Place, were from the 1940s to the 1960s. Cecil de Mille's very popular film The Greatest Show on Earth, running at Plaza when this picture was taken, was released in 1952.
Press Information Bureau, New Delhi

aunts, grandparents and children, to escape the formidable heat. Simla, Mussourie, Manali, Ranikhet, and Nainital too, were overflowing with plainspeople through those months till the rains broke in early July. It was not very common to go overseas.

In 1947, when India liberated herself from Colonial rule and became a democratic nation state, Lord Mountbatten, the last viceroy, descended the grand steps of what is today the Rashtrapati Bhavan, making way for the new incumbent, the first governor general of independent India, C. Rajagopalachari (fig. 136). The Indian Civil Service administered and operated from North and South Blocks, and the former residence of the British commander-in-chief, christened Teen Murti House, became the official residence of the prime minister of India, Jawaharlal Nehru.

The baton had been passed on.

2011. One hundred years down the road, from the day the foundation stone of the new imperial capital was ferried from Old Delhi to Raisina Hill, the core area of New

Fig. 131: THE CONSTRUCTION OF THE ASHOK HOTEL IN NEW DELHI.
It epitomizes the traditional grandeur and hospitality of the historic capital of India, and was among the first 5 star hotels of Delhi. Set in a prime location in New Delhi's Diplomatic Enclave, it is a distinctive landmark.
Press Information Bureau, New Delhi

Delhi, overlooking the evergreen Ridge, this city has grown into a one that is home to over sixteen million Indians. Lutyens Delhi, as it is referred to now, has managed to keep and preserve its early character and sensibility. It remains an insular space for the rulers and their administration! My personal memory of Delhi goes back fifty years. From a laid back, happy and quiet 'government' and 'cantonment' town, with broad shady avenues, fenced-in residences sitting on two and three acres of garden, sparse traffic, clean air and rarefied lives to a now sprawling, vibrant, and energetic metropolis. In my childhood years, South End Road was the extreme end of the new city beyond which lay ruins of past dynasties, isolated, standing amidst dense undergrowth where jackals howled at night, often wandering towards the closed gates of the scattered bungalows that housed the bureaucracy and political class.

Land on the periphery of the Ridge, now Diplomatic Enclave, was sold to the many embassies that had come to New Delhi post 1947. One of the first to put down its foundations was the Embassy of China, marking the great Hindi-Chini Bhai Bhai days

Fig. 132: SUPREME COURT BUILDING, designed by architect Ganesh Bhikaji Deolalikar. The construction of the Supreme Court of India was one of the biggest contributions to the Indian political system. Built on a triangular plot of 17 acres, the design of the building is in the shape of a balance with a pair of Scales of Justice. The Supreme Court commenced its sittings in the Chamber of Princes in the Parliament House in 1950 until it acquired its present premises in August 1958.
Press Information Bureau, New Delhi

of unquestioned 'friendship'. Chanakyapuri, named after the great political strategist, became a sought-after residential area with many a contemporary architectural delight from I.F. Stone's Embassy of the United States to Satish Gujral's design of the Belgian Embassy. Some plots were auctioned to private individuals and very quickly Malcha Marg, Kautilya Marg, Panchsheel Marg, and Kitchener Road, now Sardar Patel Marg, became the exclusive addresses for the new Delhi 'settlers', people who came here post partition, and chose to make Delhi their home, putting down their roots here, in this new city.

In Old Delhi, Civil Lines remained a coveted address but gradually as the capital expanded in the 1950s, the centre of social, political and administrative 'power' rested in Lutyens Delhi and some areas along its periphery. The government of independent India soon began to allocate 'colonies' to different professional groups and auctioned residential plots at reasonable rates. Defence Colony for the armed forces, Niti Bagh for the legal community, Vasant Vihar for the administrators, EPDP colony for the East

Pakistan Displaced Persons, Mayfair Gardens for the Sindhi refugees who had come to settle in Delhi, and more, all of which transformed the landscape and the skyline of the city as Delhi spread out into the 'hinterland'.

Back in Lutyens Delhi, an area 'walled in' without a wall, abode of the present-day elected rulers and their administrative arms, a favoured municipal zone peppered with homes of the families that built New Delhi and a few 'early' residents of this new capital built in the early and mid-nineteen hundreds, the contrast with the rest of the city is sharp and dramatic. With the exception of some rather senseless and displeasing high-rise buildings constructed to house the offices of a large and unwieldy government, this part of town, the centre of New Delhi, remains 'privileged' and protected. The government office blocks that rose up into the sky alongside Rajpath, with two spectacular vistas at either end, sadly had no connect whatsoever with the architectural style of the city that Lutyens had built. This new genre of aesthetics belonged neither to our traditional, secular, hybrid vernacular styles, nor to a Western import. Concrete blocks without any lyricism, devoid of grace or movement and simply not compatible with the extremes of temperature that descended upon Delhi through the year, this post-independent government architecture, cast in stone by the Public Works Department, the development authorities, the municipalities, came together to kill the age-old sensibilities of our civilization that had been absorbed, modified and digested diverse styles and forms over centuries. A profound dilution set in and a strange, haphazard, culturally rootless and anonymous Delhi was beginning to proliferate.

Connaught Place, once the hub of all social and retail activity, was steadily deactivating and local markets, attached to the burgeoning colonies, fed the needs of their immediate residents. A kind of 'segregation' ensued as 'colonies' closed in separating them from the outside, unfamiliar space. Crazy taxation laws compelled landlords and owners of old properties to neglect the upkeep and restoration of their buildings thereby allowing for complete degradation of what should have been deemed heritage structures, held in trust for future generations. Soon CP, as it was affectionately referred to, looked tired and shabby. Then suddenly one morning, its name changed, and an edifice in the round, with outer, middle and inner circular roads embracing it, was re-christened Rajiv Chowk. Chowk in Hindustani means a square, making the new name meaningless, one of the most inappropriate, unthinking decisions that triggered off many more such changes of historic names of Delhi streets that had kept alive by gentle suggestion, its multi-cultural soul.

In the good ole sixties, bands had played in restaurants in the afternoon and young men and women flocked to weekend jam sessions, dancing to the songs of Sinatra and Elvis, snacking of chicken patties, cheese and tomato sandwiches, and chocolate éclairs. On weekdays the Tea House in Regal Building served delicious, greasy mutton cutlets, a forgotten delicacy, comparable to the great chicken curry served by the railway cooks on the Frontier Mail! India's first ever discotheque, The Cellar, replaced the Tea House and became the non-alcoholic watering hole for the young. In those days everyone knew everyone, aunts and uncles, cousins and brothers! There was a sense of 'safety' in that extended family of friends and acquaintances. Midnight was 'lights out' time. Life was carefree and happy. Delhi was safe.

As the city grew, it became more and more impersonal, almost alien. That sense of knowing people on the bus, in the park and in restaurants, at the movies, soon changed and the earlier comfort of 'community' and 'friendship' began to melt away, into a set of treasured 'memories'. The renamed streets were suddenly unfamiliar – Ratendone Road with its old flowering laburnums became Amrita Shergil Marg, destroying the past in one fell swoop. Many such 'anchors' infused with history, were unceremoniously removed making some of us Dilliwallahs proud of our layered and plural history, feel rudderless. It was sad to see King George move from under the cupola specially designed for him, to Coronation Park in north Delhi, enclosed in a garden of many busts and statues of the kings, queens, and viceroys of India.

One of the radial roads that extended out of the circle and circus of Connaught Place, led to Irwin Road, later renamed Baba Kharak Singh Marg! The fruit and vegetable vendors who were a city fixture for decades, carefully arranged along the road opposite the famous Hanuman Mandir, were marched into an ugly, horrendous concrete structure called Mohan Singh Place. It was symbolic of the destruction of the soul of Dilli and the intrinsic DNA of India, comfortable with her vibrant open-market places. The 'colour' soon began to fade into shades of grey and the city started to lose its unusual tactile strength. The Coffee House, adda to three generations of Dilliwallahs, was decapitated and erased from memory in a 'beautification' drive! A dark and dank underground shopping centre specializing in selling 'grey-market' products in what was then a 'controlled economy' was a pock-mark on the landscape. An unappealing grey concrete structure, to house officers of the New Delhi municipality rose high to dwarf the ancient Jantar Mantar, Delhi's famed observatory.

Decades later, as the city spread into outlying areas of the Greater Capital Region, a network of flyovers were constructed to link this octopus-like metropolis. A state-of-the-art airport, bland, glass-fronted buildings, shopping malls, multiplex cinema theatres, self-contained residential blocks of apartments, all sanitized and without character but infused with modern amenities and services, have monopolized the fast changing landscape.

Through the many contortions, often painful, in this ongoing metamorphosis, the historic walled city of Shahjahanabad and Lutyens Delhi, have fortunately managed to withstand, to some extent, the onslaught of unreasoned, unregulated growth and development. They are the oases that are manifestations of a rich and extraordinary legacy that reinforces the belief that Dilli has, forever, been the priceless jewel in many a crown!

Fig. 133: A PRESS CONFERENCE IN REVERSE – the annual reception in the courtyard of the Legislative Assembly by members of the Indian press for the Speaker, party leaders and members of the Viceroy's Executive Council.
Imperial War Museum, London

Facing page, Fig. 134: CENTRAL SECRETARIAT COURTYARD: The original caption for this photograph from the 1940s read 'A majority of Government servants in India go to office on cycles. A typical scene five minutes after office-opening time in one of the Central Seretariat courtyards' – a nostalgia-provoking contrast to the scene today of hosts of white official cars struggling for parking space.
Imperial War Museum, London

237

Fig. 135: INDIRA GANDHI, LORD MOUNTBATTEN, LADY MOUNTBATTEN, AND JAWAHARLAL NEHRU at a performance in the Mughal Gardens at the farewell party for the entire staff. The entertainment included various performances, watched by the Mountbattens, surrounded by staff and friends, June 1948.
Private collection

Fig. 136: LADY MOUNTBATTEN AND 'RAJAJI' (RAJAGOPALACHARI): An emotional farewell from the new Governer-General.
Private collection

Fig. 137: THE FIRST REPUBLIC DAY IN INDIA. Republic Day commemorates the date on which the Constitution of India replaced the Government of India Act 1935 as the governing document of India on 26 January 1950.
Press Information Bureau, New Delhi

Bibliography

Ahmed Khan, Syed, *Asar al-Sanadid*, Delhi, 1847, 2nd ed. 1852

Archer, M., *British Drawings in the India Office Library*, HMSO, London, 1969

Archer, M., *Company Drawings in the India Office Library*, London, 1972

Archer, M., *Company Paintings: Indian Paintings of the British Period*, London, 1992

Archer, M. and W.G., *Indian Painting for the British 1770-1850*, Oxford University Press, London, 1955

Archer, Mildred, and Toby Falk, *India Revealed: the Art and Adventures of James and William Fraser 1801-35*, London, 1989

Bahura, G.N., and C. Singh, *Catalogue of Historical Documents in Kapad Dwara, Jaipur, Part II Maps and Plans*, Jaigarh Historical Trust, Jaipur, 1990

Bayly, C.A., ed., *The Raj: India and the British 1600-1947*, National Portrait Gallery, London, 1990

Beach, M.C., E. Koch, and Thackston, W., *King of the World, the Padshahnama*, Azimuth, London, 1997

Blake, Stephen P., *Shahjahanabad: The Sovereign City in Mughal India 1639-1739*, Cambridge University Press, Cambridge, 1991

Dalrymple, W., *The Last Mughal: The Fall of a Dynasty, Delhi, 1857,* Bloomsbury, London, 2006

Ehlers, Eckart, and Krafft, Thomas, *Shahjahanabad/Old Delhi: Tradition and Colonial Change*, Stuttgart, 1993

Frykenberg, R.E., ed., *Delhi through the Ages: Essays in Urban History, Culture and Society*, Delhi, 1986

Gadebusch, R.D., 'Celestial Gardens: Mughal Miniatures from an 18th Century Album' in *Orientations,* vol. 31/9, 2000

Gole, S., 'Three Maps of Shajahanabad,' in *South Asian Studies*, v. 4, 1988, pp. 13-27

Gole, S., *Indian Maps and Plans: From the Earliest Times to the Advent of European Surveys*, Manohar, New Delhi, 1989

Goswamy, B.N., and C. Smith, *Domains of Wonder: Selected Masterworks of Indian Painting*, San Diego Museum of Art, 2005

Gupta, Narayani, *Delhi between two Empires 1803-1931*, Delhi, 1981

Gupta, Narayani, 'The Indomitable City,' in Ehlers and Krafft 1993, pp. 27-42

Howes, J., *Illustrating India: The Early Colonial Investigations of Colin Mackenzie (1784-1821)*, Oxford University Press, Oxford, 2010

Hurel, R., *Miniatures et Peintures Indiennes*, Editions BnF, Paris. 2010

Kattenhorn, P., *British Drawings in the India Office Library, vol. 3*, British Library, London, 1994

Kaye, M.M., *The Golden Calm*, Exeter, 1980

Koch, Ebba, *Mughal Architecture*, New Delhi, 2002

Koch, Ebba, *The Complete Taj Mahal*, Thames & Hudson, London, 2006

INTACH, *Delhi: the Built Heritage*, 2 vols., Delhi, 1999

Lafont, J.-M., *Chitra: Cities and Monuments of Eighteenth Century India from French Archives*, Oxford University Press, New Delhi, 2001

Lafont, J.-M. and R., *The French & Delhi: Agra, Aligarh and Sardhana*, India Research Press, New Delhi, 2010

Leach, L.Y., *Mughal and other Indian Paintings in the Chester Beatty Library*, London, 1995

Leach, L.Y., *Paintings from India: The Nasser D. Khalili Collection of Islamic Art*, vol. VIII, London, 1998

Losty, J.P., *The Art of the Book in India,* London, 1982

Losty, J.P., *Indian Book Painting*, London, 1986

Losty, J.P., 'The Great Gun at Agra', *British Library Journal*, v.15, 1989, pp. 35-58

Losty, J.P., *Calcutta City of Palaces*, British Library, London, 1990

Losty, J.P., 'The Delhi Palace in 1846: A Panoramic View by Mazhar 'Ali Khan', in *Arts of Mughal India; Studies in Honour of Robert Skelton*, ed. Rosemary Crill, Susan Stronge, and Andrew Topsfield, Ahmedabad and London, 2004, pp. 286-302

Losty, J.P., *Delhi 360° Mazhar Ali Khan's View from the Lahore Gate*, Roli Books, New Delhi, 2011

Losty, J.P., and L.Y. Leach, *Mughal Paintings from the British Library*, London, 1998

Nath, R., *Monuments of Delhi: Historical Study*, Delhi, 1979 [a free translation and adaptation of Syed Ahmed Khan's *Asar al-Sanadid*]

Pal, P., and others, *Romance of the Taj Mahal*, Thames and Hudson, Los Angeles County Museum of Art, London and Los Angeles, 1989

Pal, P., and V. Dehejia, *From Merchants to Emperors – British artists and India 1757-1930*, Ithaca and London, 1986

Parkes, Fanny, *Wanderings of a Pilgrim in Search of the Picturesque*, London, 1850

Polier, Antoine, *A European Experience of the Mughal Orient: The I'jaz-i Arsalani (Persian Letters 1773-79) of ... Polier*, trans. and ed. by Muzaffar Alam and Seema Alavi, Delhi, 2001

Rohatgi, P., and G. Parlett, *Indian Life and Landscape by Western Artists: Paintings and Drawings from the Victoria and Albert Museum*: V&A and The Museum, Mumbai and London, 2008

Russell, Ralph, ed., *Ghalib: the Poet and his Age*, London, 1972

Roy, M., *The Artist Mihr Chand son of Ganga Ram (fl. 1759-86): Idiosyncrasies in the Late Mughal Painting Tradition*, Ph. D. thesis, School of Oriental and African Studies, University of London, 2009

Roy, M., 'Origins of the late Mughal Painting Tradition in Awadh' in Markel, S., and Gude, T.B., *India's Fabled City: The Art of Courtly Lucknow*, Prestel Publishing, New York, 2010, pp. 165-86

Sharma, Y., *In the Shadow of Empires: Delhi 1707-1857,* Asia Society, New York, 2012

Sharma, Y., 'From Miniatures to Monuments: Picturing Shah Alam's Delhi (1771-1806)' in K. Leonard, and A. Patel, eds., *Indo-Muslim Cultures in Transition*, Brill Publications, 2011.

Spear, P., *Twilight of the Mughuls*, Cambridge, 1951

Stronge, S., *Painting for the Mughal Emperor: The Art of the Book 1560-1660*, Victoria and Albert Museum, London, 2002

Tieffenthaler, J., *Description géographique d'Hindoustan*, Berlin, 1786-89

G. Tillotson, *Robert Smith (1787-1873), Paintings of the Mosque at the Qutb Minar, Delhi*, Indar Pasricha Fine Arts, London, 1992

Titley, Norah M., *Miniatures from Persian Manuscripts: A Catalogue and Subject Index of Paintings from Persia, India and Turkey in the British Library and British Museum*, British Museum Publications, London, 1977

Welch, S.C., *Room for Wonder*, New York, 1978

Welch, S.C., *India: Art and Culture 1300-1900*, Metropolitan Museum, New York, 1985

Welch, S.C., et al., *Gods, Kings and Tigers: The Art of Kotah*, Prestel, Munich, New York, 1997

Zafar Hasan, *Delhi Province: List of Muhammadan and Hindu Monuments*, Calcutta, 1916-19

Notes
Delineating Delhi: Images of the Mughal Capital

1 Losty 1986, no.13; Stronge pls.33 and 53.
2 Beach, Koch and Thackston 1997, no.29.
3 *Ibid.*, nos. 12-13, 23-24, 25-26, 27-28, 45.
4 *Ibid.*, pp.131-32.
5 Blake 1991, p.xiv. Sharma, forthcoming, prefers a more mundane explanation, citing European military engineering manuals as the exemplars.
6 For example one of the Agra Fort also c. 1750 acquired by Richard Johnson 1780-82 (Falk and Archer 1981, no. 191).
7 Gole 1988; Archer 1992, no. 100; Lafont 2010, figs 28 and 30.
8 A German edition had been published previously in 1786.
9 In the Montigny archives in Quimper, Brittany – Lafont 2010, fig. 86. The archives also contain a very interesting sketch by Montigny himself (or a draughtsman who was with him) showing the east elevation of the Red Fort from across the river. A copy of it may have been retained by an Indian artist to inform later 'picturesque' depictions – see fig. 29.
10 Add.Or.3263-65. The James Chicheley Hyde Collection (mostly unpublished) formerly in the Coram Foundation and now in the British Library, was collected 1806-37 and consists of 87 drawings from Bengal, Bihar, Lucknow, and Delhi (Add.Or.3188-3274) and two albums of natural history drawings (NHD50/1 and 50/2).
11 Gole 1989, no. 95; Bahura and Singh 1990, no. 180, Koch 1991, fig. 129.
12 Inscriptions on some of the drawings suggest that the artist was an architect who worked for Nawab Shujauddaula of Avadh: Lafont 2001, pl.47; Hurel 2010, no. 287, 2.
13 Catalogued in Hurel 2010, no. 287, all reproduced in Lafont 2010. Also Victoria and Albert Museum AL 1764 (the Emperor's zenana and garden).
14 For the mansions of the Mughal nobility in Delhi, see Blake 1991, pp.71-82.
15 Lafont 2001, pl.48.
16 Lafont 2001.
17 Lafont 2001, pl.47.
18 For Polier's letters to Mihr Chand, see Polier 2001, *passim*. For Mihr Chand's authorship see Roy 2009, pp. 176-79, and Roy 2010, followed by Markel and Gude 2010, figs 130 and 131.
19 Koch 2006, fig. 356.
20 For Faizallah, see Welch 1985, no.186.
21 Phillimore 1946-58, I, pp.364-65; Losty 1990, pp.36-39.
22 Some later copies of these originals leave out the surroundings, making the buildings appear to be tilting upwards towards the sky.
23 They were seen by the Daniells on 23 January 1789 according to the manuscript of William

Daniell's journal (British Library WD 4147), omitted from the printed edition of 1932. He makes no comment about them.

24 For Stewart as a surveyor see Phillimore 1946-58, I, p.346. The drawings are in the Braybrooke Collection and are now (in part) at Audley End House, Essex (Archer 1992, p.129). Some are on loan to the Victoria and Albert Museum.

25 See Archer 1972, pls.60, 62-65 and Pal 1989, ch. 2, for some of the finest examples of the paintings of Agra monuments.

26 A plan of the Agra Fort in the British Library (Add.Or.4392) c. 1812-15 is inscribed in Persian as the work of Shaikh Ghulam Ahmad *naqsa navis* or draughtsman (Losty 1989, pp.35-38).

27 Archer 1972, no.44.

28 Archer 1969, pp.244-46; Kattenhorn 1994, pp. 204-05; Rohatgi and Parlett 2008, pp. 196-07

29 Drawings in the Victoria and Albert Museum and British Library respectively. Compare Rohatgi and Parlett 2008, p.196 with Archer 1972, pl.62.

30 E.g. in the Wellesley (Archer 1972, no. 44) and Hyde Collections (unpublished) in the British Library.

31 British Library, Board's Collections, IOR F/4/274 no.6111.

32 British Library, Board's Collections, IOR F/4/620 no.15492.

33 Archer 1972, no.131.

34 British Library, Board's Collections, IOR F/4 296 no. 6819.

35 British Library, Board's Collections, IOR F/4 312 no.7126.

36 British Library, Board's Collections, IOR F/4 312 no.7137. Both the well and the gates were repaired under the direction of a M. Gascoin, described as a Frenchman resident in the city and a pensioner of the Company.

37 Nath 1979, p.58.

38 Blake 1991, p.171.

39 E.g. Archer 1972, p.179; Archer 1992, no.103.

40 *Oriental Scenery*, I, 23, published 1797 and V, 24, published 1808.

41 Archer 1969, pp.472-552; Howes 2010, p.201.

42 From the Wantage Album in the Victoria and Albert Museum. See Stronge 2002, pp.145-49. The many later versions of early imperial paintings in the Wantage and Kevorkian Albums are products of this phase.

43 The *Padshahnamas* of Qazwini and Lahauri and Muhammad Salih Kanbu's history known as *'Amal-i Salih* were the favourite texts.

44 Titley 1977, nos.281-82 (misdated to the eighteenth century); Losty 1982, nos.107, 137.

45 Losty 1982, no.107.

46 Archer 1992, no. 124 (19-60) as well as the set in the Metcalfe Album (see below).

47 See for example Losty 1989, pl.I, the Taj Mahal from across the bend in the Yamuna, and Bautze 1998, no. 82, then unknown, but in fact the gate and mosque at Motijhil outside Murshidabad.

48 See Archer and Falk 1989.

49 *Ibid.*, pp.37-38.
50 Archer 1972, no.175.
51 Bayly 1990, no.180; Sharma, Y., forthcoming.
52 This is in a private collection, see Sharma 2012
53 Archer 1972, no.143.
54 Dalrymple 2006, p.32
55 Losty 2004 explores this concept in detail.
56 Spear 1951, p. 65, relying on Major Archer, *Tours in Upper India*, 1833. Mirza Babar's coach and horses may sometimes be seen in the panoramic processional scenes of Akbar II (e.g. Sotheby's London 25 May 2005, lot 136, a precession datable 1827-30).
57 Nath 1979, p.14.
58 *Ibid.*, p.15.
59 Archer 1972, pp,184-5, pls.66 and 67.
60 Archer 1972, pp.185-7, pl.61.
61 *Oriental Scenery,* I, 23 published 1797.
62 *Oriental Scenery,* I, 3, published 1795.
63 Archer 1992, p.149.
64 Gupta 1981, p.8, and 1993, pp.37-8.
65 Inscribed on a painting dated to 1855 now in San Diego (Goswamy and Smith 2005, no.120).
66 Explored in Losty 2004.
67 Gupta 1993, p.38.
68 Partially published with his daughter Emily Clive Bayley's recollections in Kaye 1980.
69 Archer 1992, pp.145-9.
70 Losty 2004 and 2011.
71 Gupta 1981, pp.26-31.
72 Published and discussed in Ehlers and Krafft 1993.
73 British Library Add.Or.4391.
74 Now in the collection of Dr David Khalili.
75 R. Burton, *Personal Narrative of a Pilgrimage to El-Medina and Mecca*, London 1852, p.112. These drawings are stylistically actually more akin to those from the previous century such as those connected with Gentil (figs 16-20).
76 British Library Add.Or.5476; V & A 03563(IS).
77 Archer, M. & W.G., 1955, pp.70-71.
78 Welch 1978, no.44.
79 Welch 1985, no.285; Welch 1997, no.65.
80 For their work see Archer 1969 and Rohatgi and Parlett 2008. Also Pal and Dehejia 1986.
81 Bayly ed. 1990, no. 257; Tillotson 1992.
82 *Delhi, Agra and Rajpootana*, London, 1865.

Index

360° panorama 59, 71, 72, *180*
Abdali, Ahmad Shah 104, 125, *127*
Agra artists 34, 36, *48*, *53*, 58, 59
Agra Fort 15, 19, 35, 125
Ajmeri Gate 108, *115*, *116*
Akbar 11, 15, 35, 106, 119, 141, 149, 152, 153, 154, 161, 165
Akbar II *2*, 35, 40, 43, 58, 64, *65*, *84*, 87, *107*, *109*, 110, 113, 117, 120, 125, 182
Akbar Shah II 132
Akbarabadi Gate 104, 108, 155
Akbarnama 15
Ali Mardan Khan canal *27*, 35, 104, *173*
Amal-i Salih 64, *107*
Asad Burj 44, *45*, *48*, *49*, *61*, *69*, 82, *83*
Asar al-Sanadid 60, *70*, *71*, *172*
Ataga Khan's Tomb 149, 153
Baburnama 14, 89
Bahadur Ali Khan *28*, 59
Bahadur Shah II (also Bahadur Shah Zafar) 58, 64, *71*, 85
Baker, Herbert *169*, 202, 214, *219*, *221*, 222
Beato, Felice *75*, 85, *105*
Begum Jahanara's Garden 104, 158, 178
Begum Samru 73, 104
Begum Zinat Mahal 85
Bourne, Samuel 85
Bu Ali Qalandari 45, 59
Burton, Richard 74
Calcutta 11, *12*, 13, 31, 33, 34, 35, 37, 41, 43, 85, *135*, 191, 196, 200, *205*, 215
Carpenter, William 84, *95*, *96*, *101*
Chandni Chowk 17, 19, *27*, 30, *36*, 40, 43, 73, 74, 89, 102, 104, *105*, *107*, *123*, 148, *153*, 155, *159*, 161, 166, 178, 179, 190, 224, 224
Chatta 43, *58*, *67*, 71, 161, *167*
Chaunsath Khambha 149, 154, 161
Connaught Place 155, 215, *230*, *231*, 234, 235
Correa, Charles 203
Council House 203, *221*, 222
Daniell, Thomas 35, 36, *42*, *44*, *53*, *59*, 82
Daniell, William 34, 35, 36, *53*, *59*, 82
Dara Shikoh 102, 108, 125, *188*
Dariba 89, *95*, 104
Deen Dayal 85, *157*

Delhi artists *12*, 13, 30, 37, 43, 45, 58, 59, 74
Delhi Durbar
1877: *191*
1903: 85, *191*, 189
1911: *12*, 85, *205*
Delhi Gate *28*, *42*, 44, *58*, 73, 74, *75*, *91*, 155, *165*
Dinpanah 149, 154
Diwan-i Am 19, 40, 58, *65*, 65, *70*, 74, *107*, 108, 141, 155, 160, *166*, 177, 190
Diwan-i Khas 19, 35, 37, *39*, 43, 44, 45, *48*, *51*, 59, *60*, 65, *83*, *84*, 109, 110, *120*, 141, 160, *161*, 167, 170, 178, *182*, 190
Faiz Ali Khan 60, *70*
Faiz Bazaar *27*, *28*, 30, 74, *91*, 155, *172*
Faizabad artists *27*, 34, *186*
Faizallah 31
Fatehpur Sikri 107, 110, 149
Firoz Shah's Kotla 37, 59, 73, 141
Firozabad 149
First War of Independence 104, 134, 161, 178
Forrest, Charles Ramus 82
Fraser, James 43, *122*
Fraser, William *2*, 33, 43, *81*, *98*, 141
Gentil, Col. Jean-Baptiste *27*, *28*, 30, 31, *33*, 33, 34, 35, *186*
Ghulam Ali Khan 37, 41, 43, 44, 45, 58, 59, 60, *65*, *69*, *102*, *121*, 125, *138*, *139*, 141, *161*, 185
Ghulam Murtaza Khan 33, 125, 141
Ghulam Qadir Rohilla 104, 131, 132
Havelis 102, 104, *145*, 171, 177, 178, 179, 190, 200
Hayat Baksh garden *8*, 35, 40, *64*, *71*, 158, 170, 179
Hodges, William 34, 41
Hulas Lal 43
Humanyun's Tomb 33, *40*, 41, 58, 59, 73, *73*, 88, 116, 135, 141, 149, 152, 168, 169, 171
Hyde Collection 37, 44, *61*
Hyde, James Chicheley 30
Impey, Eugene 85
India Gate 203, 227
Indraprastha 202
Ismail Khan 74
Itimaduddaula 153

Jahanara Begum 102, 104, 155, 158, 171
Jahangir 11, 14, *14*, 40, 58, *132*, 141, 149, 153, 154, 161
Jahangirnama 14
Jama Masjid 11, 13, *17*, 30, 31, *33*, 34, 35, 36, *36*, 37, 42, *44*, 45, *48*, *53*, 58, 59, 73, *75*, 82, 89, *95*, *96*, 104, *105*, 106, 110, 132, 138, 139, 141, *151*, 155, 170
Jogmaya Temple 115, 117
Kabuli Gate 104, 108, 116, 155, 158
Kashmiri Gate 108, 132, *140*, *143*, 155, *207*
Khairallah 33
Khusrau, Amir 110, 116, 142, 170
Khwabgah *19*, *27*, *48*, *50*, *61*, 65, *83*, *84*, 110, 167
Lady Hastings *17*, 41, *62*
Lady Irwin 205, 214
Lahore Fort 149
Lahore Gate (of the Red Fort) 13, *17*, 19, 42, *48*, 59, *61*, *67*, 71, *75*, *107*, 160, 161, *167*, *180*, 199
Lahori Gate *36*, 73, 74, 108, *145*, 158
Lal Kot 148
Lallji 43
Latif 36, 37, 45, *48*, *52*, 58, 59
Lodi, Ibrahim 88, 89
Longcroft, Thomas 34, *44*, 45
Lord Hastings *17*, 41, 42, *62*, 72, *93*, 115, 151, *175*
Lutyens, Edwin 13, 102, 148, 152, 155, 168, 202, 203, 205, *210*, 214, 215, *217*, 219, 232, 233, 234, 235
Mackenzie Collection 37
Mackenzie, Colin 37, *60*
Madrassa of Ghaziuddin Khan *115*, *125*
Mahabat Khan ki Reti 110, 117
Mahtab Bagh *8*, 170, 179
Masjid, Akbarabadi *26*, *76*, 188, *172*, 178
Masjid, Fathepuri *27*, 40, *36*, *75*, 104, *107*, 138, 155, *159*
Masjid, Moti *48*, *51*, 65, *109*, *113*
Masjid, Sonehri 59, *172*
Mazhar Ali Khan 59, 64, 65, *70*, 70, 71, 72, 74, *75*, *79*, *80*, *81*, *95*, *108*, *111*, *120*, 140, 141, *153*, *159*, 161, *173*, *180*, *184*
Mehrauli 74, *93*, 108, *109*, *113*, 114, 117, *135*, 143, 148
Menpes, Mortimer 196, 197
Metcalfe House 64, 71, 73, *79*
Metcalfe, Charles *2*, 33, 42, 64, 83, *98*
Metcalfe, Sir Thomas Theophilus 61, *135*, 141
Mihr Chand 31, 36, *36*, 39, 72, *130*

Mirza Ali Gauhar 33, *127*
Mirza Babar 58, *61*, *70*, *132*
Mirza Fakhruddin 84, *101*
Mirza Ghalib *100*, *101*, 102, 104, 106, 117, 139, 142, 143
Mirza Salim 43, 132
Mirza Shah Rukh Beg 60, *70*, *71*, *172*
Montigny, Col. Deshaies de 30
Mori Gate 108
Mughal artists 14, 19, 37, *99*, *100*, *137*
Mughal Garden 149, 158, 238
Murray, Dr John 85
Musamman Burj *19*, *27*, 31, 35, *39*, *48*, *61*, *83*, *84*, 110
Nadir Shah 104, 110, 125, *129*, 132, 141, *182*
Nahr-i Bihisht *64*, 160, 167, 170, *173*, 179, *182*
Naubat Khana 160, 161
Nehru, Jawaharlal 13, 115, 231
New Delhi 160, 168, *169*, 190, 201, 202, 203, 214, 217, 219, *222*, *226*, *227*, *230*, *231*, 232, 234, 235
Nidhamal 19, *19*, 30
Nizamuddin Auliya dargah (also shrine) 59, *111*, 116, 142, 149, 153, *157*
Ochterlony, David 33, 34, 35, *80*, *132*, *137*
Oriental Scenery 34, *42*, 59, 84
Padshahnama 19, 125
Peacock Throne 37, 110, 132, 167, *182*, 200
Polier, Col. Antoine 31, *39*
Purana Qila 73, 149, 168
Qadam Sharif 59, *114*, 116
Qila Rai Pithora 148, 149
Qudsiya Begum *42*, 59
Qudsiya Garden 59, 141, 191
Queensway 215
Qutb Minar 11, 35, 36, *52*, 58, 59, *70*, 74, *91*, *93*, *111*, *175*
Qutb Sahib 70, 74, *93*, *108*, *109*, *113*
Quwwat al-Islam mosque 11, 37
Raisina Hill 143, 202, 203, 219, 226, 231
Rajpath 148, 202, *213*, *229*, 234
Rang Mahal *39*, *48*, *50*, 58, 61, *70*, *83*, *84*, 110, 132, 170
Red Fort (also *Qila-a Mubarik*) 11, 19, 43, 44, 45, *45*, *48*, 58, *58*, 59, *60*, 61, *67*, *69*, 71, 72, 73, *75*, *81*, *82*, *83*, 85, 89, *100*, *102*, 106, 107, 109, 110, 125, *126*, *134*, *135*, 138, 141, 143, *145*, 149, 152, 154, 155, 158-61, 165, 166, 167, 171, 173, 176, 177, 178, 179, 180, 188, 190, 191, 196, 199, 227
Reminiscences of Imperial Delhi 64, 141

Roshanara Begum's garden 158
Ruby Madden 196, 197
Sadatallah Chowk *28*, 104, 138, *172*
Sadatallah Khan *91*, 106, 107, 110
Safdar Jung's Tomb *72*, 141
Salim Shah 31
Salimgarh Fort *19*, 30, 35, *52, 58, 61, 75*, 107, *145*, 154, 160, 178
Select Views in India 34
Seton, Archibald 33, 35, 37
Shah Alam II 31, 33, *39, 109, 113, 127*, 132
Shah Burj *27*, 31, 40, 44, *48, 52, 61, 64*, 65, *145, 173*
Shahjahan *8, 10*, 11, 14, 19, 37, 40, 44, *48*, 58, *60*, 64, 65, *65, 70, 82*, 89, *91*, 106, 107, 107, 109, 117, 119, 125, 148, 149, 153, 154, 158, 169, 160, 161, 165, 167, 170, 171, 178, 179, 190
Shahjahanabad 11, 13, 14, 30, 59, *75, 80, 82*, 89, 102, 106, 114, 143, 148, 149, 154-58, 170, 171, *172*, 176, 178, 179, 190, *191*, 196, 200, 202, 203, 224, 227, 235
Shalimar Gardens 42
ShalimarBagh (Lahore) 149
Shepherd, Charles 85, *134*
Shujauddaula 30, *41*
Simpson, William 84, 85
Sir Sobha Singh 214, 227

Siri 148, 149
Sita Ram *17*, 41, 42, 43, 59, *62, 67, 72, 73*, 74, 85, *93, 109, 113, 115, 151, 175*
Skinner, James *2*, 43, 61, *80, 98, 119, 121, 123, 138, 139*, 141, *143, 145, 185*
Smith, Col. Robert 35, *53*, 84
St. James Church 61, *75, 80, 81, 143*, 178, *184, 185*
Steell, George 34, 35
Stewart, William 31, 33, 34, *40, 41*
Syed Ahmed Khan 58, 60, 61, 64, 65, *70, 71*, 72, 125, 142, *172*
Taj Mahal 19, 31, 34, 35, 89, 149, 152, 153, 154
Tieffenthaler, Joseph 30
Tis Hazari Bagh 104, 158, *207*
Tomb of Ghaziuddin Khan 116
Tripoliya Gate 31
Tughluqabad 149, *175*
Tytler, Robert 85, *134*
Viceroy House (also see Rashrapati Bhavan) 152, 158, *217, 219*, 231
Zinat al-Masajid 34, *45*, 59, 138, 141, 171
Zoffany, Johan 34